# THE RIVER THAT MADE TEXAS

# THE RIVER THAT MADE TEXAS

## A Forgotten History of the Trinity

SCOT McFARLANE

The University of North Carolina Press
CHAPEL HILL

This book was published with the assistance of
the Authors Fund of the University of North Carolina Press.


Manufactured in the United States of America

Designed by Lindsay Starr
Set in Dante by codeMantra

Material in chapters 3, 4, 5, and 6 previously appeared in
"The Wet Frontier of Slavery: Plantation Slavery and Freedom on Texas' Trinity River," *Slavery and Abolition* 42, no. 4 (2021): 733–54.

Cover art: Henry Clogenson, *Trinity River at Its Height, Dallas Texas*, 1908.
Courtesy of Library of Congress, https://lccn.loc.gov/2007660628.

Library of Congress Cataloging-in-Publication Data
Names: McFarlane, Scot author
Title: The river that made Texas : a forgotten history of the Trinity / Scot McFarlane.
Description: Chapel Hill : The University of North Carolina Press, 2026. |
Includes bibliographical references and index.
Identifiers: LCCN 2026015743 | ISBN 9781469698359 cloth alk. paper |
ISBN 9781469698366 paperback alk. paper | ISBN 9781469692739 epub |
ISBN 9781469698373 pdf
Subjects: LCSH: Trinity River (Tex.)—History | Texas—History
Classification: LCC F392.T83 M34 2026
LC record available at https://lccn.loc.gov/2026015743

For product safety concerns under the European Union's General Product Safety Regulation (EU GPSR), please contact gpsr@mare-nostrum.co.uk or write to the University of North Carolina Press and Mare Nostrum Group B.V., Doelen 72, 4831 GR Breda, The Netherlands.

For Nana, who taught me that love
is more powerful than history

# CONTENTS

## INTRODUCTION

# THE STYX

I first saw the Trinity River from a car seat as my dad drove around its bottomlands shooting at animals out of his truck window. My earmuffs dulled the sound of gunfire but not the bright colors of the muzzle flash or the puddles of blood contrasted against the autumn landscape. Due to my young age at the time, or perhaps wanting to forget, I can only speak about the deaths of those deer, coyotes, and crows as a historian might, from a distance, relying on photo albums or the stories my father told me.

History is not so different. So much happened before our lifetimes. Even within living memory, trauma and violence are often unconsciously buried. In my ten years of research, however, I have seen how memories of Texas's Trinity River keep rising to the surface like the hundreds of corpses that have floated in its waters. Underneath this silence, many are desperate to talk about and share their personal history of the river. Every Texan's story fits into the larger story of Texas. Everywhere there is evidence of human history, even in the water.

My childhood on the river was marked by goodbyes. When I was five, I accompanied my father on squirrel hunting trips to Red Town, a 6,900-acre tract on the middle section of the river in East Texas. But two years after I was introduced to Red Town, our host sold it to a timber company. We lost access to the land, and soon enough the new owners clear-cut the hardwood forest and made it into an unrecognizable wasteland.

The loss of Red Town prompted my dad to start buying property of his own, to have a place to hunt and a right to the Trinity. By the mid-1990s no one saw much value in East Texas bottomlands. An acre without marketable timber on the Trinity River sold for around $300. My dad kept buying until he owned thousands of acres. He funded some of these purchases through the sale of mitigation credits. Organized by the US Army Corps of Engineers, these credits enable developers to permanently fill and destroy wetlands that might have impeded a strip mall in exchange for planting trees and placing a conservation easement on another property. So, in part, my dad built his Trinity holdings through the payments that legally allowed for the destruction of other Texas wetlands inconvenient to the state's relentless growth.

Shortly after he began acquiring this land, my mom brought me and my twin sister to Concord, Massachusetts. The move gave us an opportunity for a better education than the schools of Palestine, Texas, offered; in Palestine I'd spent much of my time bored in the classroom with my head on the desk or scolded in the principal's office. New England private schools prepared me to pursue a PhD in history, but it was the stories I heard about the Trinity whenever I returned to Texas that fueled my drive to become a historian. Every holiday I stayed with my father along the river. Living between rural East Texas and suburban Massachusetts meant that I did not fit in either place. I was alternately too educated or too feral. As the poet Czeslaw Milosz wrote, "When it hurts we return to the banks of certain rivers," and my river was the Trinity.[1] Watching the flow of water, sticks, and trash, I felt the comfort that I belonged here, as the one constant and familiar place in my life.

After a big rain, a stream of garbage flows on top of the Trinity. Bright yellow oil jugs, clear and green soda bottles, and—this being Texas—footballs travel down from Dallas and Fort Worth. As a boy target-shooting in the river, I appreciated the trash—hitting plastic containers would make them pop into the air, whereas sticks would bob undramatically in the water. Visible pollution from the Dallas–Fort Worth region has been a part of the river for over a hundred years. While the water itself has become significantly cleaner than it once was, this floating trash testifies to the neglect of the Trinity, and of rural East Texas, through which the lower half of the river flows.

Whenever I returned to Texas from New England, I observed the inexorable march of development during my flight's descent into Dallas Fort Worth International Airport. Driving through the urban sprawl with my father, I could hardly see the Trinity as I rode over its tall levees and high bridges. At Corsicana, we left the bright lights of Interstate 45 and turned onto US Route 287, formerly the edge of Texas's population boom, though now new subdivisions reach right up to the wooded border of East Texas. Shortly after crossing the Richland-Chambers Reservoir, built to supply the Dallas–Fort Worth region with water, we reentered the Trinity floodplain. Without slowing or saying a word, my dad would roll down the windows as we approached the main channel so that I could smell the Trinity and know I had come home. Even in the winter, the river's rich odor of life and death is distinctive. And in the summer, the cacophony of owls, frogs, and insects competes with the noise of the wind rushing over the truck at seventy miles an hour. With the windows rolled back up, we continued on in hushed silence till we turned off the highway in Tennessee Colony, heading toward our property.

In the first years after I left, the Trinity sometimes flooded and made Route 287 impassable—an event that, if one was caught unprepared, would easily add an hour of travel.[2] By this time, state engineers began to raise the road and the smaller bridges in the floodplain to prevent the highway from flooding. The river continued to inundate the blacktop until finally, in the first decade of the 2000s, the highway department began hauling in countless loads of earth from an old woman's property on the eastern bank, creating gullied scars that still mark the topography decades later. For now, the Trinity has largely been kept at bay by the state's efforts. People and goods flow unimpeded down Highway 287. This raising of the road to bypass the river's mercurial nature is one of the numerous reasons many Texans simply forget the Trinity exists.

***In 2011 an entire waterway*** turned red as it flowed into the Trinity River. A meat-packer had piped blood from slaughtered livestock directly into the water. Were it not for a software engineer flying a drone during his lunch break, this violation of state and federal law might have continued unnoticed. Major news outlets across Texas reported on this story as a shock, but such actions were once commonplace, stretching back to the early twentieth century when Fort Worth slaughterhouses killed more livestock than any other place in Texas and a good portion of their waste ended up in the Trinity River.[3]

The river stank so badly by the early 1920s that it became the subject of a state study. In Fort Worth and Dallas, the report affirmed what everyone already knew: The Trinity was terribly polluted and unable to support life. Oxygen levels were close to zero in several sections. Carp, a species that can thrive with oxygen levels much lower than most fish, suffocated in the river. Near the outflow of sewage from South Dallas and Fair Park, toilet paper and "frothy sudds" covered the Trinity's dark water. And of course, the "odor

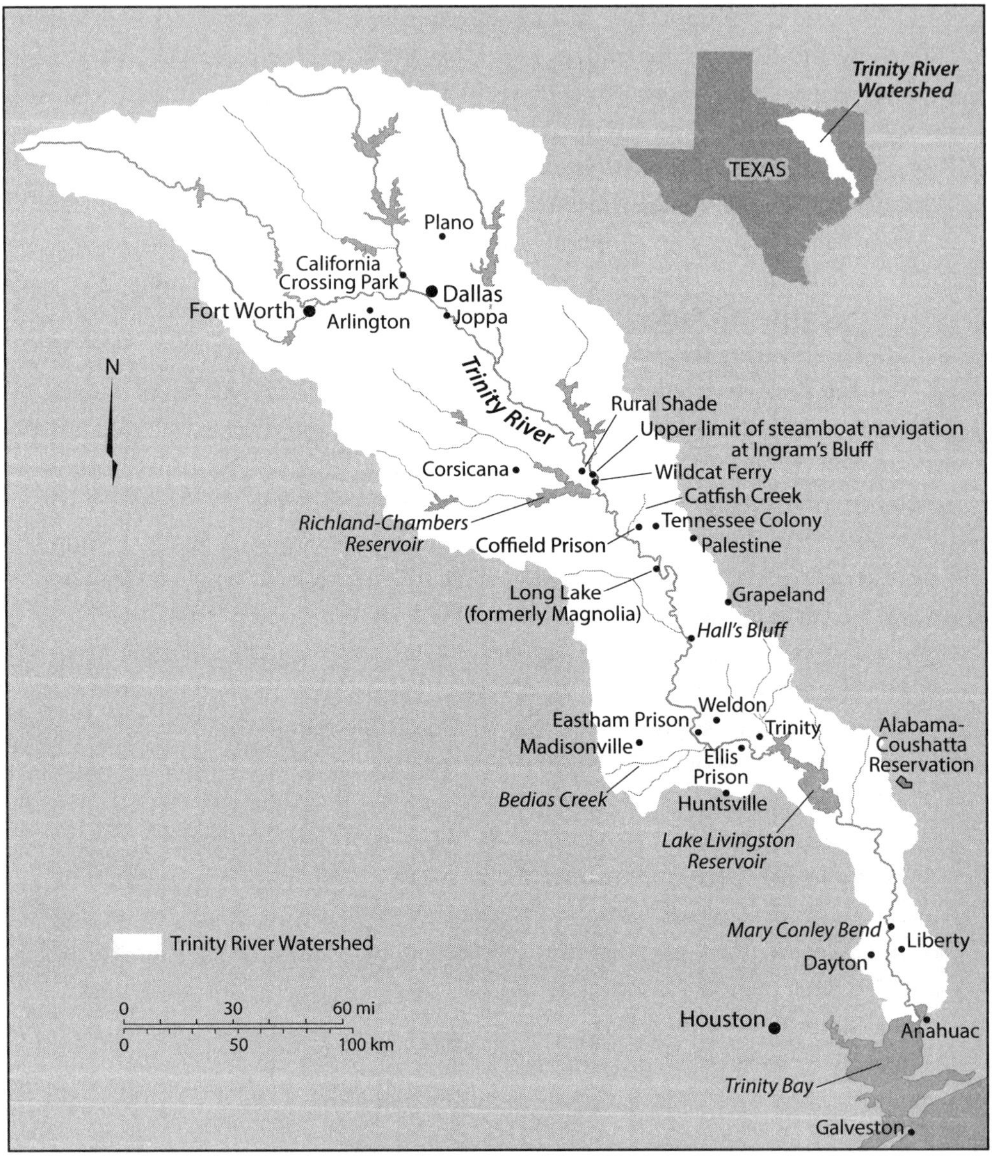


Present-day map of the Trinity River.

was extremely bad." Just upstream from this outlet, a dead, bloated mule lay in the grass. And downstream, a similarly swollen cow also died from drinking river water.[4]

The state research team learned that this degradation did not stop at the city limits. Forty-eight miles below Dallas, a witness described his attempts to revive loads of sick fish, including an eighty-pound catfish. Farther away at Wildcat Ferry, the ferryman said that in the previous summer the Trinity reeked so intensely that the stench traveled for miles. At this location, people had to contend with two major sources of pollution. First, floods carried a wall of filth from the cities of Dallas and Fort Worth, but a rural oil boom did its part too. Whenever oil flowed past another ferry, lots of dead fish soon followed. Oil, cattle, and cities—three pillars of the booming Texas economy—fouled the Trinity. For the river's inhabitants, dirty water and dead fish made for life and death consequences. Residents in the middle stretches of the river got sick from malaria. Fifty miles south of Dallas, the fish abruptly disappeared and people abandoned a once popular fishing hole.[5] The Trinity had provided sustenance to communities living along its banks for thousands of years, but an increasingly eerie silence spread farther and farther down the river after it flowed out of Dallas.

Figure 0.1. This picture of a dead, bloated mule was included in Texas's 1925 sanitary report on the Trinity River. Courtesy of Dallas Municipal Archives.

Published in 1925 by the State Health Department of Texas, the *Trinity River Sanitary Survey* included over 250 pages of testimony, field data, and charts. As part of its investigation into river pollution, the authors documented the "daily killing capacity" of the major packinghouses in Fort Worth, where factories could process 4,650 cattle, 11,250 hogs, 3,500 sheep, and 3,000 calves. Several sewage treatment plants already existed and more were on the way, but they were poorly matched to the scale of the task. While the report is largely focused on data, the authors used the introduction to suggest that the waterway's degradation was not a matter of course but a disturbing violation of environmental stewardship and the public trust. Pollution had transformed a beautiful river into "some mythological river of death"—a River Styx, full of "hideous danger." Understandably, these lines are the report's most quoted, but arguably the more important lines are in the following paragraph: "The people along the stream are entitled to a clean river," suffering neither a loss of "health or happiness, or economic embarrassment in order that Dallas may save dollars."[6]

This was ultimately the crux of the matter. What happened on the Trinity was not an isolated abuse of natural resources but an existential question about whom Texas belonged to. And for that reason, as much as any other, the history of the Trinity is the history of Texas.

***The Trinity River*** has been a friend and foe to many Texans—among others, the Trinity has been home to the River People, the Coushatta, enslaved people, freedpeople, prisoners, small farmers, and millions of urban residents. On the South Fork of the Trinity, archaeological findings from burial sites have revealed that human habitation began on the river over thirteen thousand years ago. These burials included red pigments to honor the dead. At least one of those buried died from arrow wounds in combat—not because the Trinity was a river of death but because it has always been a home worth fighting for.[7] The modern story of Texas has emphasized how its people and environment have been shaped by force, but Texas's relentless growth has been defined by rivers and their people, neither of which passively accepted domination. Tracing the Trinity's human dimensions over the centuries shows how crucial the river has been in creating Texas and why this particular history has been hidden for so long.

Today roughly half of Texans depend upon the Trinity River. Dallas–Fort Worth, the fourth-largest metropolitan area in the United States, relies on the river for most of its water, as does the city of Houston. More Texans live nearer this river than any other. Yet so much of the Trinity's history is dirty, and the river is uniquely neglected in Texas history and culture as a result. Other than a single promotional book published in the 1930s, no one has written at length about its history. Meanwhile, there are multiple books about the Neches to the east and the Brazos to the west, including John Graves's celebrated classic, *Goodbye to a River*. Even the city of Austin's relatively tiny Barton Creek has had several books published about it. A recent collection of writings on Texas rivers spanning over three hundred pages included only six pages on the Trinity. Such is the neglect of the biggest river in Texas whose watershed—the area from which rain flows into the river—is solely within the boundaries of the state. How this vital river has become so invisible to the millions of Texans who depend on it deserves an explanation.[8]

Parts of the Trinity's story are similar enough to those of other rivers with bigger followings, like the Rio Grande's role as a border, the Brazos and Colorado Rivers' place in the founding of the Republic of Texas, or the San Antonio River's vibrant River Walk. The Trinity's role as a main artery of development and explosive wealth accumulation also makes a compelling comparison to the Mississippi, a river crucial to the growth of the United States, but its hidden history surely offers more surprises.

In Texas, the Trinity has the third-highest average volume of water flowing through its channel, and because of changing water-use patterns it could someday have the highest flow of any river in the state. The Dallas–Fort Worth area extracts water from multiple rivers and aquifers. Once in the sewage system, the spent water doesn't go back to its watershed of origin; rather, all this water flows into the Trinity, enough to make it the only Texas river with increasing summer flows despite rising temperatures. In the hot and dry Texas summers, nearly all the water flowing down the river comes from wastewater treatment plants, much of which is then reprocessed and turned into drinking water. The needs and whims of our civilization dictate its flow, even though no single jurisdiction can claim complete control.[9]

Seen on a map, the river takes a northwest-to-southeast route across the demographic heart of the state. Rising from the ground and splitting into forks near the Oklahoma border where the yearly rainfall is around thirty inches, the Trinity flows 710 miles before emptying into its coastal bay, where annual rainfall is about fifty inches. Though there is no precise dividing line, the Trinity flows primarily within two regions whose names have become synonymous with their landscapes, culture, and history: first in North Texas, a mostly open and increasingly urban place, and then, approximately seventy miles below Dallas, through East Texas, a place that remains mostly wooded and rural to this day.

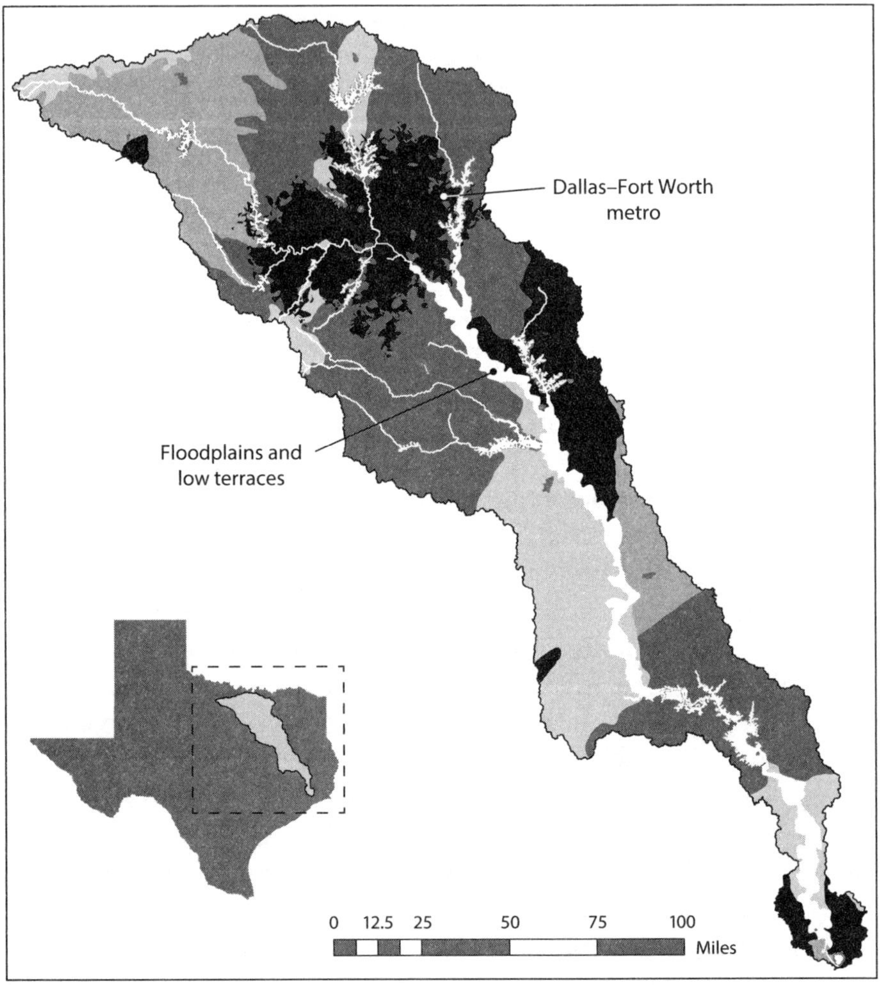


This map shows the varied ecological regions the Trinity transects. The river's flow is especially defined by the Dallas–Fort Worth metropolitan area, its many reservoirs, and its wide floodplain. The gray areas indicate various eco-regions. Map by Jackson Fitzgerald, courtesy of Trinity River Authority.

The Trinity has its own ecological habitat and landscape, called a hardwood bottomland forest, where a mix of trees, including oak, pecan, and cottonwood, grow old in its occasionally wet floodplain. The Trinity's bottomland forest is the largest in the state.[10] During periods of greater rainfall, the Trinity's muddy waters spread into the wooded floodplain and enrich the soil. While the mechanisms of renewal are the same along the length of the river, it is hard to overstate how unpredictably and unevenly they are applied. In peak dry summer, children playing on the river could once jump from one side to the other, as if it were a smaller stream or creek rather than a mighty river. When flood season comes, the Trinity swells nearly to the horizon, measuring more than five miles across at its widest. As one resident described looking at the Trinity during low flows, "You wouldn't think to look at the river, when it was down that it would ever get that high."[11]

The distant geological history of the river can be described in millions of years; comparatively, its human history is short, volatile, and epochal. But just as geologists can explain the natural history of the Trinity by studying shifts in its flow and sediments, this book shows how a historian can tell the river's human history by tracing the flow of people and the force they exerted to shape the river—and, in turn, how they were changed by their relationship with the river.[12] When examined by satellite, the Trinity's floodplain is dotted by both natural and manmade histories. Curved lakes, called oxbows, mark where the river once flowed before cutting a new path.

The forests tell stories, too. On my family's property in the floodplain, a dense forest is divided across and down by fields, reminiscent of a checkerboard pattern. This geographic feature is a result of my grandfather's one and only foray as a real estate agent in the 1960s: a single transaction to obtain twenty-thousand-plus acres for Texas's prison system to ultimately build Coffield Prison, still today the largest unit in the state. The Coffield warden ordered that all the forests on this acreage be cleared so that cattle could graze in open fields. George Watts, the prison farm manager, dutifully led the clear-cutting of these forests. However, by the time he approached the main river channel, Watts lost his appetite for such destruction and found that he always had another pressing task to do when the warden would remind him of his order to clear the remaining trees. As a compromise, to make the woods less hospitable to escaping inmates, he cut the remaining forest into blocks so that if a prison break happened, a guard could be posted on a corner of the woods to spot an inmate running across the fields. Without my father telling me George Watts's story, the creation of the checkerboard woods might have remained a mystery.

Figure 0.2. An oxbow lake (*bottom of the photo*) recently formed from the Trinity River. Courtesy of the US Geological Survey, https://earthexplorer.usgs.gov/.

Figure 0.3. An aerial image of the blocks of forests, called the checkerboard woods, next to the Trinity River and Coffield Prison. Courtesy of the US Geological Survey, https://earthexplorer.usgs.gov/.

Today, my family maintains our property's upkeep by renting out lodging to hunters, who stay for a long weekend while they hunt ducks, deer, and wild boar. The checkerboard woods, purchased by my father from the Texas prison system as it downsized its farms at the turn of the millennium, have been particularly fruitful. Wildlife love the plants that proliferate in the fertile black soil and the extensive edge habitat—where the forests meet the fields. Long, clear sight lines from towering hunting blinds allow even the wisest pigs to be tracked through the tall grass. Like much of the still wooded Trinity bottomlands, the checkerboard feels like a wilderness, a place shaped by the rhythm of the river and its ecology. The area is also, in no small part, shaped by the whims and desires of human beings: the decisions of a prison farm manager over half a century ago, or of the developers endlessly constructing new roads and houses upstream.

***When I enrolled in*** Columbia University's history PhD program, I returned to the Trinity, my first home, as the focus of my dissertation. On research trips to Texas, archivists and local contacts almost always asked for an explanation as to why someone living in New York City cared about the river. Telling them where I came from cleared up their confusion, but the question revealed a widespread suspicion that the Trinity could not genuinely matter to any outsider. During my more than ten years of research on the Trinity, my work has taken me far from its waters. I have spent time in local historical societies, state archives, and university libraries across Texas, each containing countless sources about life on the river. Thousands of miles away, at Cornell's University Archives, I read correspondence from one of Texas's largest slaveholders describing how enslaved people relied on the bottomlands for sustenance. Meanwhile, Yale University holds the diaries of a French naturalist and a Mexican general who explored the Trinity in the 1820s.

I was able to illuminate the river's history in modern ways, too. I dug through digitized census records and newspapers from across the country, looking for any mention of the Trinity, which were more often than not about drowning. In the beginning, I kept detailed records of every drowning event on the Trinity. Eventually I stopped counting and accepted that it was a lot. On my research blog, I estimated that at least a hundred people had drowned in the river. A former resident, who once lived near the mouth of the Trinity "in a little neighborhood called Snake River," wrote to correct me. He had never "heard of another river as bad . . . of eating people the way that [the Trinity] does" and felt my estimate was "far too low." The river terrorized his community: "That river took many of my friends and tried to get every member of my family at one time." Another commenter wrote about a gruesome murder in which the victim was bashed on the head until he sank underwater. The anonymous commenter closed by asking me, "Does any of this ring a bell?"[13]

Even before I publicly shared my research on murders and drownings on the Trinity, individuals reached out to me with their own stories about this river of death. I learned about Geraldine Harris from one of the first readers, who emailed me within a week of my site's launch to share her great-grandmother's tragic story and ask what role the Trinity played in her death.

In the spring of 1923, Geraldine Harris, her husband, and some friends went on a fishing trip to the Elm Fork of the Trinity, just northwest of Dallas near the California Crossing. While the rest of the party angled, Harris explored the surrounding woods in the early morning light. When one of the men heard a rustling sound from the bushes, he did not hesitate to protect his friends from a potential wolf or "booger" and fired two shots into the dense vegetation. Harris's husband and one of his friends armed themselves before investigating what they thought was a wounded animal. Once they went into the bushes, they discovered a terrible mistake: Harris lay dead in a pool of blood and mud. Her husband rushed toward her and exclaimed to his friends, "My God! You've killed my wife!"[14]

The shooter never faced charges. The reputation of the Trinity as a place of fear made for a strong defense. Nor would this be the last time that someone would be acquitted of murder primarily because of the Trinity's bad reputation; Texas judges and jurors have repeatedly agreed that fears of the Trinity River constitute legitimate grounds for self-defense. The day after Harris's death, two separate Trinity-related headlines appeared in the same issue of the *Dallas Times Herald*. The first noted the demise of "Woman Bullet Victim"; just below, the next headline read, "Heavy Rains May Cause Trinity to Overflow Again."[15] Two years after Geraldine Harris was killed, state officials called the Trinity "some mythological river of death" in their official report.[16] In the subsequent decades, big levees rose, walling off settlements from the river and the river from sight, which made what lay on the other side of the earthen wall even scarier and more unknown. Ignorance of the Trinity and its people has had life-ending consequences.

Even in its neglected state, there is beauty in the river: its brown water contrasting with red or sometimes sandy white banks; prehistoric alligator gar rising to the surface; ancient cypress trees draped with Spanish moss. Eventually the beauty gives way to the river's natural perils, as the water oaks and willows closest to the bank fall into the river and become snags, bobbing and threatening passing boats. Rather than look away from these snags, let us study the Trinity closely. Doing so can transform fear into awe at an impressive, unexpected history of the river and the people who made Texas.

## CHAPTER 1

# THE RIVER PEOPLE

In 2001, Dallas police brought the bones of an unidentified woman to the local coroner's office. Long buried under layers of sediment, her body had appeared on the banks of the Trinity. But these remains were unlike others that typically arrived at the coroner's office—they were over a thousand years old. After a brief visit by an archaeologist, her skeleton was removed to an unknown location, meaning neither other archaeologists nor tribespeople could study the bones or anything about her history: not her origins, not her name, not what led her to her final resting place on the river's banks, certainly not things about which we can only guess.[1]

The history of Texas's name begins with a story about the region's Native people and rivers. The story goes something like this: "Texas" comes from a late seventeenth-century encounter between Spanish soldiers and the Caddo people who dominated what is now East Texas. The Caddo referred to themselves as *tayshas*, meaning "friends," which morphed into "Tejas" and later "Texas." It's a good story, except that it might not be true. Spanish maps referenced Tejas before the Spaniards ever met with the friendly Caddo. Instead, the name Texas may come from what the Spaniards saw along the region's waterways: bald cypress. The iconic trees of Southern swamps and rivers with knobby knees and branches often covered with Spanish moss (named by the French) were given the Latin name *taxodium*—"yew-like," or *teja* in

Spanish. After seeing enough *teja*-like trees on Texas's eastern rivers, the Spaniards bestowed it as a name.[2]

When the Spanish entered Caddo territory, they were following in the footsteps of a Frenchman named René-Robert Cavelier, Sieur de La Salle. La Salle had explored the Great Lakes and the Ohio River before traveling down the Mississippi to claim the whole watershed for France, naming it Louisiana after King Louis XIV. But on a subsequent trip meant to start a colony at the mouth of the Mississippi, the Gulf currents washed La Salle and his crew ashore in Texas. In 1686, as they traversed most of Texas's major rivers, La Salle gave the Trinity its first European name—La Rivière de Cenis, a reference to the Hasinai Confederacy of the Caddo. A year later, La Salle's party killed him in a dispute over buffalo meat. The remaining Frenchmen returned to La Rivière de Cenis. They found the river changed. Previously, the men had waded across, but on their return the water levels had risen too much to risk crossing without a boat. As they constructed a canoe out of buffalo skins on the bank, they found the three fleurs-de-lis—Louis XIV's coat of arms—that La Salle had carved into a sweet gum tree during their last visit. The carving smelled, potently, with sticky, fragrant sap.[3]

It was on a 1690 Spanish expedition—the same one where "Tejas" was once thought to have originated—that the Trinity acquired its current name. Alonso De León's party came upon a forest with "a large deep river" that they named "Río de la Santísima Trinidad."[4] The Spanish quickly learned that the river, like the tripartite deity of the Christian faith, had multiple personalities that changed regularly. Returning to the Trinity two weeks after naming it, they found it swollen with floodwaters, like the French group before them. They waited for the flood to recede. It did not. Several days later, left with few other options, they built a raft and eventually crossed.

The western edge of Caddo settlement abutted the middle stretches of the Trinity, but the Caddo people's influence flowed wherever the river ran. Shards of Caddo pottery have been found on the open plains on the uppermost reaches of the river, evidence of trade with other tribes. On the larger rivers in their territory, the Caddo traveled and traded on dugout canoes—a seven-hundred-year-old example, some thirty feet long, has been found in the banks of the Red River, another Caddo river.[5] Only the bald cypress—that is, the *teja*—had the size and water resistance to make these boats.[6]

***Between the late seventeenth century*** and the early nineteenth century, the Trinity was a central, disruptive character in a Texas drama. While France and Spain—and later Mexico and the United States—have taken most of

Figure 1.1. Alexander de Batz, *Desseins de Sauvages de Plusieurs Nations*, 1735. The painting depicts New Orleans; on the far right is an Ishāk man. Gift of the Estate of Belle J. Bushnell, 1941. Courtesy of the Peabody Museum of Archaeology and Ethnology, Harvard University, 41-72-10/20.

historians' attention, this story includes multiple, evolving Native nations. The river was a vital trading route and resource for its Native inhabitants. It was not a question of how successfully they resisted European colonizers but of which Native groups held power and how they used it. Natives' success rested on their embrace of a fluidity that enabled adaptation in a rapidly changing world.

On the far right of a 1735 French painting of New Orleans, a man stands tall with a black tattoo down the middle of his face (fig. 1.1). In one hand he holds a large feathered calumet, or peace pipe, and in the other, a plain pipe for personal use.[7] In block letters, the painting identifies him as Atapakas. The Atapaka tribes—or Ishāk, as they call themselves, meaning "people"—lived in the watery region that spanned from the west side of the Mississippi River to present-day Houston. The Trinity has been home to two distinct bands of the westernmost Ishāk: the Orkokisak ("Trinity River people") on the lowest reaches of the river, and the Bidai ("brushwood," according to their Caddo neighbors) farther upriver.[8] In the era of exploration and colonization, the feathered calumet played a key role in the Trinity Ishāk tribes' diplomatic negotiations, as the Orkokisak and Bidai embraced alliances, diplomacy, and trade rather than warfare.[9]

The Orkokisak and Bidai cultures changed after Europeans arrived, but they retained sought-after knowledge of their wet homelands. The Trinity may have been a new world for many entering it, but the Orkokisak and Bidai knew its crossing points, fishing holes, and traps and dangers. They knew the river intimately, and they leveraged that knowledge. And to know the river gave them power over the relatively clueless Europeans.

Take the alligator, for example, which has historically thrived on the Trinity. Spanish explorers called this terrifying creature "the lizard." Alligators can grow to an enormous size, like the fourteen-foot alligator captured in the Trinity floodplain in 2016. They draw deep breaths into their cavernous bodies, which can be heard from quite some distance away. To the Orkokisak, these predators were a resource. Not only did the alligators provide meat, but their grease repelled mosquitoes, which carried diseases like malaria following the arrival of Europeans.[10]

Spanish colonists, other tribes, and—much to the consternation of the Spanish colonial officials—French traders bartered with the Orkokisak on the Trinity. One such Frenchman was Joseph Blancpain, who had set up a trading post among the eastern Ishāk before arriving on the Trinity in 1754. His operation there proved short-lived; he was arrested on the Trinity riverbanks by the Spanish government, skittish about French incursions into its claimed territories. And Blancpain's wares, which included seventeen guns, four barrels of powder, twelve dozen knives, and thirteen hundred powder horns, gave those officials further cause for alarm.[11] The Spanish worried that weapons like these could be used against them by Native foes. And so they seized them, together with their Native allies, who claimed several canoes tied up along the Trinity.

When the Spanish carried Blancpain away, some Native people tried to prevent his arrest, but Blancpain, speaking Ishākkoy, told them to let him go. He misjudged how quickly he could resolve this dispute and return to his life as a trader, though; sent to a prison in Mexico City, Blancpain died in suffering that winter. He had not been alone, either; his party included two enslaved Black men. They also languished in the jail until the authorities sent them on the ship *La América* to Spain, where they spent the rest of their lives imprisoned in a dungeon.[12]

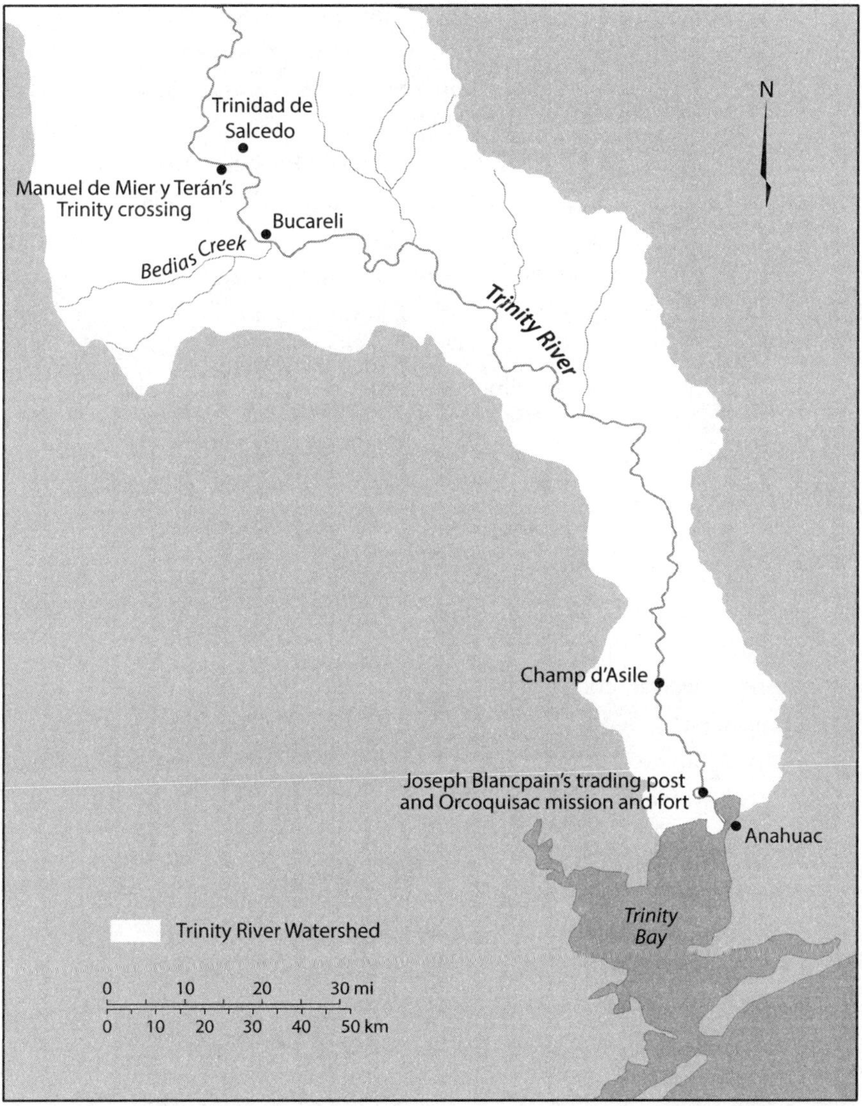


A colonial-era map of the Trinity River.

This was the beginning of a pattern. French incursions threatened Spain's tenuous grasp on the territory. The Spanish were already unsure of the strength of their Native alliances, and a French post on the Trinity would cut the Spaniards off from their missions in East Texas. Despite the instability, the Trinity was a logical trading post for the Spanish: Rather than continue building settlements only for the purposes of dealing with "infidels," as one official put it, they should invest in their first "seaport" to export their products.[13]

And so the Spanish founded Mission Nuestra Señora de la Luz del Orcoquisac (Our Lady of the Light of the Orkokisak) and an adjoining military fort near Blancpain's trading post. The two friars of the mission struggled to connect with the Orkokisak while enduring dysentery and a plague of flies, ants, and mosquitoes, and both died before the next year was out. A hurricane did not improve the site's prospects. A visiting Spanish official reported that its inhabitants subsisted on wild foods and deemed it "useless."[14] Shortly thereafter, the Spanish abandoned the site and the Trinity.

But only for a short while. The Spanish returned three years later in 1774 to the river that had defeated them, in part to monitor a handful of Anglos coming in from the British colonies far to the east. The new but poorly equipped outpost of Nuestra Señora del Pilar de Bucareli neighbored the Bidai Ishāk (for whom nearby Bedias Creek is named) and included several cannon that no one knew how to operate. While Bucareli had a primitive chapel for Spanish settlers and Native converts, the Bidai would ultimately be the Spanish colonists' saving grace. Bidai knowledge of the Trinity was crucial after the colonists lost their corn crop to a flood in the first year. The Bidai taught them to plant on the opposite side of the river where it was higher, enabling a successful harvest.[15]

The Bidai's position on the Trinity was a key node in a larger trading network. French traders like the unfortunate Blancpain brought goods and guns to the Trinity that the Bidai traded farther west with the Lipan Apache—enemies of Spain—in exchange for horses. Diseases, sometimes devastating, came with trading.[16] In late 1777, a smallpox epidemic that had begun during the 1775 outbreak of the American Revolution in Boston reached New Orleans and then quickly spread through these well-worn paths to the Trinity.[17] The Bidai experienced catastrophic losses. Bucareli officials estimated that half of the Bidai died during the outbreak.[18]

Smallpox hurt the tiny Spanish colony, but it would be the Comanche that brought them closest to ruin. The Comanche had fought and raided the Spanish and other tribes since the early 1700s. They had quickly established military supremacy, shooting muskets from the backs of Spanish horses, which they rode with an unsurpassed level of skill.[19] By the 1770s the Comanche had arrived at the upper Trinity, including what is now Fort Worth, from their more western and northern territory. Like the Spanish, the Comanche referred to the river in threes, albeit for different reasons. The tribe named the river Pih-heet Pah-e-hoona, which translates to "three rivers"—the three most prominent forks of the upper Trinity.[20] Texas's northern plains, more conducive to the Comanche people's mounted strategies for buffalo hunting and raiding rival settlements, formed the core of their territory rather than the denser wooded environment of the middle and lower Trinity. But Bucareli happened to be located adjacent to a prairie that broke up the forests—what one Spaniard described as "a spacious plain bathed by the voluminous Trinity River."[21] In the spring of 1778—as peace negotiations were set to begin between the Spanish and the Comanche—Bucareli residents mistakenly fired at a party of the Natives. In retaliation, the Comanche raided across the region, with their greatest wrath directed at Bucareli.[22] That fall, the tribe effortlessly seized most of the horses and cattle grazing in the adjacent prairie. Afterward, the Bucareli settlers grew so afraid of the Comanche that they refused to leave their homes to tend to crops or go fishing and hunting.[23] Starvation followed, and so did the end of Bucareli. Most of the Spanish left that winter in such a reckless hurry that they accidentally burned down half the town's structures.

What fire did not accomplish, the Trinity finished. That year, the river experienced its first major flooding since the founding of Bucareli. The buildings spared by fire were covered with muddy water, and horses and cattle drowned. Separated by the floodwaters, it took days for Bucareli's remaining soldiers and families to reunite as a single group. As they gathered, the Comanche returned, seizing the last of the surviving livestock and killing six Spanish-allied Native Americans. The Spanish hurried across the swollen Trinity in canoes. They did not look back.[24] Abandoned by its stewards, Bucareli washed away, any evidence of its existence carried away by the Trinity.

Bucareli's only archaeological clue reveals the layers of history on the Trinity. In the 1960s a rusted musket was discovered not by an archaeologist but by an inmate at Texas's Eastham Prison, on the opposite, eastern side of the river from where Bucareli stood. In colonial Texas, guns were highly valuable objects—if this weapon had been dropped in combat, it is likely that it would have been recovered by one side or the other. But if instead it was dropped as an act of desperation, weighing down its owner frantically wading through the bottomlands, then it could have been left behind, lost for nearly three centuries.[25]

Defeated after Bucareli, the Spanish officially withdrew from their territory along the Trinity. In their absence, traders seized the opportunity to operate without oversight. The Bidai, reduced by smallpox and Comanche attacks, also remained. In the aftermath of the devastation, they had to find new ways to rebuild. Sustaining themselves with the same trade routes that had brought them smallpox, they intermarried with other tribes.[26]

In the early nineteenth century, the Spanish returned to the Trinity once more. Like the last time, illness and floods continued to challenge them. At Trinidad de Salcedo, on the opposite bank from Bucareli, the Spanish tried to police the contraband trade and prevent unauthorized settlers. When the American explorer Zebulon Pike passed through Trinidad in 1807, he met a number of Black freedom seekers, Frenchmen, and Irishmen. Meanwhile, about a hundred Spanish soldiers were "all sick, one scarcely able to assist the other."[27] Six years later, during the Mexican War of Independence, a Spanish lieutenant colonel pursued rebels to Trinidad. Over several days he executed at least seventy-one men before burning the town to the ground.[28] And so once again the region's population of any non-Native groups dwindled to next to nil.

***All migrants encountered the Trinity*** as something novel, a densely vegetated and usually wet world. The flooded Trinity, several miles wide, makes an imposing border, but even in dry times it divides ecological regions. Along much of its length, there are entirely different landscapes and climate zones across opposite sides of the bottomlands. The differences could be stark for newcomers: For travelers arriving at the lower half of the Trinity from the east, the opposite side of the river might have been the first time they would have seen open country. This meant that staying on one side or the other of the Trinity offered different groups more or less familiarity and safety. And it also meant that the river's ecological diversity made it a meeting place for different cultures.

In the late eighteenth century, the Bidai encountered an additional wave of Native people who, unlike the Spanish, would remain on the Trinity. Following their 1763 defeat alongside their French allies in the Seven Years' War, the Alabama and Coushatta tribes of the Upper Creek Confederacy migrated west from present-day Alabama. Within three decades, some Coushatta lived along the Trinity River, with most arriving a decade later in the aftermath of

Figure 1.2. Ambroise Louis Garneray, *1ère Vue d'Aigleville, Colonie du Texas ou Champ d'Asile*, 1820. This is a romanticized illustration of the short-lived Champ d'Asile colony on the Trinity, with no evidence of the Native people the French colonists depended on. Aquatint and etching with applied watercolor, $9\frac{3}{8} \times 13\frac{9}{16}$ in. Amon Carter Museum of American Art, Fort Worth, Texas, 1968.46.

the 1803 Louisiana Purchase, having negotiated their resettlement with the Spanish governor of Texas. The Coushatta chose the Trinity in part because it resembled the Alabama woodlands that they had long known; just fifty miles farther west, they would have encountered a drier, more open landscape.[29] For the Coushatta, Spanish Texas offered refuge from the United States' slave-economy-driven expansionism.[30] Even though the region was ecologically similar to the American Southeast, it was not yet home to a rapidly growing system of plantation slavery.

It was a successful migration, in large part due to its fortunate timing. The Coushatta arrived when the Bidai were recovering from depopulation and open to forging links with other tribes. Intermarriage between the Bidai and Coushatta facilitated a transfer of knowledge about the Trinity and the Bidai's expansive and evolving trade networks. The Coushatta traded south down the Trinity to the Gulf of Mexico in Galveston and on paths to the east and west to places like San Antonio.[31] They learned the foodways of the Trinity, fishing in the oxbow lakes, gathering turtle eggs from sandbars, and hunting bears in the dense woods. The Coushatta used the Trinity as a source of power over the Spanish, whose inability to settle on the river meant the Coushatta could sell their services as vital correspondents.

That was exactly what happened in 1818, when the Coushatta alerted the Spanish to a new French colony on the lower Trinity called Champ d'Asile, meaning "Field of Asylum." French colonists, veterans of the Napoleonic wars, built over twenty wooden structures along the river for their hundred-plus adventurers. The location was chosen because it was, in the words of one historian, "a no man's land" contested by Native people, the French, the Spanish, and the United States.[32] In reality, though, it was Native land, and the French quickly discovered why waves of European settlers had failed in previous colonizing efforts and abandoned the Trinity. Mostly made up of Bonapartist military officers, the colonists were more prepared for battle with the Spanish than for long-term survival. Like so many of the European visitors before them, they suffered through the hot, humid, pestilential weather of a Texas bottomland summer, all while depending on aid from the Coushatta.[33] Facing a Spanish blockade, the adventurers returned to Galveston in July and, after enduring a hurricane, left for New Orleans. They had lasted only six months.[34]

## CHAPTER 2

# FLOODED EMPIRES

Though the French colony of Champ d'Asile failed on the Trinity, it underlined the urgency for clearly defined borders between Spanish and United States territories in the years after the Louisiana Purchase.[1] And so in February 1819, the United States and Spain signed the Adams–Onís Treaty, named for US Secretary of State John Quincy Adams and Spanish Ambassador Luis de Onís, setting the border between Spanish Texas and the United States at the Sabine River, east of the Trinity.[2] The Adams–Onís Treaty meant the Trinity now unambiguously flowed through Spanish Texas, yet the river would continue to interfere with the goals of whichever empire claimed to control it.

While Manuel de Mier y Terán's impressive career began under the flag of the Spanish Empire, his life-defining accomplishments, including a survey stemming from the Adams–Onís Treaty, would be under the flag of a newly independent Mexico. Handsome and intelligent, Terán began his upward trajectory at birth in 1789. A graduate of the College of Mines in Mexico City, he played a key role in defeating the Spanish in the Mexican War of Independence. He later served in the Congress of Mexico and then as minister of war and obtained the title of brigadier general. The war had postponed an expedition meant to study the new boundary between Texas—now the territory of Mexico—and the United States. But after the end of hostilities, the Mexican government appointed General Terán to survey the boundary and to report back on the extent of both Native and Anglo settlement in

Texas. The proximate cause for concern: a botched attempt at rebellion near the border. It was a glorious opportunity for the general, who had thus far experienced few professional setbacks.[3]

Terán believed that the Trinity was the linchpin to maintaining control of the province of Texas. That control, he believed, was slipping away, in part owing to the mistakes of what he called "the mindless Spanish government." Shortly before his expedition's departure, he drafted a letter blaming Spanish idiocy for severely constraining the population of Hispanic residents (called Tejanos) in Texas. The massacre of the revolutionaries at Trinidad de Salcedo on the Trinity River had not helped matters in this regard, he added. Meanwhile, a ceaseless flow of Anglo settlers, Black enslaved people, and displaced Native tribes was arriving in Texas. Suspending "settlement by North Americans" and implementing Mexico's own plantation economy by sending five thousand Yucatán settlers to the Trinity would be "the greatest and most beneficial enterprise for the [Mexican] federation." Terán offered to dedicate himself to this task. Mindful of his boldness, however, he never sent this letter to its intended recipient—President Guadalupe Victoria.[4]

On his survey expedition, the setbacks began almost immediately. By the time Terán and his party reached the western bank of the Trinity on May 25, 1828, they had already been delayed crossing high water on the Brazos River to the west, but at the Trinity he saw the river had transformed into "a sizable lake."[5] Jean Louis Berlandier, a French naturalist accompanying Terán, noted their poor timing, since the Trinity was known to overflow every May or June.[6] The expedition stalled; there was no way for the wagons to cross the strong current. For a naturalist like Berlandier, this delay was at first a gift: He could linger among the banks, studying the "many nut trees, oaks, maples, elms, and pines." But before long, the mosquitoes that swarmed the bottomlands had proved more than a nuisance, and several members of the group, including Terán, were ill. So was Berlandier, who in the throes of illness came to view the river differently. "All the simplest natural phenomena, which I had always seen in the wilderness as majestic, appeared to me there much more disagreeable," he grumbled.[7]

Following three days on the riverbank, Terán realized the Trinity had foiled his plans for a thorough survey. He sent back most of the expedition, including Berlandier and the wagon of scientific instruments. Berlandier would never return to the Trinity; years later he died attempting to cross another river, possibly with some sense of his regret for having turned around at the Trinity. Terán, meanwhile, continued east on horseback with a much smaller force. Jettisoning so much of his expedition meant Mexico's ownership of the land beyond the Trinity would be much more tenuous. Given his engineering background, Terán understood that knowledge is power. With fewer instruments, the maps and surveys lost precision, and without a naturalist who could identify plant and wildlife species, the expedition could not accurately catalog them. Terán would have to return to Mexico City with less information than he had hoped to bring for his country through which it could claim the land.[8]

Terán and his diminished party finally crossed the main channel on a flatboat. Then, because the craft could not pass through the trees, they transferred to a small canoe and paddled "through a flooded forest." The men dodged falling trees, crossed a flooded prairie, and then remounted their horses to travel through another flooded prairie.[9] Of the approximately ten miles they traveled, Terán estimated "only about a sixth of it is free from floodwaters." At its worst, the river's peculiar flooding patterns made it impossible to choose one method of transit, particularly when the river was "half flooded and there is not sufficient water to handle the boat, but too much to travel on horseback or in wagons." The bottomlands could become fully submerged or almost dry, but the muddy in-between made travel the most difficult. Terán and his men—wet, muddy, and trembling with exhaustion—had encountered no enemy except the Trinity itself. Eventually, the general did cross the river. But his struggles did not bode well for his government's ability to police borders or quell unrest beyond the treacherous river.[10]

Terán returned to the Trinity that winter, learning about the river and eating bear and deer with Alabama and Coushatta guides. After staying at a Coushatta village on the Trinity for several days, he discovered a home encircled by floodwaters, concealing it and its denizen from the world beyond. Concealment, claimed Terán, was exactly the intent of this migrant from the United States who surrounded himself with the Trinity's forest and floodwaters because he was an evil thief who had "sought this lair to hide what he steals."[11] Such a location enabled privacy and protection from outsiders unfamiliar with the Trinity's bottomlands and, if Terán is to be believed, from the law, too. It was an instructive example; the more he learned, the more it seemed the Trinity was destined to hinder the Mexican government's ability to quantify, control, and tax those living along its banks.

Near the mouth of the Trinity, Terán discovered more settlers from the United States—a colony, he noted, that had "been created without the authorities' knowledge."[12] But a lack of proper authorization had done nothing to stop the Anglo settlers from importing slaves and raising cattle and sugarcane. This was an unhappy discovery for Terán, but he understood how it had come to be: The devastation from the Mexican War for Independence, Native foes (especially the Comanche), and limited control of rivers like the Trinity had weakened the Mexican government in the province of Texas.

When the first American settlers—the authorized kind, that is—arrived from the United States in the early 1820s under empresario Stephen F. Austin, they settled between the two major rivers directly west of the Trinity. The colony between the Brazos and the Colorado included several cotton plantations, the largest holding ninety slaves. But the Trinity, conspicuously, was not where Austin's group settled. Shortly after Stephen's father, Moses, gained initial approval for the colony, he, along with Richmond, an enslaved man, were attacked by a panther on the Trinity. When Stephen carried on his father's legacy, he had no desire to become further mired in the Trinity.[13] And so with no Mexico-approved colonies, the Trinity was settled not by formal processes but by chaotic, dangerous settlements like the one Terán had found at the mouth of the Trinity.[14]

Terán crossed the river for the last time in 1829, relying on a local settler to ferry him across.[15] Though he would not return, the Trinity continued to torment him. The failure of his survey complicated Mexico's efforts to govern Texas, and the river's behavior made monitoring and controlling the trade that took place on its waters difficult, if not impossible. The Mexican government established a customs fort on the Trinity to prevent smuggling among the growing population living along its banks. In November 1831, Terán arrived in Galveston and ordered the fort moved downriver to Anahuac, at the Trinity's mouth, where a customs collector would collect duties from boats on the Trinity and Brazos.

Settlers and merchants were outraged by these new tariffs—and by the Mexican government's more enlightened attitude regarding slavery. The matter came to a head in 1831, when Juan Davis Bradburn, commander of the Anahuac garrison, accepted two Black men who had fled a Louisiana plantation. Slavery was technically illegal in Mexico, but Anglo settlers were allowed to import slaves as long as they were referred to as "indentured servants" rather than as slaves. In this case, Bradburn granted the men asylum, rebuffing slave catchers' efforts to return them to Louisiana. In May of the following year, their former slaveholder hired two local lawyers to help recapture them. One of the lawyers was William Travis, who would achieve more fame as the commander who died at the Alamo. Travis tried to fool Bradburn by claiming a large militia force was marching from Louisiana to re-enslave the runaways.[16] In response, Bradburn had both of the lawyers arrested.

The arrests caused an uproar and led to an insurrection of Anglo-Americans in Mexican Texas, which started on the Trinity and spread to the Brazos.[17] This uprising, known as the Anahuac Disturbances, preceded the Texas Revolution by three years and resulted in several major clashes, including the Battle of Velasco, at which more than ten people died.[18] One week later, Terán feared the loss of "the northern provinces." The Trinity had thwarted his plans for a complete survey, and now the migrants living along it threatened to rise as their own nation. It was too much for the depressed general. The morning after his prediction, Terán ended his own life by impaling himself on his sword.[19]

***Unlike Spain and then Mexico,*** knowledge of and adaptation to the Trinity had empowered Native tribes. The border between Mexico and the United States seemed to offer protection from the expansion of cotton plantations in the Deep South. Yet one moment in this early history of the Trinity foreshadowed how a similar proliferation might eventually occur in Texas: At the site of the doomed Bucareli settlement, where the Bidai showed Spanish settlers the safe side of the river to grow their crops, the settlers had experimented with sowing a few cotton seeds. The cotton plants grew very well, surprising the Spanish.[20] For slaveholders moving west in the early 1800s, this would not have been a surprise. Native tribes like the Coushatta had arrived on the Trinity at the perfect time to increase their leverage over the first anemic waves of settlers, but soon they would have to use their skills to survive the westward march of the cotton frontier.

The expansion of slavery on the Trinity created new political instability in Texas. The river that had thwarted empires became a lure to planters looking to exploit accessible and fertile soil within a weakened Mexico. When global cotton prices rose in the 1830s and the reward finally outweighed the risk, thousands of Anglo settlers, including many slaveholders, came to northern Mexico, concentrating along the region's river valleys. The Trinity, which had long vexed settlers, suddenly became a promising navigation route and farmland ready for development. The proslavery newcomers were hostile to Mexico's position on the matter, and the pressure built to the point of rebellion. Though the goal of the Texas Revolution—to become a semiautonomous state or an independent nation—was not clear at first, the rebels agreed that whatever law was established should protect their right to property in slaves.[21]

Slaveholders rebelled to strengthen this right, but the disruption created by the Texas Revolution initially weakened their control over enslaved people.

The rebel commandant of Galveston Island fretted about the possibility of a slave insurrection on the Trinity. "The negroes high upon the Trinity," he wrote in March 1836, "have manifested a disposition to become troublesome & in some instances *daring*." The slaveholders killed one enslaved man and whipped another. But that was not a sufficient response, according to the worried commandant; troops needed to be deployed to stabilize the situation.[22] Even though slavery had been one of the primary causes of the Texas Revolution, every reapportionment of resources to maintain control over slaves meant fewer resources to fight the Mexican government.[23] Worse for the rebellion, concern was rising over a possible alliance of enslaved people and the Coushatta that could open another front.[24] Even if the rebels could acquire more guns and soldiers, the Coushatta people's intimate knowledge of the Trinity bottomlands would have given the rumored alliance an advantage over the overextended Texan forces.

In reality, the Coushatta negotiated neutrality with both sides of the conflict and a guarantee to the land already granted to them by the Mexican government.[25] Despite rebels' initial fears of the Coushatta during the Texas Revolution, families fleeing Santa Anna—the general and former Mexican president leading the troops—found the Coushatta to be invaluable allies. Following General Sam Houston's decision to retreat from central Texas in March 1836, a mass exodus of settlers, later labeled the Runaway Scrape, streamed out of the Colorado and Brazos River Valleys and headed east toward the safety of the US border. Reports of massacres at Goliad and the Alamo increased Anglos' fears that they would be next. As the first major river after the Brazos, the Trinity would have provided safety if the refugees could have made it to the eastern bank. Unfortunately, the river had begun flooding; rather than a more manageable one hundred to two hundred feet wide when below flood stage, they saw a five-mile-wide stream.[26]

Just as the Trinity had delayed Terán's expedition eight years earlier, it threatened the safe passage of the Runaway Scrape refugees. Memories of the Spanish officer who had massacred over seventy Tejano rebels on the flooding Trinity at Trinidad de Salcedo in the Mexican War for Independence two decades earlier heightened the stakes even more. On the banks of the Trinity, the secretary of state of the newly minted Texas Republic reached the point where he did, finally, "despond."[27] Refugees hurried to the Trinity's western bank only to find themselves stuck and vulnerable. The ferry could carry them and their belongings across the river, but service was first come, first served, and they would have to wait up to a week on the unprotected western bank for their turn.[28] An outbreak of disease led the ferrymen to prioritize families with sick children. One young woman accompanying her sick sister jumped to the head of the line, but her terror did not end once she boarded the ferry. Her family spent "several hours surrounded by water," and it took eight men to direct the boat through the treacherous floodwaters. The men struggled against the strong current and the dense forest of trees and briars that slowed their passage. As this woman later wrote, "The horrors of crossing the Trinity, are beyond my power to describe." Meanwhile, another five hundred people remained on the west bank waiting for their turn to cross.[29]

Other families caught in the Runaway Scrape followed Native trails like Long King's Trace seeking help from the Coushatta. When the tribespeople, led by Chief Colita, found the refugees, the Trinity was "a wide and muddy barrier between Texans and the territory they considered a haven. . . . The heavy, rich black land of the bottoms was a veritable mire." The Coushatta rode to the western bank to lend their aid, felled trees and tied them to the settlers' wagons so that they could float across, and guided them through the flooded woodlands to dry land.[30] Shortly thereafter, the Texas Revolution ended swiftly in the nearby Battle of San Jacinto on April 21, 1836. A messenger paddled across the Trinity in a canoe to tell the refugees that Texas had won its independence.

Many of the leaders of the Texas Revolution remembered the aid from the Coushatta during the nadir of the rebellion and attempted to repay the people's generosity. But theirs were not to be the voices that carried the day. Instead, land-hungry Anglos who cared little for the recent past used their newfound independence to displace the Coushatta by taking their land.[31] In 1839, three years after the Runaway Scrape, settlers killed five Coushatta, leading many of the tribe to abandon their homes. Chief Colita wrote to Mirabeau Lamar, president of the Republic of Texas, to protest. "Times was, when we could have driven the White man off—but we were their Friends and did not want to hurt the White man." He wanted assurances that "I will live here till I die which cannot be long and I want to know what is to become of my people."[32]

Previously, Lamar had waged a war of extermination and displacement against virtually every other tribe in Texas, but in this instance, he changed tack and admonished the greedy settlers.[33] The memory of the aid provided by the Coushatta and the gratitude it engendered among the saved settlers was powerful. Going further at Lamar's behest, the Texas Congress passed a law for the creation of a reservation for the Coushatta and Alabama tribes the next year.[34]

Unfortunately, the Coushatta would be betrayed once more, this time by the Trinity. While the tribe's ability to navigate the river had helped them avoid the Texas government's policy of annihilation, destructive floods made it impossible for the reservation lands proposed by the government to be mapped out. "I selected the lands intended for the Indian," the exasperated Indian agent appointed by the Texas Congress to conduct the survey wrote, "but owing to the high waters at the time, we could then procede [*sic*] no farther."[35] And so they did not. By the time the mapping was completed, all the reservation land had been claimed by Anglo settlers. This was the second time the Coushatta had appealed to governments to affirm their right to the land. In the 1830s, the Coushatta had been in the process of receiving a land grant from the Mexican government, but Manuel de Mier y Terán's untimely death, partly due to the frustrations wrought by the Trinity, unraveled that plan.[36]

Many of the Coushatta stayed on the river even after the planter Alexander Hamilton Washington usurped their land in 1840 and refused a Texas official's order to return it. While enslaved people worked most of the plantation, the Coushatta continued to live on the east bank, growing corn, peas, and potatoes.[37] Steamboat operators on the Trinity referred to Washington's plantation as "Shirt-tail Bend" because of the long deerskin shirts the Coushatta wore that "looked like shirt-tails flapping in the breeze."[38] Though the Coushatta were unable to retain legal ownership over any of their river land, they, along with the Alabama tribe, eventually obtained land twenty miles to the east of the Trinity—the only Texas reservation created in the nineteenth century that still exists today.[39]

# CHAPTER 3

# THE MOAT

Summer, 1848. Several miles downstream from Shirt-tail Bend, Thomas, Charles, and Goodwin were building a road along a bluff on the Trinity River and sweating in the humid Texas heat. The men were enslaved, each from one of three nearby plantations, and had been impressed into service on the county road crew under the watch of an overseer. Each had been brought to Texas by migrant slaveholders, coming from places like Mississippi or North Carolina.[1] Earlier that year, the United States and Mexico had signed a treaty to end the Mexican-American War, closing another chapter in the westward expansion of the United States. But Thomas, Charles, and Goodwin looked east, toward the loved ones they had been forced to leave behind, longing for a more familiar world than this plantation frontier.

To go home, they first had to cross the Trinity. The record is unclear about what happened next. Perhaps Thomas, the oldest at twenty-five, led the way, waiting until the overseer's back was turned before jumping into the turbid waters, Charles and Goodwin close behind. Escaping together would improve their chances. In summer, the river channel narrows but maintains a strong current. Did they hold hands or take their chances on their own? Either way, they all went under, drowning in the same brown water they'd hoped to cross toward freedom and family.

Word spread quickly to all Native, enslaved, and slaveholding residents on the river: Thomas, Charles, and Goodwin, working on the county road crew, had drowned in the Trinity. On the three plantations where they lived, their friends and what family had been brought to Texas with them suffered a devastating loss. But there was a wider message for all recently arrived slaves: Whether they dreamed of heading west to freedom beyond the Mexican border, where slavery was outlawed, or east to their homes and families, rivers like the Trinity were the moats around their plantation prisons.

Three years after their deaths, Thomas, Charles, and Goodwin's former slaveholders petitioned the Texas legislature for compensation, despite their wealth made manifest in thousands of acres near the Trinity and at least eighty-five surviving slaves.[2] The petitioners valued the three men as property worth between $800 and $900 and claimed that the state constitution entitled them to government funding. They argued the county had taken these men without remuneration, only for them to be "accidentally (or for want of proper care and attention) drowned in the Trinity River."[3]

Just as government officials like General Manuel de Mier y Terán had been hindered by the Trinity and other Texas rivers, so were enslaved people. The deaths of Thomas, Charles, and Goodwin demonstrated the deadly consequences of trying to cross the powerful river. High water funneled freedom seekers onto ferries, where they faced a greater risk of capture.[4] Both enslavers and the enslaved understood the ways in which the Trinity served as both a barrier and a route to freedom. Across Texas, rewards for runaways sometimes varied based on the river crossed.[5] In 1854, a sheriff placed an advertisement in the *Texas State Gazette* after capturing two young men near Robbins Ferry on the Trinity River.[6] Fourteen years earlier, a planter had instructed a county surveyor to put up signs for three escaped slaves, specifying his belief that they may try to cross at Robbins Ferry, so a sign at the ferry "would be the most important."[7] In 1864, an advertisement appeared for a man named Harry who had last been spotted at a ferry on the Trinity on his way to Louisiana.[8] Given ferries' role in surveilling enslaved people, slaveholders encouraged the government to finance sentries at the state's major ferries.

In rare cases, the Trinity was a route to freedom. When the river flooded, its waters extended from the narrow channel into a wooded floodplain several miles wide, allowing travel in smaller craft without being seen by other boats or by people on the shore. Isaac "escaped from his home at the mouth of the Trinity River," taking clothing, weapons, and a boat.[9]

Enslaved people hoeing cotton and loading steamboats in the bottomlands developed a close understanding of the Trinity's unique environment and trade networks but had to weigh their familiarity with the river against their awareness of slave patrols. In the aftermath of events like the deaths of Thomas, Charles, and Goodwin, news about the river and its people traveled along a clandestine network of shared knowledge about resisting slavery.[10] This information, passed from plantation to plantation whenever the enslaved would meet, was essential.

The dangers of the river paled in comparison to those posed by the slaveholders. Mintie Miller recalled an incident from her childhood on a plantation: An eight- or nine-year-old girl swam across the Trinity to flee her enslaver. She attempted this escape in winter, and her feet froze. When the man caught her, he thawed her feet in the fire and burned them. When Miller shared this story decades later, reliving the moment when she, also a child, heard those terrible screams, her point was not to emphasize the river and cold winter but an inhumane man in an inhumane era.[11] In their minds, Trinity slaveholders could not accept the humanity of the enslaved. When a plantation mistress wrote to her son about a person named Ike fleeing her plantation, she claimed not to know why Ike had departed, declaring that he did so without any reason.[12]

The specific motivations of Goodwin, Charles, and Thomas for swimming across the river are lost to time, but the risk they took was shared by many freedom seekers who desired to reunite with their families. Even if a family had not yet been torn apart, separation remained a constant threat. For example, in his will, Goodwin's former enslaver wrote that his daughter could take four enslaved women, named Little Ginney, Emma, Sandy, and Henrietta, "into her possession at any time."[13]

Thus, in order to reunite with their families, not all who escaped from the Trinity's plantations headed far away; an untold number found ways to stay on the river. A fugitive slave advertisement for a man named Rip suggested he was heading for a river landing about ten miles downstream from the plantation he had escaped.[14] The slaveholder assumed Rip would go there because of prior escapes or family ties. Another advertisement from a plantation north of the Trinity made this assumption explicit. The pursuer wrote, "I believe that there [*sic*] intention is to go [to] the Trinity, as they have relations there."[15] Freedom held little value if it meant never seeing one's family again.[16] An advertisement from a county bordering the Trinity River described finding a deceased fugitive who had dug a hole and concealed it with wood and dirt. The structure collapsed during a heavy rainstorm and killed him. Family explained the man's decision to remain since his wife lived close to the deadly shelter.[17] With so many people enslaved along the Trinity, not everyone chose to leave the river, especially if it meant abandoning their family.

In other cases, freedom seekers were not running toward family but away from cruel overseers and slaveholders. A man named March left a Trinity River plantation, traveling hundreds of miles toward the Mexico border before being captured in Fredericksburg, Texas. An advertisement announcing his recapture reveals evidence of March's torture: The thumb and a finger on his right hand were "crippled."[18] The tormentor he fled and to whom he was forcibly returned even beat people owned by other Trinity slaveholders. Even after slavery ended, this sick man continued to attack Black people, refusing to accept emancipation. March's recapture shows how difficult it was to escape; at most five thousand freedom seekers crossed into Mexico to claim their freedom.[19] Countless examples of cruelty occurred on or near the Trinity. A steamboat clerk recalled how a slaveholder's son went duck hunting as they traveled from Galveston Bay to the Trinity. After the enslaved child paddling the skiff accidentally dropped an oar, scaring the ducks, "Young Morgan, mad, his gun ready for the ducks, deliberately emptied the load into the shoulder of the colored boy."[20]

The lack of publicized torture by some slaveholders should not be mistaken for decency. Laura Cornish described her life as one of over thirty enslaved people on a Trinity plantation owned by Isaiah Day, where they planted cotton and tended his large herd of cattle. He insisted he be called "Papa" rather than "master," a detail that has been interpreted to suggest he was benevolent toward those he enslaved.[21] On closer examination, however, he was the very embodiment of the nightmare of slavery: He was called Papa because he repeatedly raped one of the women he enslaved, Amanda Cribbs. Though he continued to treat them as legal property rather than as family, at least nine of these enslaved individuals were his children: Aaron, Francis, Theophilis, Milton, Loren, Wilena, Leana, Cora, and Henderson.[22] Like March's abuser, Day later refused to accept the end of slavery, beating Amanda Cribbs to death with a wooden bucket after she repulsed his attempts once she was a free woman.[23]

Facing a wicked work regime, enslaved people used the Trinity as a temporary refuge from the whip. Hiding nearby, even for a few hours, was a frequent tactic. An overseer discovered one close hideaway, returning the individuals and their supplies to his Trinity plantation. However, eight days later, perhaps in response to losing their hideout, two enslaved men, Bob and Gus, headed west, covering about one hundred miles of ground until they were recaptured. But undeterred, less than a week after returning to the Trinity plantation, Bob broke his chains and "fled to parts unknown."[24]

***Work on the plantation frontier*** was relentless because nearly all the wealthiest planters settled along Texas rivers. Threatened with whippings and being sold, enslaved men, women, and children labored ceaselessly, replanting crops after floods and clearing land during the winter once the cotton had been harvested. Dave Byrd recalled how his former enslaver woke him at 4:30 a.m. to begin working.[25] While scattered prairies existed around the lower Trinity, most of the bottomlands consisted of dense hardwood forest. This wooded land had to be cleared in order to grow cotton. As soon as the rush of picking season diminished, enslaved laborers went to work creating more cotton fields. One overseer had men cutting trees and women burning the brush and felled wood. On a single cold winter's day, his journal documented the labor clearing land, building ditches, and loading boats to transport goods downstream.[26] There was always work to be done on the Trinity even when the growing season had ended—in this environment, slaveholders expected an unending cycle of toil.

The Trinity's floods made fertile soil. An Englishman traveling through Texas described this pattern of plantation development and flooding. Plantations needed to grow cotton in the bottomlands since these were the richest lands. In warmer Texas, he suggested, planters had the added benefit of planting weeks earlier than in Mississippi. However, they faced greater costs in getting their cotton to New Orleans, not to mention flooding. "With the present low prices, the planter loses by his crops," he wrote, "particularly those who are near some of the rivers and whose lands are subject to overflows."[27] These lands were so fecund precisely because the floods deposited fresh sediment. This fact usually went unrecognized by Trinity planters, who wanted to reap a profit from the land but thought little about the source of its fertility or how it might be replenished in the future (since, after all, they could simply move to new lands once more as they had already done in moving to the Trinity).[28]

Floods meant extra work for those who labored on the river's plantations. In more established plantation regions elsewhere in the South, planters might construct levees to hold back floodwaters, but on the Trinity, they were too busy clearing land. One formerly enslaved man recalled how the river frequently overflowed in the spring, noting that it generally happened early enough that cotton could be replanted after the floodwaters abated.[29] Planters could accept flooding if they had time to grow another crop and profit from the enriched earth. After all, it was not the slaveholders but enslaved people who had to do the extra work of replanting.

The rapid pace of settlement now meant learning about the extent of the Trinity's floods through trial and error rather than via Native expertise. Newcomers could survey the highest bluffs and observe the mud lines on trees (the mark of past flooding) to gauge the area's propensity to flood, but other locations yielded few clues. Misjudging the landscape led to waterlogged fields and moldy homes. One traveler found a house near the Trinity that had been inundated with four feet of water, forcing the inhabitants to retreat from the river.[30]

***Until the abolition of slavery,*** the lower half of the Trinity was a key economic region in Texas, with more planters and fewer small farmers compared with the rest of East Texas. When Sally Banks Chambers remembered how her former enslaver had sought out a Trinity plantation, she explained the practical need to "find a place on the river bottom." The location was "just suited for the quantity of slaves he had."[31] The Trinity was the most promising steamboat route of all the Texas rivers. The river's connection to global cotton markets via the Gulf of Mexico, as well as its remarkable fertility, meant plantations defined life on the Trinity. However, two additional reasons also explain why there were so few small farms compared with most of East Texas: One needed money to buy the relatively expensive land, and one needed a big property to handle flooding.

Land along the Trinity cost more than most land in Texas. An economic depression caused by the Panic of 1837 led to increased immigration to the Republic of Texas because of its generous land grants and the chance to escape creditors in the United States.[32] Few of these grants were on the lower Trinity because most of that land had been claimed by private landowners; latecomers would have tough luck finding high-quality parcels "within ten miles of the river."[33] This was true across the South, where much of the best riverfront land had been claimed well before the region became part of the United States.[34]

Possession of Trinity River land depended on the wealth and political power of the planter class. Old land claims did not guarantee ownership, as Spanish land grants could be preempted by wealthier Anglo settlers with access to lawyers. In 1853, the planter and doctor Pleasant Kittrell sold 1,300 acres of Trinity land to a Mississippi planter for $6,500. Kittrell had originally cobbled the purchase together from several sellers who had squatted on undefended Spanish claims and did not actually hold title.[35] Usurping land allotted by a deposed foreign government gave enterprising speculators and early migrants the chance to get Trinity land at low cost, if money was exchanged at all. But even with this advantage, the costs of improvements and establishing legal ownership made the Trinity land more expensive than the abundant unclaimed land elsewhere in Texas. And landowners knew it: Otis Wheeler, for example, received an unsolicited offer to buy his Trinity plantation for $18,000 in 1855, but the offer left him cold. The sum would have been a fortune, but Wheeler insisted that he would sell for no less than $20,000.[36] Paying higher prices for Trinity properties meant purchasers expected greater profit from it. Their economic survival depended on their ability to simultaneously farm and improve the land, in a race to make money and protect profits before the floods came.

Most Trinity plantations had a layout that helped them minimize crop losses from drought and floods. The typical plantation stretched from the wet banks of the river channel and bottomlands into the mostly dry uplands, a gradient of moisture that decreased with elevation. The moisture held within the bottomlands persisted long after floods, nourishing crops during drought. Planters benefited from the enriched soil and slowly percolating groundwater that floods left behind, which could sustain their crops through dry summers.[37] Nearly all original Spanish land grants extended in elongated rectangles from the banks of the river. Though not as narrow as the land grants in South Texas where settlers depended on rivers for irrigation, these long grants increased the number of landowners who had access to the Trinity (see figure 3.1).[38] This layout of both bottomlands and uplands allowed planters to avoid losing an entire crop to flooding or drought by utilizing the full length of the plot. Planting in the uplands prevented flood damage, but it came with its own risks like reduced yields from less fertile soil and greater potential to suffer from drought. The lower Trinity received more than forty inches of rain annually, unevenly distributed throughout the year, with hot, dry summers often threatening the cotton crop.[39] The wetter bottoms provided planters with a hedge against Texas summers. An overseer whose cotton crop had been lost to the flooding Trinity had the opposite experience during a later drought when the crop on "low places" was fine but the upland crop "entirely ruined."[40] Smaller farmers with less varied properties were unable to diversify their plantings in the same way.

Few planters tried to prevent flooding by building levees along the Trinity.[41] Aside from the scattered prairies that broke up the woodlands along the Trinity, they had invested in clearing the land and focused on adding to their enslaved property rather than on building levees. In contrast, on the Mississippi River, planters built substantial levees to protect their investments in the land and the people who worked it.[42] Yet on the Trinity, the planters spread

TRINITY CO.
A. G. Van Fradelles.
E. Clements
R. Barrow
Thomas Cartwright
Writts.
Geo. Smith.
Polly Ryan 1. 153 ptd.
M. de Lejarza by Pierre Blanchet
A. M. de Lejarza by Pierre Blanchet T. July 5/34. B. 39. P. 1036.
R. Lynch 1- 141. ptd.
J. Johnson
John Burges.
Esther Clark.
Michael Chavenne.
M. Garcia.
G. Hodges.
C. Devore.
G. W. Miles.
J. Ratliff. T. June 30/35 B. 20. P. 71.
Thomas Burrus. T. Febr. 5/35 B. 20. P. 143.
James Smith.
Ann D. Criswell. T. March 28/35. B. 20. P. 225.
Daniel Wilburn. T. June 2/35. B. 20. P. 651.
Jno. Lindsey. T. March 18/35. B. 20. P. 143.
J. D. Burks.
M. L. Choate.
William Johns.
J. Bland.
LIVINGSTON
Morgan.
Thomas Stubblefield.
John T. Pinkney. T. April 30/35. B. 21. P. 247.
SWARTWOUT.
T. Bradley.
William Pace. T. May 3/35. B. 20. P. 375.
J. D. Thomas.
Isaac Parker.
J. M. Dikes.
H. B. Prentiss agent for AUGUSTINE VI
AUGUSTINE VIESCA
J. S. Garner
William Beasley
Calvin Barco
TRINITY RIVER.
SAN JACINTO CO.
Long King Cr.
n No 101)

their crops over areas more or less prone to flooding and took their chances; having the ability to plant in both bottomlands and uplands would not have been an option along the Mississippi, with its much larger floodplain. Ultimately, the decision to avoid confronting the Trinity through levees may have saved planters from greater losses, since later efforts to successfully construct them often failed. The planter Otis Wheeler wrote his mother, "We always start a crop in hope sometimes end in dispair."[43]

On the Trinity, landowners made few efforts to control the landscape, and when slavery ended, there were few levees for the river to erode; instead, the river would continue to flood the same fields it had before the Civil War, a fact that would have serious consequences for freedpeople. While Trinity planters did not embrace the flooding, they could recognize that growing cotton—or rather, having their slaves grow cotton—required them to do so "with patient perseverance."[44]

***For planters,*** access to the bottomlands provided a major source of wild and semiwild foods, especially fish, hogs, and cattle. Depending on where one lived in the South, the laws and customs differed regarding the open range, where livestock and hunters could legally roam across property lines. Places like Virginia, with a longer history of plantation slavery, sometimes placed limits on free-range grazing. Meanwhile, on the Texas plantation frontier it was essential.[45] Compared with most places east of Texas, the Trinity was relatively isolated, with fewer opportunities to purchase foodstuffs, making its abundant supply of animals all the more important.

Hunting, fishing, and herding were other forms of work for the Trinity's enslaved population. Dave Byrd, who described rising at 4:30 every morning to work, received much of his sustenance from rabbits, deer, and lots of fish.[46] Byrd's brother credited the abundance to the Trinity directly: "We always had plenty [of] fish on the table as we lived close to the river and it was not any trouble to get all the fish we wanted."[47] Between the fish, wild game, and pecans—not to mention the corn and livestock—the bottomlands provided a substantial portion of the food for both free and enslaved residents. Hogs were everywhere, fattening themselves on the vast acorn crops and anything else they could consume. Frederick Law Olmsted, who reported

Figure 3.1. An 1871 map of Polk County illustrating the contrast between the lengthy rectangles along the Trinity and the square plots in the rest of the county. Polk County 1871, #3957, General Map Collection, Archives and Records Program, Texas General Land Office, Austin.

for the *New York Daily Times* on slavery in the South before making his career designing Central Park, called the hogs on the Trinity "dirty persecutors," setting up his tent inside a fence to protect himself.[48]

Otis Wheeler used the river as a place to keep his livestock. Writing to his mother in Lincoln, Massachusetts, he described a place he named Hog Rancho on the banks of the Trinity where an elderly enslaved man tended to hundreds of hogs, sheep, and horses. The fact that an enslaved man labored solely in tending to Wheeler's livestock illustrates the bottomlands' extensive uses beyond cotton production. Sustenance also came from the river channel itself. Wheeler continued to explain how he kept all his fishing supplies at Hog Rancho, and "if we want fish or turtle it is only to send a little Negro at night & he returns in the morning with a horse packed."[49]

In some cases, livestock provided additional income alongside cotton production. At the Day plantation, Isaiah Day owned 1,500 cattle and 4,500 unimproved acres. Henderson Day, Isaiah's enslaved son, later testified that he worked with these cattle "from the time he was large enough to sit on a horse." Henderson Day's testimony was pivotal in a court case regarding the Trinity River that reached the Texas Supreme Court. His story highlights how the plantation frontier was changing. Born in 1853, he had not been marched there from some other part of the United States but was part of a second generation born on the Trinity. His familiarity with the river bottom could empower him only so much before emancipation, but learning to read such a wild landscape gave Day a crucial set of skills in a place often feared and avoided by newcomers. Living upriver from Henderson, Dave Byrd made this point more directly: He was not allowed "to learn how to read or write." But despite rules requiring passes for enslaved people to travel between the Trinity plantations, he was one of many whose knowledge of the landscape allowed him to "slip off," even if he was almost caught one time.[50]

The work performed by enslaved laborers contrasted with the leisure of the planters. Plantation mistress Elizabeth Gaines Smith expected her enslaved workers to gather the fruits the bottomlands provided. Large pecan trees grew in the Trinity River bottoms and provided a source of food for the plantation. She described how on Sunday, typically a day of rest, "the negroes went after pecans." Meanwhile, Smith relaxed on the riverbank and perfected her fishing technique. She monitored the river levels; a rising river increases the number of bites, because fish begin feeding on whatever they find in the freshly flooded land. She caught as many as twelve fish at a time, sharing the fish with her daughter, who lived near the plantation. Though catching fish to eat may have explained part of her motivation, she also simply wanted to be close to the river—an entry for April 9, 1859, reads, "Went to the river & eat dinner on the Bank."[51]

Sometimes, Smith had no luck fishing. One such entry reveals how the worlds of free and unfree people differed. On a very cold day she "went fishing but caught nothing." Meanwhile, all her enslaved workers went to a neighboring plantation to pick cotton.[52] Smith had the luxury of enjoying the river as a place to fish and contemplate, whereas the enslaved people she possessed labored ceaselessly on the Trinity.

CHAPTER 4

# THE COTTON HIGHWAY

In the early 1800s, a transportation revolution transformed the United States: Steamboats that could travel against the current meant journeys that used to take weeks could be completed in days. Goods, people, and information moved much faster than ever before, whether on navigable rivers or on an expanding network of manmade canals. And by the 1830s, railroad construction, especially in the Northeast, took off, but Texas risked being disconnected from these swifter routes. In the South, planters near the coast relied on faster oceangoing vessels, and in the interior, many depended on the Mississippi River to ship through New Orleans. The Mississippi connected thousands of miles of navigable streams, but the network only reached the northern edge of Texas via the Red River. An 1857 map presenting the rates of travel to New York City shows how dramatically movement slowed upon reaching the Texas border (fig. 4.1). Without faster travel, Texas would fall further behind the rapid transformations that fueled the United States' rising economic power.[1]

*Early Bird*, *Lone Star*, and *Trinity Planter* were among a long list of steamboats that headed up the Trinity. Navigation had begun in the 1830s, and the boom times arrived in the 1850s, when the enslaved population in several counties abutting the Trinity grew by over 50 percent.[2] River trade had been central to the expansion of the United States since its creation, and the Trinity tied Texas into a national, and increasingly global, economy.[3] Advertisements promoting towns or counties featured the Trinity in their claims to future commercial success.[4] In Anderson County the newspaper was named the *Trinity Advocate* because of the Trinity's importance to commerce.[5] County seats miles away relied on the Trinity for trade. Merchants waited to hear the bells heralding arriving ships ready to carry thousands of cotton bales each year.[6] Boats headed upstream bringing coffee, clothing, and other staples from merchants in Galveston, New Orleans, and adjacent plantations. Captains relied on the Trinity's environment to feed their crews and fuel their boilers with thousands of cords of oak and other hardwood trees. A white crewmember described his amazement at the game-filled region on his first trip up the Trinity, where he saw lots of alligators and they regularly purchased deer to eat.[7]

The term "sold down the river" most famously applied to the Mississippi River, but this also occurred on the Trinity where men, women, and children were treated as property and separated from their families. The planter Otis Wheeler, who had shipped cotton and human beings from Texas to New Orleans to settle his debts before moving west to the Trinity, mockingly wrote to his family in New England that he lived in a "semi-barbarian

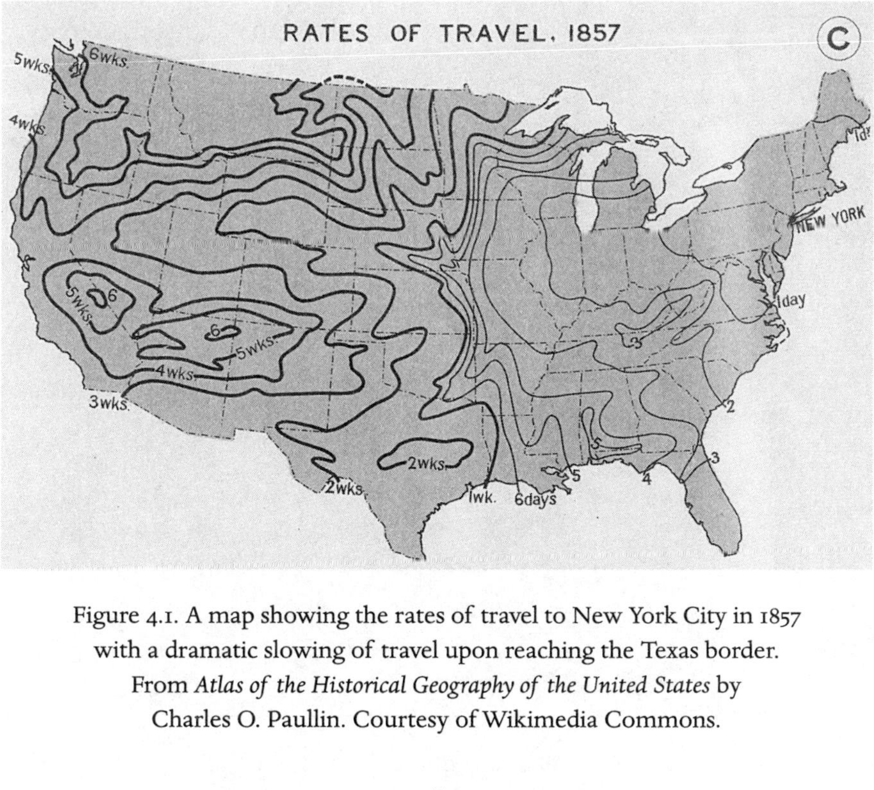


Figure 4.1. A map showing the rates of travel to New York City in 1857 with a dramatic slowing of travel upon reaching the Texas border. From *Atlas of the Historical Geography of the United States* by Charles O. Paullin. Courtesy of Wikimedia Commons.

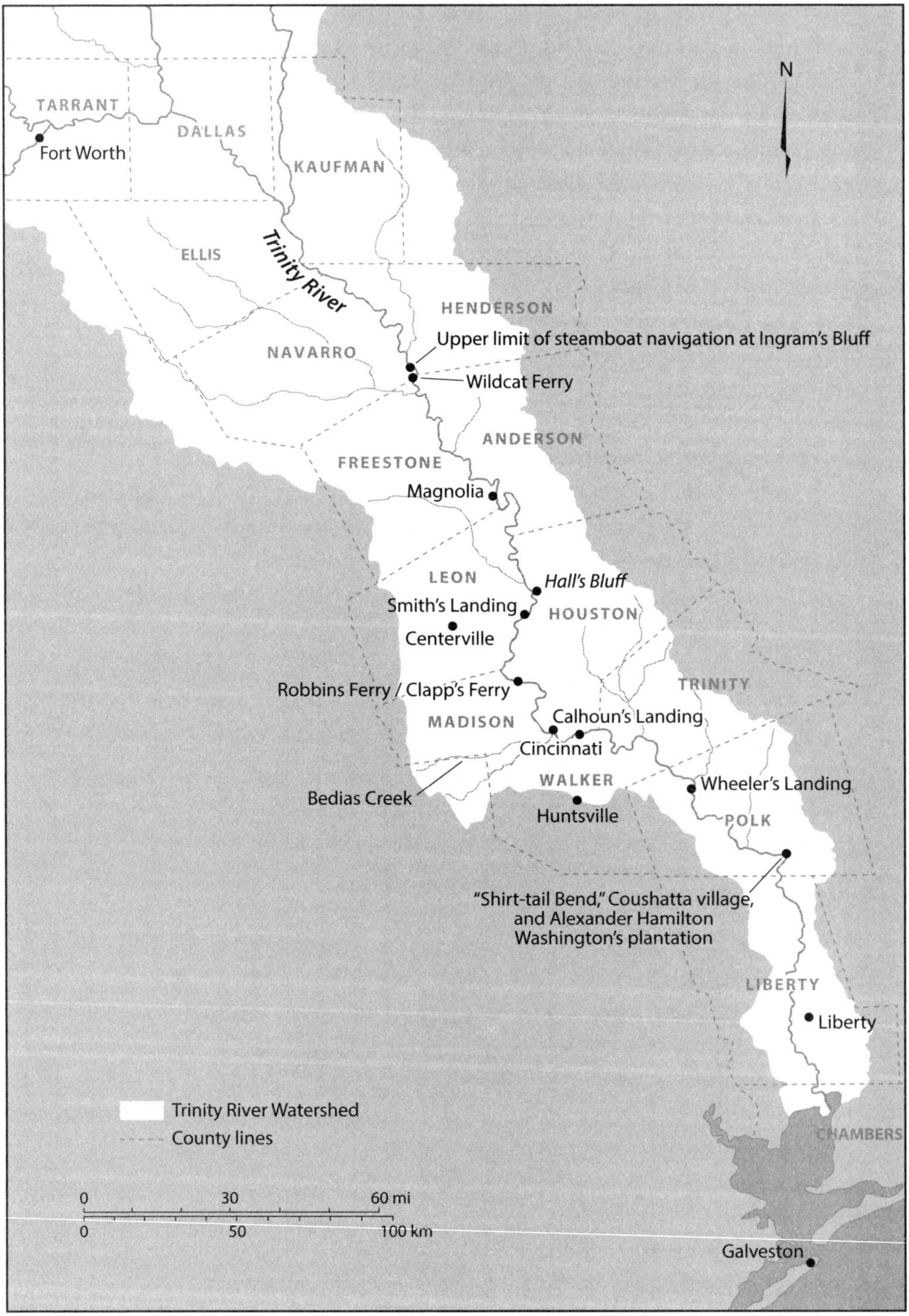


Circa 1860 map of the Trinity River.

slaveholding country."[8] He was right, though probably not how he meant it. The Trinity had become a stygian plantation region. While most planters marched their slaves overland and onto ferries to cross rivers, a new era of technology in Texas now meant some enslaved people arrived at their plantations via steamboats.[9]

Slave sales highlighted the terror of slavery as slave traders traveled along the Trinity.[10] Slaveholders used such transactions to profit from their human property and as a threat against them. During his Texas tour in the 1850s, Frederick Law Olmsted noted how common such events were among the "almost nomadic" slaveholders: "The very word 'sale,' applied to a slave," he argued, "implies this cruelty."[11] William and Dave Byrd described how their former slaveholders would wash and grease individuals before they were auctioned off. William Byrd explained that some slaveholders withheld the identity of a child's parent so they could separate children from their families with less difficulty.[12] However, Dave Byrd remembered, nothing could dull this pain. When a slaver trader ripped someone from their family, never was such torment heard since "they probably would not see them again."[13]

Freedom seekers occasionally used Trinity steamboats to escape slaveholders' attempts to divide their families.[14] But unlike on the Mississippi River, few were able to find freedom via the river channel. On the Mississippi, the volume and regularity of steamboat travel made escapes a regular occurrence, with enslaved steamboat laborers using their knowledge of the industry and its routes to deliver themselves and their fellow slaves to freedom.[15] Trinity steamboats were smaller—whereas the Mississippi steamboats could carry upward of ten thousand bales of cotton and hundreds of passengers, the Trinity boats were a tenth as large and rarely had more than ten passengers on board. The crews were smaller, too, with perhaps two enslaved firemen fueling the boiler out of a total workforce of four or five.[16] Except for the busier city of Galveston at the Gulf of Mexico, enslaved workers on steamboats encountered a homogeneous world of scattered landings and plantations on the lower Trinity. The smaller Trinity steamboats provided less privacy and fewer places to hide unnoticed. Local ownership of most boats meant heightened surveillance as slaveholders or captains had a better sense of who did not belong on a given craft.

But this familiarity worked both ways, and the river's connection to the plantations along its banks enabled the exchange of vital information. Enslaved workers on the boats or docks were invested in helping other known enslaved residents escape the plantation frontier.[17] Wayman Williams recalled living close to the boat landing where his father labored whenever "he was not working in the fields."[18] Williams's father would have learned and shared information with the crew as he loaded and unloaded supplies. The people who labored on steamboats connected plantations, bringing enslaved people who had been separated from their relatives news of their families—knowledge that might spur them to run away. As in the case of Thomas, Charles, and Goodwin—the three young enslaved men who died crossing its waters—the Trinity could be a threat to life. In her entry describing the loading of a flatboat at her plantation landing, Elizabeth Gaines Smith wrote of an enslaved person's drowning as if such deaths were a regular occurrence.[19]

The Trinity was one of the state's most important routes, and Texans watched the river levels and passing steamboats carefully. People came to the landings not just for business; the arrival of a steamboat was a social occasion. When steamboats docked at Texas Governor George Wood's plantation, everyone came to join the excitement.[20] In the once bustling riverfront town of Cincinnati, Texas, a young man complained of the steamboat *Mustang*, whose noisy late-night loading prevented him from sleeping. "I think man in general ought to be considerably more obliging and accommodating to each other than they are wont to be," he wrote grumpily the next morning.[21] His statement rang true in more ways than one on the plantation frontier's most navigable river.

Just as earlier methods of trade had brought disease to the Trinity's Native people, steamboats navigating the river often carried illness. Cincinnati, Texas, a thriving river port 350 miles from Galveston, was vulnerable to yellow fever because the Trinity was both a highway to market for every settlement along the river and a vector for disease. Once yellow fever arrived there, it spread easily due to the abundant mosquitoes. Hundreds died during the 1853 epidemic, and many more permanently fled the river town.[22] The journal entries for the plantation mistress Elizabeth Gaines Smith abruptly end after her husband left on a boat for Galveston loaded with cotton. Within a week her daughter and mother had died from yellow fever, and then Smith herself succumbed.

Planters came to the Trinity believing Black people were less likely to become sick—an idea that played into their racist justification for slavery.[23] A traveler's report from the early 1840s characterized the lower Trinity as especially unhealthy, claiming the land was "suited rather to Negro labour" because of the risk of fevers in the bottomlands.[24] Deaths due to disease contradicted such statements, as when a woman described the fever on her Trinity

Figure 4.2. A typical small steamboat on the Trinity River, circa 1870. Courtesy of Palestine Public Library and the Portal to Texas History, University of North Texas Libraries, https://texashistory.unt.edu/ark:/67531/metapth26549/.

plantation that quickly took the life of "poor little Flora."[25] Otis Wheeler sometimes left his plantation as illness spread and made primitive attempts to vaccinate enslaved children.[26] Dave and William Byrd recalled relying on a Black woman's expertise in the life-saving potential of their environment to nurse them back to health. This nurse gathered herbs in the woods, including a plant that contained quinine, to create a tea that effectively treated their chills. Malaria, which caused these chills, was introduced to North America following the arrival of Europeans and Africans, but this woman relied on native Texas plants to cure her patients.

Cotton formed the basis for the economy of the plantation frontier. The root of this plant, however, could be used as a source of resistance to the trade in cotton and human beings. On the Trinity, Black women chewed on cotton root so they would not give birth. No matter how closely slaveholders scrutinized them, the women could leave at night to gather enough cotton roots "to do what they wanted it do."[27] In a world where their choices were so often constrained, the cotton root empowered them to prevent pregnancy and abort fetuses, whether they worried about a jealous mistress who would sell them off the plantation or the possibility of having their future offspring stolen from them and shipped down the Trinity alongside the cotton bales they produced.

***Before railroads came to Texas,*** the Trinity was the most promising route from the state's interior to the coastline. As planters flocked to Texas, the Trinity's population began to catch up to the other plantation regions, such as the original Austin colony between the Colorado and Brazos Rivers or the Sabine River on the Louisiana border.[28] The Trinity was the best option for selling cotton from the interior of Texas, but it was unpredictable. Christopher Columbus Goodman, a farmer living three miles from the river, complained to his brother that he hated having to depend on a river that could be "low enough for a horse to walk across it," whereas in floods it could be five miles wide. Goodman was a farmer rather than a planter, and he grew crops mainly for subsistence and for bartering with neighbors. The exception was cotton, for which he could get a much better price by shipping it down the Trinity to Galveston than what a local merchant would offer him.[29] When Frederick Law Olmsted crossed the Trinity while on assignment for the *New York Daily Times*, it had not been high enough to navigate for six months. When he returned later that spring—which was usually the wet season—it remained too low for steamboats. "None of the Texan rivers can be said to be permanently navigable," Olmsted remarked, "as is evident, when this is called the best of them."[30]

River captains regularly misjudged the navigability, hoping for an upriver storm to salvage their naive decisions. Fannie Gooch came to Texas in the 1850s, booking a steamboat for the 512-mile trip from Galveston to Magnolia, close to the upper edge of the Trinity's navigable range. She made it only about seventy-five miles upriver. Her family spent weeks on the boat as they waited for the waters to rise, depending on wild game once the boat's provisions ran out. When the fall rains failed to arrive, they abandoned plans to take the steamboat any farther and headed to shore to walk through the woods instead.[31] Still, compared with the other major rivers in the wetter eastern half of the state, the Trinity remained the finest option for navigation. For example, a boat originally built for the Colorado River had to be transferred to the Trinity since it drew too much water on the shallower Colorado.[32]

A single cotton bale weighed a quarter of a ton, enough to bog down wagons on Texas's relatively unimproved roads, so floating large cargoes downriver worked better than overland routes. A visitor made this exact point regarding a seventy-mile journey that took a group of wagons three months to complete, exclaiming, "Water navigation forever! Hauling is no go!"[33] Until better wagon roads and eventually railroads appeared in Texas, the Trinity River was the finest route. The relative paucity of railroads and canals throughout the South meant that Southerners had to do more of their trade on rivers large and small, not all flowing as consistently as the Mississippi.[34]

Most of the wealthiest planters followed a basic formula of choosing a river site to grow cotton on and ship it from, but in doing so they overlooked what made Texas different from the Deep South from whence they came. While rainfall on the lower Trinity was similar to that of places to its east, its unforested headwaters received about half that.[35] These geological differences made the water levels of the Trinity more extreme and unpredictable than those of the rivers to its east. While water levels on any river are inherently variable, people were consistently surprised by the extent to which they were on the Trinity.

Whether they fretted about the arrival of a steamboat, planting times, or fishing prospects, everyone paid close attention to the river level. If the water was too low, no steamboats could come upriver to trade for deerskins, cotton bales, or human beings. The overseer for one of the largest plantations rejoiced in his journal that the river had been in "fine boating order" so that he could send and receive goods at the plantation's docks.[36] Yet shortly thereafter he lamented that the river had risen too high and ruined his cotton crop.[37] Everything had to be perfect, and thus the Trinity frequently meant disappointment for those who settled there in order to profit from it. Fertile soil allowed the cotton plant to flourish, but it was not worth anything if it could not be shipped and sold to mills in the Northeast or across the Atlantic Ocean.

Even with ideal water levels, navigation could be treacherous. Steamboats regularly encountered snags along the heavily wooded river. These dead trees were often completely submerged and hidden from a pilot's watchful eye. In a narrow river like the Trinity, they would have been unavoidable at times. For example, on its first trip upriver, the steamer *Brazos* ran into a snag, delaying the trip for two days while the crew rigged a temporary repair.[38] Boats often struck snags and sank in shallow water, where at least they and their cargo could be saved.[39] If the water was deep enough, snags could completely sink boats like the *Brownsville*, which went down almost instantly, resulting in the drowning deaths of three men. Fortunately for the people who shipped their goods on the *Brownsville*, most of the cargo had been insured.[40]

In an 1853 report to Congress, an Army Corps of Engineers lieutenant noted that the Trinity's main obstacles—snags, a sandbar at its mouth, and overhanging trees—could all be dealt with at low cost to significantly improve the speed and safety of transportation. To explain to Congress how the Trinity worked, especially in relation to the distribution of sediment and the growth of sandbars at its mouth, this lieutenant compared the Trinity to the most famous American stream. "The analogy *on a small scale* as to nature of the banks, character of alluvions, forces of current, great depth of stream, extent and shoalness of bar, and form of delta between this and the Mississippi," he wrote, "is almost perfect."[41] While the goal of the Mississippi analogy was to make the Trinity understandable, his point may also have tempered enthusiasm for improving the river, since many Americans believed the Mississippi was impossible to control. Mark Twain, who experienced the Mississippi as a steamboat pilot, wrote, "One who knows the Mississippi will promptly aver—not aloud, but to himself—that ten thousand River Commissions, with the mines of the world at their back, cannot tame that lawless stream, cannot curb it or confine it, cannot say to it, Go here, or Go there, and make it obey."[42] The artistry and skill of Mississippi River pilots that Twain memorialized—how they memorized every bend and read the water for hidden obstructions—would have been all the more necessary on the Trinity, whose narrower channel left less room for error. No matter how skilled or experienced a Trinity River captain was, mishaps were inevitable.

As a result, navigating the Trinity posed risks that raised freight and insurance costs. Shipping rates varied based on the point of departure, with the lowest rates coming from below Liberty.[43] In the 1840s, it cost four dollars to ship a bale of cotton from Magnolia, the primary head of navigation on the river, to Galveston.[44] Volume affected pricing, too; as river plantations and traffic increased dramatically in the 1850s, the cost was halved to two dollars.[45] Sometimes the same locations caused repeated wrecks, leading area newspaper editors to complain that "these losses call loudly on the people interested in trade, for cleaning of the river."[46]

Planters, merchants, and steamboat captains understood the need to engineer safer passage on the Trinity. They believed improving navigation would be cheaper than building railroads and sought state and federal support for their vision. However, due to rising tensions between the North and South over slavery, Congress stopped appropriating funds for this purpose in the 1850s. Local politicians, often Trinity planters themselves, lobbied state officials to ensure the Trinity received its share of funding.[47] Eventually, Texans funded their own river improvement bill, with the legislature apportioning $300,000 for all the state's waterways in 1856.[48] The state engineer contracted to have the sandbar at the mouth of the Trinity dredged, an operation merited by the Trinity's status as one of the state's "first class rivers."[49]

In the spring of 1860, the Trinity planter Otis Wheeler wrote to his mother in Massachusetts to inquire about an old friend he not seen in over two decades. Wheeler wanted to reconnect but only on the condition that his Northern friend not oppose slavery. "If he is an abolitionist," Wheeler exclaimed, "any other country would suit him better than this."[50] Texas had been at the center of the political crisis of slavery since its annexation as a state triggered the Mexican-American War, which then left the question of slavery in much of the newly obtained territory unresolved until the Civil War. If Texas's mercurial eastern rivers represented a limit to the westward spread of cotton plantations, then Southern planters faced an uncomfortable truth: The expansion of slavery had met environmental, in addition to political, constraints. For planters, encouraging the continued spread of slavery required them to attempt to improve the navigation potential of "first class rivers" like the Trinity.

Cotton grown along the Trinity traveled to the mills of Lowell, Massachusetts, and Manchester, England, but cotton was not the only tie between the plantation frontier and centers of industry. The Trinity's steamboats came from the bustling shipyards of Cincinnati, Ohio, and Pittsburgh, Pennsylvania. Planters shared stories of their wealth with all who would listen. Put away concerns over the morality of slavery, they said, and instead focus on the opportunity to gain wealth in the nation's newest plantation regions. One Pittsburgh-based family heeded this call by commissioning the construction of two steamboats. Named after Trinity River slaveholders John F. Carr and Colonel John Stell, these gilded, nearly two-hundred-ton boats were built to transport cotton and people on the river.

Timing mattered, and when he arrived in Texas on the eve of war, Franklin Gearing worried that his family had erred in borrowing so much money to build the *John F. Carr* and *Colonel Stell*. "The times here are very hard," he wrote. Following the election of Abraham Lincoln, uncertainty over a potential conflict between the North and South chilled commerce. To make matters worse, the cotton crop failed on the lower Trinity. Farther upriver there was cotton to carry, but water levels were too low for steamboats to reach it. Franklin wondered whether they could retreat from the Trinity and sell the boats in New Orleans. However, by this point he realized that even on the more established Mississippi River, few would have the means for his family to recoup their investment.[51] The Gearings' dashed hopes were part and parcel of the particular challenges of the Trinity's plantation economy as it collided with the outbreak of the Civil War. In their eagerness to get rich in the cotton South, the Gearings failed to recognize that not all plantation regions were alike. With no good options to sell, the Gearings used the two steamboats to transport cotton bales as best they could on the Trinity until the Confederacy eventually took possession of the boats.

## CHAPTER 5

# TEXAS'S WAR WITHIN

When a steamboat traveled up the Trinity, it potentially could stop at over eighty towns and landings. Most were named for the bigger plantations, such as Wheeler's Landing after Otis Wheeler; Smith's Landing after Elizabeth Gaines Smith and her husband; Day's Landing, home to Henderson Day; or Calhoun's Landing, where Dave Byrd had been enslaved. Only a handful of these names endured on maps for more than a few decades after the brief era of the plantation frontier. Hall's Bluff was named for the Hall family, who owned twenty thousand acres along the Trinity River starting in the 1830s. The landing became a small, bustling community with a warehouse and store run by the Hall family.

By the start of the Civil War, forty-two-year-old James Madison Hall had already witnessed his share of drama and death, not only during his time as a soldier in the Mexican-American War but also from events at home. A thick, red-bearded man, Hall had stabbed a close friend to death in a dispute over his daughter's marriage to someone living across the Trinity in 1859. In that same turbulent year he divorced his wife and promptly remarried his much younger stepsister.[1] His social world shrank and his reputation suffered as a result of these actions: The Freemasons evicted him and the local credit office condemned him. Still, when Hall stood trial for murder in the neighboring Trinity County the next spring, the jury acquitted him of the charges. In response, he treated the jury to all the champagne he could purchase.[2] That fall the informant for the local credit-rating office summed up the recent events in Hall's life, including "a divorce from his first wife & a division of ppty. [property] with her. His subsequent marriage to another, a charge, trial & acquit[t]al of murder render in some degree his true position somewhat uncertain." The only thing that was "certain" was that James Hall needed "to be watched closely."[3] To distance himself from his enemies close to home, Hall spent a good portion of the next few years living downriver in Liberty, working for and in partnership with a merchant there while still maintaining his farm and mill along a creek not far from Hall's Bluff. Hall depended on the river for his livelihood, buying and selling goods and people he transported on boats.[4]

Secessionist fervor had increased in Texas, and fears of a slave insurrection reached their peak in the summer of 1860, when a number of fires broke out in North Texas. The editor of the *Dallas Herald* claimed that he had uncovered an abolitionist plot "to devastate, with fire and assassination, the whole of Northern Texas"; this claim led to the hanging of three enslaved men on the banks of the Trinity.[5] Meanwhile, along the plantation frontier, residents purportedly discovered a plan to poison the drinking water, and two white men were hanged.[6] One week before the Battle of Fort Sumter heralded the start of the Civil War, James Hall went to the Trinity River to demonstrate his allegiance to the Confederacy. Hall and his neighbors hoisted the new Confederate flag up a thirty-foot pole on top of his warehouse, where, he said, "it now floats to the breeze, the emblem of the free." To emphasize the natural world's response to his actions, and his anxieties, Hall wrote, "The river commenced rising very fast."[7]

In wartime, the Trinity presented new risks. The muddy water was the same as it ever was, stubborn and unpredictable, rising and falling depending on its moods. The same old questions, like whether the crops might flood or the steamboats could make it up the river, gained new importance and more consequence. A flood could plunge the region into starvation. The Trinity also offered a way to ship enemy soldiers deep into Texas, if the Union could find a way to exploit the state's most navigable river.

During the Civil War, the clashes between the enslavers and enslaved, on the one hand, and between the planters and the nascent Confederacy, on the other, were just as consequential as the few, relatively small battles that occurred between the US Army and the Confederacy on Texas soil.[8] In this stronghold of slavery far south of the Mason–Dixon Line, most of the Trinity region's white male voters approved of secession by a wide margin. While fears over the fate of slavery under a Republican ticket drove secession, the

Confederacy was in a war for its existence and sometimes chose expediency over property rights to achieve a military victory. From the outset, slaveholders clashed with their own state and Confederate governments to protect their rights to their property—centrally, slaves—and to commerce.[9]

Once the Union navy began attacking Confederate ports and rivers, many white Texans worried that the state's navigable rivers would allow Union gunboats to penetrate its interior. Shortly after taking office in 1861, Texas Governor Francis Lubbock ordered residents to secure their cotton to prevent Union forces from taking away what many believed was the Confederacy's strongest advantage: King Cotton. The South produced three-quarters of the world's supply, and planters supposed that their monopoly on this vital commodity would win them international allies, especially the cotton-hungry United Kingdom. To protect this advantage they had to continue—or rather, enslaved people had to continue—producing cotton, and they would have to find a way to safely get this cotton to international purchasers. Governor Lubbock's order specifically noted that there should be no cotton stored below a certain point on the Trinity.[10] The following year, he urged Confederate forces to act quickly to protect the river by building obstructions along the bars of Galveston Bay. "If it is practical," Lubbock wrote, "it would insure the safety of the Trinity."[11]

Trinity slaveholders agreed with government officials on the importance of cotton production and that the Union navy was a threat, but they disagreed on whether this threat should be addressed. Planters depended on river navigation for their wealth and thus did not think that the river should be obstructed. A Union blockade along the Gulf Coast impeded trade throughout the Confederacy and made the rivers flowing through the interior of Texas all the more important. Knowing that the Trinity would be an even less reliable route to market in war, some river residents turned their focus to "home products" such as grains and meat rather than cotton.[12] Though planters attempted to make their plantations more self-sufficient, they continued to plant cotton that would have to be carried down the Trinity.

There was one exception to planters' reluctance to defend the river: Alexander Hamilton Washington. He was born in Virginia in 1805, five years after the death of his cousin once removed, former President George Washington. By the start of the war, forty-seven enslaved people labored on his plantation. In addition, the land he claimed had already been home to the Coushatta, who continued to live there and do work such as picking cotton. Washington took on a Confederate commission as major for the defense of the Trinity River, an effort that would link the competing interests of slaveholders, the Coushatta and Alabama tribes, Confederate deserters, and enslaved people.

Washington understood that on a practical level, defending the Trinity should be relatively easy because it was already challenging to navigate. When a Confederate navy officer surveyed the mouth of the Trinity to prepare barriers to navigation, he discovered the remains of military fortifications from Manuel de Mier y Terán's efforts to control access to the river. This officer also recognized that the river had done much of the work for him. The mouth of the Trinity consisted of four separate outlets, three of which were already obstructed by logs, while the one passable outlet could be guarded with a battery placed on the shore.[13] Should the Union gunboats push past the battery at the mouth of the river, they made plans to defend the Trinity farther upstream. In the fall of 1862, a naval base was established on Washington's plantation because it offered both a ready source of subsistence and a good location to defend against incoming boats.[14] These efforts took on added importance since Union forces had just seized Galveston.

Even with Union gunboat cannon within earshot of the lower Trinity, the Confederacy found few people willing to contribute to its efforts. The Gearings' steamship *Colonel Stell*, now the property of the Confederacy, arrived upriver in search of enslaved men who would build fortifications at the mouth of the Trinity.[15] James Hall expected to attend a large meeting regarding plans to obstruct the river. However, this meeting had to be canceled due to "the lukewarmness of the people." Hall lamented that "every body appeared to be resigned to their fate if the enemy should come."[16] He worried about an invasion happening via the Trinity, but he too did not volunteer any of his slaves for government service. Confederate plans to obstruct the Trinity represented a dual threat to slaveholders by taking away their enslaved property and their ability to sell the goods their remaining slaves produced. Eventually, another meeting was held but without success for those in favor of this work, and the *Colonel Stell* left empty-handed.[17]

Upriver from Hall, Washington was the only slaveholder who actively contributed to the river's defense. He provided a Confederate naval officer with nine enslaved men who cut timber and built boats and relied on his relationship with Native people for a planned military unit.[18] When the Confederates commenced obstructing the river, white residents complained about the military's insistence on defending it, calling this effort "a foolish business."[19] In letters to his commanding officer, Washington described the "difficulties" he had with getting other planters to contribute—at the very least they wanted to first plant cotton before considering helping.[20] Meanwhile,

Confederate officers made plans to require the Trinity River's residents who had not headed east to fight to defend the river.[21] These efforts to fortify the Trinity earned the "constant derision of the people" who believed it was a waste of time.[22]

Ultimately the Trinity itself played a role in shaping the outcome of this debate in favor of the vast majority of white residents who wanted nothing to do with defending the river. By February 1863, the Trinity began to flood, contributing to the spread of disease, carrying away bridges, and halting the mail coming into the naval base on Washington's plantation. With greater need for troops elsewhere, the Trinity's Confederate naval base shut down in the spring of 1863.[23] The debates over the river and the use of slave labor to defend it reflected the self-interest of the Trinity planters but also differing views of strategy. In Texas, so far from the major battles, planters wanted to focus on producing cotton rather than on protecting an unruly river.

In contrast with his gloomy private letters about disorder on the homefront, Washington wrote several songs to raise morale and support Confederate efforts. In one titled "Texian Appeal," he used a river metaphor:

> Planters! Cease your garner'd stores to swell with bootless toil,
> While on the invading torrent pours to sweep you from the soil!
> Your homes, and land, and treasures all, entrust to boy and slave;
> And hasten on at duty's call, from ruin all to save![24]

Texas planters did not want to entrust their plantations to those whom they had enslaved. Plantation owners received preferential treatment from the Confederate leadership to leave the battlefields. The widower of the plantation mistress Elizabeth Gaines Smith, who had died two years earlier from yellow fever, temporarily resigned his position as an officer to return to his plantation along the Trinity River and attend to his daughter's plantation after her husband had been killed in the war. Mr. Smith wrote that no one "except the Negroes" remained to manage both plantations. Seeking leave from his post in the Confederacy, he asked the postmaster general of the Confederacy for this "special favor." The postmaster complied, forwarding the letter to his superior officers by noting that this planter was "a most worthy man."[25] Indeed, this letter was written a month after the Confederate Congress passed a law permitting any slaveholder to avoid military service if he owned at least twenty slaves.[26] As did the wealthiest men in the rest of the Confederacy, Trinity River planters who served in the military expected preferential treatment from the Confederate leadership, and they got it.

Many less wealthy Texas slaveholders like James Hall felt increasingly alienated from the Confederacy. In 1863 Hall and his cousin were arrested by a group of Confederate officers looking for conscripts. They were locked up with no food and no ability to communicate with anyone. There they were kept with no charges except the suspicion that they should have been conscripted. "So much for our boasted rights as Southern gentlemen," Hall complained. He was eventually released, while his cousin was forced to enlist in the Confederate army even though he had already received an exemption. Hall believed that such coercion did not make for good soldiers, and he unironically predicted that such actions would "brake down our once happy land of freedom."[27] Following his arrest, Hall had only one decidedly unfree reason to remain loyal to the Confederacy: its defense of slavery.

***The brutality that defined*** the relationship between enslavers and the enslaved intensified during the war. There were hangings and cowardly shootings. On the Trinity, far removed from Union lines, this conflict was in part a continuation of forms of resistance that existed before the war, such as work slowdowns and freedom seeking. At his warehouse on the banks of the river, for example, Hall whipped Sam for running away.[28] The case of Bob, who was also enslaved by Hall, is illustrative. For unfree men like Bob, the war raised the question of whether slavery would ever end on the Trinity. Unlike in most of the Confederacy, until the very end it may have seemed as though slavery would never be abolished in Texas. No major battles took place in Texas, and no Union states bordered it. Though tens of thousands of Texans served in the Confederacy, the war would have felt very far from the Trinity.[29] In March 1862, Bob would have seen the Trinity through the haze of a splitting headache and a bloody bandage as he recovered from being beaten with a pistol. He was one of at least sixteen enslaved people brutally attacked by a white man who lived in the area.[30] Slaveholders who did not leave Texas to fight instead focused their violence on the state's enslaved population.

A few weeks before his assault, Bob had been at work in the Trinity's swamps with at least one other Black man. There they cut fence posts from bald cypress trees draped in Spanish moss. On warmer days they would have been menaced by cottonmouth snakes emerging from their winter dens. Cottonmouths are so named because of their white mouths that resemble a cotton boll, which they readily flash when threatened—and the choice of cotton is a telling description, since the cottonmouth's range overlaps almost perfectly with the spread of cotton plantations. While Bob hacked away at the giant cypress, he also would have disturbed less dangerous tree-dwellers such as owls and the now-extinct ivory-billed woodpeckers, often called "the Lord God bird" because of the impression it made on first sight. Laboring for his enslaver among cottonmouth snakes and the Lord God bird, Bob was not free, but his ability to work without an overseer offered a respite from the violence that defined this era in Texas. Cypress trees were prized for fence posts and other uses because of their resistance to rot and decay; it is likely that some of the stumps of the trees felled by Bob endure to this day.[31] If one looks just under the water, one might discover these hidden Civil War–era monuments that mark the resilience of men like Bob and the special shame of the slaveholders who never left Texas to fight in the war.

The psychic violence of family separation reflected both the use of slave sales as a punishment and the disruptions caused by the war. James Hall's journal details this trade in human beings on the Trinity. Four days before the first shots were fired at Fort Sumter, he sold Melinda, Laura, and Elisha for $1,700, possibly to be sent upriver on the Gearings' newly constructed *Colonel Stell*. In 1862 Hall purchased a young woman named Jemima from a sheriff living near the mouth of the Trinity River for $1,200.[32] Jemima was taken from her mother, who remained downriver. On January 1, 1863, Abraham Lincoln issued the Emancipation Proclamation that declared that "all persons held as slaves" in rebellious states shall be "forever free." However, since the Union exerted no control over Confederate Texas, it did not immediately result in emancipation. Only one week after the Emancipation Proclamation was issued, Hall paid $1,800 for Bill.[33]

Throughout the war, enslaved men and women worked to retain the connections to the people and places from which they had been severed, as well as to make new bonds. Before he was purchased by Hall, Bill had lived on another Trinity plantation. The day after Christmas 1863, Bill rode a mule back "across the river," where he spent two days visiting his friends and possibly family members.[34] In that same year, Jemima married in a ceremony described as "a general blowout." Jemima's wedding was attended by all the enslaved people living in the area, who "seemed to enjoy themselves hugely."[35] Jemima became pregnant the following year and gave birth to a daughter named Cora on June 17, 1865.[36] Throughout these wartime years, Bill, Jemima, and others performed the unceasing labor of hauling rails, plowing corn, gathering pecans, catching fish, moving furniture, salting pork, building fences, catching runaway livestock, and so on. Only sickness slowed this unpaid work for more than a few days, whether caused by brutal acts of violence or lingering fevers.

Alongside the forced movement of people like Bill and Jemima within Texas, at least fifty thousand enslaved men, women, and children arrived in Texas. An estimated five hundred thousand enslaved people gained their freedom by crossing Union lines elsewhere, but in Texas the enslaved population significantly expanded as slaveholders rushed there from other parts of the Confederacy to secure their property. One man remembered the difficulties of the trip as his enslaved family left Louisiana with hundreds more. On the way to Texas, his brother died. He had little time to mourn, as the group kept on until they came to the Trinity River.[37] The hardships of these migrations were compounded by the fact that entering Texas made the possibility of freedom more remote. Even after the Emancipation Proclamation, it was unclear whether slavery would be permanently ended in all the rebellious states, especially in Texas, which had seen minimal fighting and had a history as an independent slaveholding republic.

Initially, this movement of enslaved people to Texas was mainly the continuation of the long-term process of westward expansion. Just as the Gearings chose to invest in two steamboats for the Trinity River based on the promising reports that they read, so too did planters come to the Trinity on the basis of their hopes for continued wealth. For example, Hall's cousin came "with his negroes" on the steamboat *Ruthven* to the Trinity on March 27, 1861, after secession had occurred but before the start of the war.[38] While the secessionist crisis may have contributed to his reasons for leaving, the benefits of settling in the new region and possibilities for farming and commerce also beckoned. Unlike in most of the rest of the Confederacy, prime lands remained along the Trinity River, for those willing and able to pay. Many of the recently arrived slaveholders intended to call the Trinity home even if the war ended.[39] The circumstances of war forced slaveholders across the South to leave or risk losing their most valuable property, but with no plans of ever returning, they sought places that allowed them to put their slaves to work.

During the war, the areas around the Trinity, Brazos, and Sabine Rivers contained the majority of these new arrivals. As Union troops conquered land in the Confederacy, especially along the Mississippi River, the flood of planters and enslaved people entering Texas gained momentum, particularly by 1862. Even once the war proved the most important catalyst for migration, planters sought out properties where they could continue to grow cotton. And so these war refugees began arriving from Louisiana and then from other parts of the Confederacy like Missouri and Arkansas as the Union army began new campaigns.[40] While some slaves arrived via steamboats along the Trinity, the vast majority marched overland due to the Union blockade along the coast. For new Texas planters, the Trinity's variable navigability offered a balance between commercial possibility and security from Union gunboats.

The upper Trinity, above what had been the core plantation region, experienced some of the greatest growth in its enslaved population, more than doubling in places such as Dallas and Tarrant Counties. This area had fewer options for navigation, with no steamboats ever traveling all the way to Dallas. Being farther in the interior of the state and having a less navigable river made the region all the more appealing during the Civil War. The largest increase in the enslaved population happened along its middle section, where Freestone County added 2,616 slaves and Anderson County, across the river, added 2,275, which amounted to an 87 percent increase for Freestone and a 72 percent increase for Anderson County. In nearly every county above the mouth of the river up to Fort Worth's Tarrant County, at least a thousand slaves arrived during the war.[41] The area with the most consistently navigable channel closer to Galveston may have been considered too risky for most slaveholders, since navigability also represented a potential liability.

The fact that so many planters settled on the Trinity during the Civil War reflected divisions over slavery within the state. The majority of the state's white male residents had supported slavery and secession; however, plantations defined only a few parts of Texas, mainly along rivers. Thus, planters may have felt more secure settling among their peers in places like the Trinity River than in areas that did not already have a significant number of plantations. Planters engaged in a typical pattern of chain migration where migrants followed those who had previously left their homes from the same region. Arrivals from plantation regions elsewhere in the Confederacy settled near their former neighbors; in the last year of the war, for example, an area of the Trinity was described as being "thronged with Louisiana refugees . . . driven from their luxurious homes."[42] These patterns also highlight the general limits of plantation slavery. In the arid region beyond the Trinity and Brazos Rivers, there were few opportunities to rapidly put a large number of enslaved people to work. While concerns about free states versus slave states and the expansion of slavery played a central role in the creation of the Confederacy, the settlement patterns of these wartime migrants suggest the westward expansion of plantation slavery had run its course as the Trinity's population grew.[43]

Many of these slaveholders found themselves disappointed when reality did not meet their expectations. Arriving in Freestone County, which experienced the third-largest increase in slaves in the whole state, Gerard Brandon, the son of the governor of Mississippi, learned that one potential site would not be available to him for many months. He complained that on higher, drier ground "the land is not good" for a plantation. "Oh! How Texas has been overstated . . . poor, sandy, badly watered short of timber and grass."[44] As Brandon continued westward, he found that the greatest opposition to people like himself stemmed from his wealth in property and the idea that the war was the "rich man's was [war] & poor man's fight."[45]

Confederate leadership in Texas initially opposed the settling of refugees because they feared the disruption it might cause, but they soon realized that moving plantations to Texas could be a boon if they could grow more corn and cotton.[46] Planters took advantage of the increased opportunities for subsistence along the Trinity River while hiring out their slaves or growing cotton.

Though the plantations themselves were similar, the enslaved population encountered a new environment in Texas. Louis Love, for example, recalled how he relied on wild pigs for sustenance but also feared the panthers that lived along the Trinity.[47] Love and all who arrived in Texas transformed the landscape. Clearing forests and planting crops significantly increased erosion and sediment entering the Trinity: The river was permanently changed by their presence, making it less navigable, the sandbars higher, and the channel shallower.[48] Though Love initially returned to Louisiana after the Civil War, most of these new Black and white residents chose to remain in Texas, shaping both its politics and environment.

***After white Trinity residents*** and Confederate officers had agreed that the river should continue to be used for transport and that no more divisive talk of obstructing the river would occur, Major Alexander Hamilton Washington led the new efforts to carry goods down the Trinity. Rather than cotton, he focused on transporting corn to sustain military forces closer to the coast. Centered at Magnolia, near the upper edge of steamboat travel, Washington purchased farm products, oversaw the building of flatboats, and led the piloting of these cargoes downriver. Once again, the Trinity itself interfered with this work. In May 1864, a year after the Trinity's floods had disrupted the region, Washington wrote to his commanding officer that low water meant that boats could not get downriver. He hoped that the "ordinary spring rise may still come" so that he could fulfill his mission.[49]

A number of different groups served under Major Washington for a range of reasons. The Alabama and Coushatta people had their own cavalry company. After they floated supplies downriver, the boatmen abandoned their boats and rode back up to Magnolia on horseback to build more boats.[50] This work allowed them to serve the Confederacy while staying close to their families and home on the Trinity.

Washington also employed a significant number of deserters and put himself at risk of arrest by other Confederate officers for doing so. He believed he had received special orders to "pardon all deserters, absentees and stragglers" if he put them to work on the river.[51] Washington insisted that he needed these men as boat pilots and carpenters.[52] In 1864 the lead general in Texas issued a special order, directing two physicians to investigate some of the soldiers serving under Washington to determine whether they qualified as "cases of disability."[53] An entire company of "Pardoned Deserters" worked to build flatboats.[54] The use of deserters in service of the Confederacy in Texas highlighted the growing problem of manpower as the war dragged on and hundreds of thousands of soldiers were killed or wounded.

Throughout the Confederacy, officers turned to enslaved laborers to support their efforts as they ran out of able-bodied white men. At the outset of the war, virtually none of the Trinity's slaveholders allowed anyone to make use of their slaves. They wanted to continue growing crops and did not want to alter the Trinity or risk losing their most valuable property, but eventually they realized their opposition to Confederate oversight of their slaves was not sustainable. In 1864 the *Weekly State Gazette* argued that "a Yankee invasion would be worse than the loss of a little time by some of the negroes."[55] By the end of the war, boatyards along the Trinity were bustling as white Confederate deserters, Alabama and Coushatta soldiers, and Black men built and loaded flatboats to float downriver. At the same time, the Trinity continued to disrupt Confederate activities in Texas as it washed away railroads and slowed the flow of people, supplies, and vital information about the conflict.[56]

This final phase of the war wore down slaveholders' illusions of control. In January 1865, Bill, who had been purchased by James Hall two years earlier, went to work in one of the boatyards "in service of the Government" alongside a number of other enslaved men.[57] In February, Bill left the boatyard to visit his family without any apparent restrictions on his movements.[58] Working for the Confederacy further increased opportunities for enslaved people to gain their freedom, which was precisely the reason that slaveholders had avoided it for so long. Another man, whose enslaver had brought him to Texas from Louisiana, tried to escape after he had been "at work for the government on the Trinity River" but was recaptured.[59] Enslaved people continued to seek their freedom and reconnect with their families through the end of the war and afterward. In April 1865 Hall traveled down the river with two white men as well as "6 negro fellows" on flatboats, stopping at plantations along the way for rest and more passengers.[60] Hall recorded these events several days after Robert E. Lee surrendered to Ulysses S. Grant in Appomattox, Virginia, but this did not yet mark the end of slavery in Texas. The generals leading the region's Trans-Mississippi Department delayed their capitulation.

Disorder extended far beyond the Trinity's boatyards. Hungry, unpaid Confederate soldiers carried out raids along the river. James Hall repeatedly dealt with thieves: "So much for the soldiers of the Confederacy," he wrote. Both the marauding soldiers and the impressment of his slaves gave Hall scant reason to remain loyal to what remained of the Confederacy. Not only soldiers but even officers lost control in these final months, including a case where an officer killed another at point-blank range in Texas's military headquarters in Galveston. Well before Texas Confederates officially surrendered in June, soldiers returning home had already begun to wreak havoc along the Trinity. These men stole "every thing they could get hold of" throughout the countryside, sometimes justifying their plunder with the fact they had been unpaid for months.[61] "The reign of terror is now complete in the land," Hall wrote. "Our own soldiers are doing worse than the enemy could under any circumstances."[62]

It took the arrival of Union soldiers in Galveston to begin the official process of ending slavery in Texas. For people like Bill and Jemima, word of emancipation traveled upriver. One man who had been enslaved on a plantation along the river recalled "how the boat came up the Trinity River from Galveston bringing the news of Emancipation."[63] Hall acknowledged that he was now "deprived of nearly all my property."[64] On June 2, Confederate General Kirby Smith surrendered off the coast of Galveston, and that same day residents along the lower Trinity read the papers containing "orders declaring negroes free."[65] Then on June 19, Union General Gordon Granger issued his famous announcement regarding emancipation, now celebrated nationwide as Juneteenth.

Juneteenth was an important turning point, but in places like the Trinity it would take a sustained effort of federal forces and freedpeople to secure freedom, a process that would be distinct from that in the rest of the South. During the war an estimated three-quarters of a million soldiers killed each other, but just a few hundred did so in Texas. Hundreds more Black and white people would be killed in the first years of Reconstruction in Texas. About half a million enslaved people gained their freedom before the end of the war, but in Texas the slave population increased by more than fifty thousand people during the war. The absence of Union forces on the Trinity in wartime would have another consequence during Reconstruction: federal officials' ignorance about the environment. Federal soldiers had no experience with the seasonal patterns of the Trinity, and they would soon find its particularities to be a major impediment to the work ahead of them. Enforcing a meaningful freedom along the Trinity meant dealing with blood and mud.

As soon as emancipation occurred, freedpeople wasted no time in claiming their freedom and in using the Trinity to do so. The same river that had been used for slave trading now enabled freedpeople to rebuild their families. Jemima, taken from her family close to the mouth of the Trinity near the start of the war, reunited with her mother one month after Juneteenth by traveling on the steamboat *Lone Star*.[66] There, Jemima's mother also met her granddaughter, Cora, born two days before Juneteenth. Jemima briefly returned to James Hall's residence with her mother and daughter before leaving for good a few months later. By 1880 she and Cora lived near the mouth of the Trinity, where Jemima worked as a housekeeper and Cora attended school, an opportunity that didn't exist before Juneteenth.[67] In regions like the Trinity, the selfishness and cruelty of slaveholders who hired steamboats to carry their cotton and slaves stand in contrast to the strength and love of people like Jemima who traveled on a steamboat to rebuild her family.

Steamboats are often described in numerical terms: how much they cost, how much they weighed, or how much cotton they carried. But they are useful objects for thinking about the Civil War in Texas. Federal officers initially returned the steamboats *Colonel Stell* and *John F. Carr* to the Gearings' possession before revoking this gift and requiring payment for the current value of the boats. Then in 1867, the elder Gearing applied to the United States Court of Claims for compensation. He admitted to carrying Confederate troops on his steamboats as well as to his ongoing transactions in Texas cotton during the war. After listening to his testimony, the court ruled against him, arguing that Gearing was "in every moral, as in every legal sense of the word, a traitor."[68] That same year the *Colonel Stell* sank in the Trinity River while transporting a load of cotton—as it did in the war, the ever-changing Trinity shaped this story. In the decades that followed, traitors like the Gearings, heroines like Jemima, and the Trinity itself were overlooked by Confederate apologists who emphasized the bravery of the soldiers in distant battlefields rather than the division and disorder that defined those years in Texas.

## CHAPTER 6

# THE FIGHT FOR FREEDOM

Without much help from the federal government, freedpeople had to claim their rights themselves. In September 1865, James Hall wrote, "My negro man John or rather freedman . . . ran off and shipped on the Steamer Mary Hill." Though John was no longer Hall's property, he had signed a legally dubious contract indenturing himself to Hall. In the initial moments of emancipation, many such indenture contracts had been drawn up, limiting the freedom of former slaves. Despite the contract, John used the river to leave Hall and claim his freedom.[1]

After Jemima had departed Hall's employment for good in the summer of 1865, those who still worked for Hall redefined their relationship with him as an employer rather than an enslaver. As he had with John, Hall lacked the language to define this new era of freedom, still calling Louisa Tubbs "my negro woman" even as he recognized that she had indeed been "freed." But in what Hall described as "a rupture between us," Tubbs challenged Hall to recognize her new independence.[2] Such conflicts between freedwomen and ex-slaveholders occurred throughout the plantation South as freedwomen resisted impositions on their time and space.[3] By the end of the summer, Tubbs, like Jemima before her, quit, which forced Hall's wife to perform her own household work. The day after Tubbs left, Hall attempted to hire a new employee but failed to find anyone willing to work for him.[4] He died the following year; Louisa Tubbs outlived him by several decades. In those years, she made a home with Bill Tubbs, who had been taken by Hall from the Tubbs plantation in 1863. She also lived with Fannie, who had been a young child when she was enslaved by Hall. Records from the Reconstruction era reveal another way that Bill Tubbs claimed his freedom: On August 24, 1867, he registered to vote. Given the terror that reigned in Texas during the first years after the Civil War, the Tubbs family's survival is a testament both to their fortitude and to their luck. Hundreds of freedpeople would not survive the violence of this era.

Texas was the last Confederate state where Union forces ordered the end of slavery; Juneteenth, the emancipation holiday, is now celebrated as a national holiday. But Texas's history meant the federal government faced unique difficulties in enforcing this new freedom.[5] Violence wielded by slaveholders did not end after Juneteenth. Two months after Juneteenth, the same man who had viciously attacked Bob and many other enslaved people during the war handcuffed, beat, and kicked an older couple because their sons had left his Trinity River plantation; he also attacked another freedman who refused to work for him.[6] The federal government documented thousands of these "outrages" across the former Confederacy.[7] More than half of the total incidents in the official federal record came from Texas, the only place where more bloodshed may have occurred in the first few years *after* the war than it did during the war. The reasons for this are complex, though a key one is found in Texas geography. The state's vast and varied landscapes stretched federal troops thin. This made asserting control over former Confederates while protecting freedpeople in the eastern half of Texas, defending the US-Mexican border from French threats, and relentlessly pursuing Native nations in the Texas plains a tall order.

In the first months after emancipation, the Trinity served an important function by allowing the movement of federal forces into the part of the South most sheltered from the war. Without troops, the end of slavery in Texas was not guaranteed. Officials touring Texas found that the greater the distance from soldiers, the more likely former slaveholders were to continue the practice of slavery.[8] Fifty miles east of the Trinity, many were kept in bondage for a year as freedpeople attempting to leave were murdered along the Sabine River.[9] Conditions were so bad beyond the Trinity that it became proof of the necessity of Congressional Reconstruction. Witnesses testified about the importance of using force to restore order in Texas. One general traveled along the Trinity and then into the region to its east, an area that everyone agreed was "the very worst portion of the State." He found that most of the freedmen had never been paid for their labor since emancipation, and he also "saw freedmen east of the Trinity river who did not know they were free until I told them."[10] Given such outright refusals to recognize emancipation, the river's role in transporting troops into the state's interior helped to ensure that the practice of slavery actually ended in one of Texas's primary plantation regions. Soldiers began to arrive up the Trinity one month after Juneteenth, with several companies taking the steamboat *Lone Star*, the same boat Jemima had used to claim her freedom.[11] And so at the very beginning of Reconstruction, freedpeople directly along the Trinity had better access to the US soldiers who would help secure and protect their freedom.[12] In addition to regular military officers and soldiers, the federal government created the Freedmen's Bureau to aid and protect freedpeople as they claimed their freedom.

From the fall of 1865 to the winter of 1868, the Freedmen's Bureau made significant achievements in Texas, but its understaffed agents could not handle the violent resistance to the end of slavery, much less in the midst of environmental crises. One of Texas's postwar atrocities took place on the Cessna plantation, located near Clapp's Ferry on the Trinity River. In 1866, a Black sharecropping family, led by Thomas Holliman, had agreed to farm "on the thirds," meaning that they would receive a third of the crop they produced in exchange for the landowner providing the land and any necessary supplies. During their first year, Holliman's family farmed the land without major incident, producing some cotton but mainly corn.[13] Then, on the night of February 16, 1867, three white men known to the family attacked Thomas Holliman's house, slaying his dog and then charging through the front door aiming to kill any residents. The terrorists threw embers from the fireplace onto a bed. As the fire spread and nigh instantly consumed the house, Holliman's nephew ran out and died instantly as "bloods & brains" poured from the bullet wound to his head. The terrorists ran in the dark from house to house, spreading fire from their torches and weapons. One of the victims was shot in the back; another of them, shot in the abdomen. Mrs. Holliman hid in the underbrush "with all of my children that I could find," which, tragically, excluded one of her sons. She later testified, "I suppose I seen his remains which were lying about the place that he was sleeping. Where he was burned up in the house."[14]

Because of the scale and gruesomeness of the attack, federal military authorities sent soldiers to investigate and locate "those prowling murderers and house burners."[15] One officer essentially froze the attackers' assets, putting guards on duty at their homes to ensure their families did not hide anything of value that could be used to compensate the victims. In addition to the lives lost, the officer calculated the value of the freedpeople's beds, quilts, shoes, and Sunday clothes—precious, hard-won objects in the almost two years since emancipation—that had been lost to the fire, although the loss of the dog was not appraised.[16]

Soldiers followed the outlaws for four days until they fled "into the Swamps of the Trinity" where the horses could not follow them, causing the trackers to pause their search.[17] The Trinity provided sanctuary to those who knew it well enough to navigate its bottomlands. But luck ran out, and the assailants were finally captured. When one suspect was finally tried, he was acquitted for lack of evidence, despite the witnesses' clear statements and prior acquaintance with the three perpetrators of the attack.[18] The local newspaper referred to the devastation as "An Unfortunate Affair" and declared, "The people of the South are not yet prepared for negro equality."[19]

Though historians have studied the racist violence of Reconstruction in Texas over the last few decades, both this event and the place where it happened have gone largely unexamined. In this case, only one other published book mentions this horrific attack. The pain of this family's loss and the suffering their son experienced as he burned to death has been buried for the last century and a half.

In May, three months after the Cessna atrocity, William Sinclair, a Freedmen's Bureau inspector, filed a report from his travels throughout Texas. Despite the burning and killing that took place in Leon County, he argued that this particular county was ahead of all that he had visited across Texas and had "fewer outrages" committed against freedpeople there, a telling claim about the scale of violence across Texas. In the same report, he noted a chill over the Trinity region as the river, "4 to 10 miles wide," flooded farms. Freshly planted corn rotted under the water even as freedpeople held out hope the river would recede in time to plant their cotton crop. After all, things could not be worse than the disaster of 1866, he said, when floods destroyed so much of the cotton crop.[20]

On top of all the other troubles of the postwar years, the Trinity flooded crops, spread disease, and thwarted federal aid. Historians of the Civil War and Reconstruction have emphasized that the destruction caused by warfare made survival for freedpeople much more tenuous, but the war was not the sole determinant of freedpeople's struggles. While Texas was spared significant fighting, the freedpeople of Texas were not spared from scarcity, violence, or sickness. The postwar history of the Trinity River shows the challenges that freedpeople faced across the former Confederacy, and not just in the battle-scarred Deep and Upper South.

When enslaved laborers had been brought to the Trinity, they had cleared land and planted crops along the river, which caused substantial erosion. The Trinity could not flush out this much earth, so silt built up in the main channel and made the river shallower. The amount of rainfall could stay the same but still bring bigger floods. Before emancipation, most planters had not welcomed floods, but they were able to weather them because their holdings typically covered both uplands and bottomlands, and they could spread their plantings out to protect against both drought and floods while forcing their slaves to replant when needed. Freedpeople, who cultivated a much smaller portion of the plantation, were unable to minimize their risk in the same way. Eventually, sharecroppers began to negotiate a fairer distribution of their cropland that included less flood-prone sections of the plantation. In his memoir, a Trinity planter's son recalled how each of the thirty-five tenant families would "farm thirty acres on the hills or upland and ten in the bottom. This way, when the ever-threatening floods came and destroyed the field crops, the family would have the thirty acres to 'make the winter on.'" But these arrangements happened later and did not help those farmers who lost what little they could accumulate in the initial postwar years. In this era, freedpeople paid more for the environmental debts of plantation slavery than those who had previously enslaved them.[21]

***The life of Adolph Henry Mayer*** exemplifies the postwar challenges of the Trinity. Growing up in Ohio, Mayer belonged to a family with a storied military heritage, including a maternal great-grandfather who served as a Continental soldier in the American Revolution. Mayer's father, Elias, had served under Napoleon Bonaparte until his defeat in the Battle of Waterloo, after which he immigrated to the United States. His father might have known some of the Bonapartist refugees who attempted to establish their ill-fated Champ d'Asile colony on the Trinity in 1818. If they heard where Mayer would be stationed, they surely would have warned him about the Trinity's dangers. A few years before the Civil War, Mayer left his young family in Ohio to prospect for gold out west. At the outbreak of war, he joined the Union army through the New Mexico Volunteers with the rank of major, but illness sent him back east. Then on August 10, 1866, he received a commission as the sole Freedmen's Bureau agent stationed in the fittingly named town of Liberty along the Trinity with an annual salary of $1,200.[22]

When Mayer arrived in Liberty in the summer of 1866, the spring overflow had already drowned all the crops.[23] Coming as it did at the outset of Reconstruction, the 1866 flood brought hardships to every river resident, but the loss of the crops was devastating for freedmen. It must have felt like the Trinity itself was against them. Many freedpeople considered leaving the region altogether, but those who had lived on and learned from the mercurial river found ways to carry on after the water subsided, just as they had done before emancipation.[24] Those who persevered and replanted grew a substantial cotton crop, but this raised another issue: Could the Trinity's former slaveholders be trusted to fairly share the profits of their labor?

During the immediate postwar years, the Trinity remained the main route for exporting the region's cotton. At his post in Liberty near the mouth of the river, Mayer received widespread reports of freedpeople being swindled. Mayer wanted to take action to ensure fair distribution of crop value, but he had to be strategic. Rather than go from farm to farm, Mayer decided to take advantage of his position, stopping boats coming downriver and, in some cases, seizing their cotton if he felt that freedpeople had been cheated out of their portion. Unless shipments included proper permits certifying an equitable settlement with freedpeople, Mayer attempted to prevent the steamboats from heading to Galveston. That winter he addressed a large group of freedpeople regarding his plans to use the river as a chokepoint to force landowners to deal fairly across the region and to ensure that "for good honest labor they [the freedpeople] shall receive good honest pay."[25]

Unfortunately, Mayer lacked the manpower to fully implement his plan, and agents upstream did not always cooperate. Mayer "was nearly worn out" from trying to make sure that every planter knew the rules and proved they had abided by them.[26] Much of the cotton he seized quickly disappeared in the middle of the night, which he argued would not occur if he had enough men to guard the cotton. He wrote to headquarters requesting more soldiers, without which Mayer could not enforce the contracts that he and the upriver agents had authorized. Even as he managed to ensure a number of fair contracts and settlements that would not have occurred without his efforts, he believed that most of the freedmen upstream were still "being swindled."[27]

Despite Mayer's attempts to turn the Trinity to his advantage, in the end it did the opposite, exacerbating the scarcity of federal resources in Texas. He received a steady flow of applications from freedpeople requesting him to visit plantations in 1867 to ensure they were being treated fairly, but he could not keep up with the demand because of the conditions of the countryside, the overflowing river making it "almost an impossibility to get through."

Once, Mayer visited a plantation only three miles from the courthouse, but to get there he had to "go around through the big Prairie *eight* miles."[28]

Mayer blamed the Trinity for many of the hardships the freedpeople in his district faced. In April 1867, he wrote to bureau headquarters reporting on the problems caused by the Trinity. Even after the river had receded, the mud it left behind made the roads almost impassable, and Mayer was unable to visit all the places and people he had intended to. Plans to start schools for freedpeople were delayed. He also noted the difficulty that residents faced with getting a good crop: "First, the extreme high water prevented and now the lands are so wet that it is almost an impossibility to work them."[29] Had the farmers attempted to plant in such conditions, the mud would have stuck to their shoes and mules while they slipped around in the mire. Mayer's descriptions of the Trinity frequently included the words "impassible" and "impossible," and he attributed a good deal of the Freedmen's Bureau's difficulties to the river. In June 1867, Mayer wrote to the commanding officer in Houston requesting the help of four soldiers to arrest the thugs responsible "for inhumanely beating & mal-treating, a freedman" but thereafter admitted that with "the water being so high . . . it might be impossible to get here."[30] Officers all along the river reported similar difficulties in 1866 and 1867.

Fragmented by the flooding river, the Freedmen's Bureau and the military were unable to share their limited resources or communicate effectively. This made the agents' work not only more challenging but also more costly. Mayer once had to justify one of his receipts by explaining that his ferry bill was so expensive because the ferryman had to row over five miles "each way to reach dry land."[31] The high water even disrupted communications with agents just across the river.[32] One military official, stuck with no way to communicate with the agent across the miles-wide river, wrote desperately to the Texas bureau chief asking him for direction on how to help the freedpeople relying on him amid such a crisis. "I am all they have," he wrote.[33]

The Trinity River defined the disappointment of Reconstruction for many freedpeople, who had been given nothing after emancipation and then lost much of what they had been able to gain by their hard labor because of the flooding river. Reconstruction is often considered a brief moment of hope with major gains accompanied by federal enforcement, but the Trinity made this window of opportunity even smaller. Seventy years later, Armstead Barrett remembered the floods that came. He farmed in the first year after Juneteenth, but he "never made much cause the high water went over my crop."[34] Yet even in the summer of 1867, when freedpeople became so disheartened by the flooding Trinity, there was still hope in the air. On June 19, thousands of freedpeople gathered in Huntsville, Texas, to mark the anniversary of emancipation. In doing so they defined their freedom as worthy of celebration in spite of the incredible hardships of the past two years.[35]

Across the South, planters continued to search for new ways to exploit plantation labor, but the floods sometimes left little for them to take. The flooding Trinity was one more threat to freedpeople's survival. Reflecting on the summer floods of 1867, Mayer wondered whether the growing season could be salvaged: After months of hard work, freedpeople "look upon this as so much time & labor lost." Mayer claimed to "cheer them up" by telling them they would starve if they did not work.[36] That fall, Mayer realized that the floods had indeed created bleak outcomes: "I never saw such a condition of affairs. Every one. Employer & Employee white & black, are bankrupts. . . . What is to be done to save the freedmen with large families from starving?"[37]

Diseases and death accompanied the floodwaters and increased hardships for freedpeople trying to build new lives. Emancipation forced them to weigh the risks of plague against the cost of leaving. Throughout the South, the early years of Reconstruction were particularly lethal for freedpeople because of limited resources and insufficient federal support, ultimately contributing to the deaths of thousands.[38] But moving also proved deadly. This danger factored into the decisions many freed slaves made to try their chances along the Trinity they knew rather than relocate to the unfamiliar. Yet with their crops weakened or destroyed by flooding in the first two years after emancipation and the constant threat of being cheated by white planters, freedpeople who remained faced disease with little to sustain them. When yellow fever returned to the Trinity in 1867, it had devastating consequences. The disease hindered the ability of the Freedmen's Bureau to provide assistance and protect freedpeoples' rights at a critical moment. Hundreds of US soldiers died in Texas from yellow fever; the commander of the bureau in Texas succumbed to it in September. A former Trinity River bureau agent and voter registrar died; his replacement survived the disease but was unable to fulfill his duties during his illness.[39] Farther upriver, another agent reported that the spread of the disease was causing chaos.[40]

The yellow fever outbreak made it even harder for the Freedmen's Bureau to accomplish its mission in a region where white residents attacked agents for doing their jobs. The outbreak overlapped with a major voter registration drive in 1867, which was part of the Congressional Reconstruction that was intended to ensure that states like Texas could not disenfranchise Black people or return to some form of slavery. When Mayer asked for additional federal troops in the summer of 1867, he was denied because of the risk of their movement further spreading disease.[41] In a rare moment, Mayer complained not about the river but about the river's white residents: Those who opposed the Black vote "cannot be trusted in any way."[42] Meanwhile, Mayer's bureau colleagues were able to do little more than report on evidence of crimes they could not prevent, such as the murder of a freedman—his body, with his arms tied up, discovered floating down the Trinity River.[43] Eventually Mayer fell ill too, not with yellow fever but rather with exhaustion. That fall, his physician ordered him to leave on a steamboat to recover with his family in Galveston.[44]

At the outset of Reconstruction, the Trinity embodied the hope that accompanied emancipation as it enabled freedpeoples' mobility and carried troops intended to protect their rights, but it soon demonstrated the era's greatest disappointments. Denied forty acres and a mule or any freedom dues at all, most freedpeople had little choice except to work for former slaveholders. The river then destroyed much of their labor, year after year, making their very survival all the more tenuous. The floods left them with nothing to pay for their medical care or other needs. In the summer of 1868, a doctor serving the freedpeople of the Trinity sought help from the bureau to support his practice, since the crop failures of the last two years had left his patients "no means to pay with."[45]

In 1867 at Mayer's urging, many freedpeople had turned to chopping down trees to feed the wood-hungry steamboats traveling on the Trinity, but the steamboat traffic dwindled after the floods, making fewer and fewer trips upriver because there was so little cotton to transport due to low cotton harvests from floods, pests, and an increased focus on planting foods that people could eat. In a report to bureau headquarters, Mayer transcribed "a correct statement of the conditions" directly from the freedpeople he served. In one testimony, the freedman Sam Shaffer requested help in securing payments from the steamboat captains for the cordwood they had cut along the river. "We are in a starving condition," Shaffer said. "Our crops have failed in every particular, first the high water, next the worms, next the rains, we did our duty, we tried our best, we are now reduced, as I have stated before to starvation."[46]

Mayer resumed his duties on the Trinity much diminished, never recovering from the stress of his impossible task. Three months after returning to his post, he resigned on February 8, 1868, writing directly to Oliver Otis Howard, the first and only leader of the Freedmen's Bureau.[47] While the bureau continued to exist for several more years, it effectively became a nonentity in Texas by the end of 1868. Mayer struggled to find a new job, as "existing prejudices" in Texas meant that few white men were willing to hire a Union veteran and former Freedmen's Bureau agent. He returned to the federal government working for the Internal Revenue Department to support his family.[48] Diagnosed with consumption, he continued to decline. In this state, he wrote to his parents telling them not to worry about his poor health: "What good will worry or fretting do, you cannot help and you do yourselves no good." He told them he missed their cooking and dreamed of returning North where he could get the proper nourishment. He wondered whether perhaps he could procure some salmon when he visited Galveston, requesting their family recipe for "Saucing Pickled Salmon." He attached a check for fifty dollars, asking them to please "write me a good long letter."[49] That was likely the last his parents ever heard from their son. When he could not handle his suffering anymore, Mayer committed suicide on April 19, 1869. His remains were transported to New Orleans so that he could be buried in the Dispersed of Judah Cemetery, since it was "the graveyard of the Jewish Faith."[50] Back in Texas, the violence continued, such as a "cold blooded murder" in the Trinity River bottom.[51]

The Freedmen's Bureau played a key role in establishing schools for freedpeople across Texas, several of which were located directly along the Trinity and built in large part with funds raised by freedpeople. Despite the losses and disappointments of Reconstruction, Juneteenth remained a crucial and uplifting turning point. In the 1880 census, Louisa Tubbs, who had abruptly left James Hall's employment a few months after emancipation, now worked as a farmhand. Prior to Juneteenth, her fourteen-year-old daughter, Ann, would have had to perform similar labor, but now in this moment of freedom, Ann was "at school," learning to read and write and perhaps hearing the history of the monumental changes of the recent past.[52]

## CHAPTER 7

# THE PANTHERS' HOME

The most feared creatures on the Trinity, other than violent men, were mountain lions, which Texans called panthers. These skilled predators once ranged across the state, preferring habitats like the bottomlands, where they stalked abundant game. In the winter their tawny brown coat blended in with the dormant underbrush, enabling them to appear without warning while taking down prey such as white-tailed deer. It was on the Trinity where Stephen F. Austin's father and his enslaved man Richmond were attacked by a panther following the Spanish government's preliminary approval for a new colony. Seven decades later, a married couple made camp on the river. The man, off on a squirrel hunt, heard his wife's screams back at camp. When he rushed back to her, he found his wife "under the paws of a panther," fighting it off with her bare hands as "the animal [was] devouring the flesh of her neck and face." The gun her husband took hunting would have been her only defense.[1]

Every resident understood that survival along the Trinity required a loaded gun within reach at all times. And as the years after Juneteenth made clear to the Trinity's freed population, defense against white vigilantes was also necessary for survival. One of the men wounded in the burning and killing at the Cessna plantation testified that a soldier had confiscated his firearm before he was shot in the back. He lamented, "If I had of had my Pistol I could of protected myself."[2] The risks of panther attacks held hidden benefits for Black people seeking autonomy and safety among widespread violence. The mountain lions lurking in the bottomlands gave them a ready explanation for traveling armed in an era when Black gun ownership invited suspicion. Wayman Williams explained the importance of being armed for a panther attack: "In those days the men took their guns to the fields," because "we never knew when they were going to strike."[3] Firearms also protected them from terrorist violence.[4] At first glance, the deadly panthers suggest another reason to avoid living in the Trinity bottomlands, but they actually help explain why so many freedpeople chose to remain there: Outsiders who feared the panthers stayed away from the river, while river residents defended themselves with guns against both murderous cats and the acts of racist violence that plagued Texas.

Possessing an intimate knowledge of the river and its bottomlands could be as effective at saving one's life as possessing a gun. The river's dense woods and backwaters made it easy for visitors or pursuers to become disoriented. Indeed, even river residents could lose their bearings in the thickets of yaupons and briars: "As usual," a steamboat captain confided in his diary, he "got lost in the Bottoms."[5] Soldiers stationed near the Trinity had difficulty pursuing fugitives because they did not know how to navigate the terrain. Freedmen's Bureau agents like Adolph Mayer depended on individuals who knew the river in order to make their way through its wooded and soggy lands. On several occasions they hired freedmen to guide them through the swamps.[6] Knowledge of the terrain allowed freedpeople to turn the bottomlands into a refuge rather than a place of fear and even to command a price for it. In his fictional account of East Texas, the novelist William Goyen spoke directly to the Trinity as if it were a character, emphasizing Black residents' familiarity with the river: They "knew your bottomlands like their own rooms, knew your good fishing places and where there was white sand and safe hiding places for escaped convicts."[7]

To know a river was to have the power to disappear. In 1870 the Texas State Police were in pursuit of an accused murderer, but after several unsuccessful attempts to find him, one policeman reported in defeat, "My own impression is that he is in the Trinity River bottom."[8] As one of the rivers with the most plantations in Texas, the Trinity became a particularly important refuge, but the Trinity was also part of a statewide understanding of bottomlands. A freedwoman named Mollie Kirkland reflected on this phenomenon, saying that when someone needed to flee the "law," they would find the closest river bottom to hide out in until they could escape farther away.[9] She framed the bottomlands as a refuge for criminals, but they also provided safety when the government was unable or unwilling to protect all its citizens.

***Below Dallas,*** the Trinity serves as the principal eastern or western border for thirteen Texas counties. County governments have played a central role in the ordering of daily life and the distribution of power in Texas.[10] As Reconstruction ended, with most troops withdrawn from the plantation regions by 1870 and the Texas State Police dissolved by 1873, the power of policing returned primarily to the county level.[11] Here sheriffs controlled which laws were enforced and whom they would protect. The power emanating from these county seats was not evenly distributed across their jurisdictions, especially before good roads and automobiles were commonplace. County seats in Texas are typically located close to the geographic center of each county, sometimes reflected in names referencing their location, such as Shelby County's Center and Leon County's Centerville. This pattern meant that Trinity residents lived at the farthest edge of the county sheriff's territory. All the factors that made the Trinity a less visited place—distance from courthouses, floods that disrupted travel, fearsome panthers—also made the river into a refuge where freedpeople could pursue their independence on the margins of government power.

From 1870 to 1873 the newly formed Texas State Police force, made up of Black, Tejano, and white officers, made hundreds of arrests for murder but was unable to offer sufficient protection. Andy McAdams went to vote in Huntsville under the guard of the State Police sent by Governor Edmund Davis, the state's last Republican governor under Reconstruction.[12] McAdams soon discovered the forces sent by the governor could not shield him from the hatred of the former Confederates. "All us negroes we thought that Governor Davis would protect us," he recalled. "But Oh Son," he recounted, the vigilantes whom he called slave patrollers "went to catching negroes the first thing we knew." McAdams escaped the mob by taking refuge in the bottomlands: "But thank the Lord they never did catch me cause I went right to the Trinity River bottom and stayed there until they quit whipping negroes before I come out again." The Trinity temporarily sheltered McAdams in the absence of effective state power, but the river could not ensure the protection of his rights; he concluded his account—recorded in the 1930s—by noting, "That was the last time I ever voted."[13]

Increased representation and state-level protection for Black Texans and white Unionists was short-lived in Reconstruction Texas. The most famous of the Black politicians in this era was George T. Ruby. Originally from Portland, Maine, Ruby worked for the Freedmen's Bureau in Galveston and toured the state, giving him a detailed understanding of the challenges and opportunities in Texas. In 1868 Ruby served as a delegate to the Republican

Figure 7.1. Photograph from late 1860s of "Freedmens first vote" in Anderson County showing the federal troop presence defending freedpeople's right to vote. Courtesy of Palestine Public Library and the Portal to Texas History, University of North Texas Libraries, https://texashistory.unt.edu/ark:/67531/metapth26465/.

National Convention and then the state constitutional convention. The next year he was elected to the Texas Senate as a senator from Galveston. But after the Democrats regained power in 1873, he saw no future for his political career in Texas and left for New Orleans.

As the political path to protecting their rights closed, Black people began founding freedom colonies. Across the South, freedpeople built settlements that enabled independence, but the term "freedom colonies" was specific to Texas. These communities have been uniquely overlooked among their peer settlements; today, the Texas Freedom Colonies Project works to remedy this historical omission and has located over 550 freedom colonies across Texas, a number of which are near the Trinity. At these and other still-uncounted communities, Black families established their independence, which in part depended on being overlooked by white Texans.

After the end of the Civil War, the Trinity's main plantation region underwent a dramatic transformation in less than a decade. Once a primary trade route and center of economic importance, the lower half of the Trinity became relatively inaccessible, with growth that lagged behind the rest of the state. This transformation suited individuals like Andy McAdams just fine. As the Trinity's economic prospects appeared to dim, it allowed him to stand on relatively solid, if soggy, ground.

***At the start of Reconstruction,*** few people imagined the state's most navigable river would cease to be a vital highway into the Texas interior. Throughout the 1860s, boats built "expressly for the Trinity river trade" continued to arrive, often replacing ones that sank and could not be salvaged.[14] In 1867, for instance, a steamboat along with its 535 bales of cotton were lost to the river, and the next week two more went down.[15] Steamboat captains now faced not only the snags and sandbars of the river but also bandits who believed they could act with impunity in the region. A steamboat captain "of great energy" was murdered on the *Ida Reese* on March 2, 1870.[16] The murderers, who killed him near his home, included his former steward and another river pilot. Governor Davis offered a $500 reward for their capture, but by the time the Texas State Police investigated the murder in July, the suspects had dispersed.[17]

Even if the authorities could do little to end the violent chaos, Trinity River residents insisted that with a few incentives the government could make their river more reliable. Heeding this call, the Texas legislature passed several acts promoting navigation on the state's rivers, including one on June 3, 1873, that called for "the opening and cleaning out of the Trinity river."[18] Jules Poitevent was appointed to carry out the work and given a deadline of 1875. For every mile cleared, he would receive four certificates worth 640 acres that could be redeemed for unclaimed land anywhere in the state. Poitevent, described as sharp and shrewd, was one of the few white people to move to Texas and settle on the lower half of the Trinity in these years. He operated his steamboat, the *Early Bird*, and purchased a plantation with the intention of turning its landing into a trade center.

Like all captains, Poitevent had to be alert to avoid the river's many threats. He, however, was able to turn snags into profit by improving the Trinity and getting paid with government land grants. Poitevent and his crew on the *Early Bird* dislodged snags from the riverbed.[19] These snags had been a constant threat to the puncturable hull of a passing steamboat, but they had up to that point also been a part of the river—removing them would have its own set of consequences. When trees fall into a river they slow the flow of water; without them, water speeds up, which scours riverbanks, eroding soil, and increases the channel's instability.

Poitevent ultimately received certificates for a total of 437,760 acres of land.[20] He sold the majority of these land grants to people settling in other, more desirable parts of the state, while he stayed on as a planter and captain on his parcel of the newly cleared Trinity River. Meanwhile, much of Poitevent's Trinity work went unused. The generous land grants and improvement expenditures that the legislature approved for the Trinity and other rivers paled in comparison to those given out for the construction of railroads. Across Texas, almost 2.5 percent of its land was granted for navigation improvements, compared with nearly 20 percent of all of the state's land granted for railroads. Government subsidies and corruption fueled the construction of rail lines and river improvement, but the arrival of railroads meant that Texas's economic growth no longer had to be contained by its unpredictable and ever-changing rivers. The Texas and New Orleans Railroad was the first to cross the Trinity, which it did just before the Civil War (though its bridge was completely washed away by the Trinity when the river flooded in 1867 and had to be rebuilt).[21]

At the same time that Poitevent was clearing snags, new railroads were being built across the river, siphoning off trade. Navigation of the river ceased by the end of the 1870s as it no longer made economic sense for steamboats to tempt fate on the river. The completion of the Houston and Great Northern Railroad meant that people did not need to wait for perfect river conditions to ship cotton or travel long distances.[22] Railroads could be used year-round, and freight shipped on them did not face the same risks as those on the river steamboats. In 1876 a steamboat sank near the mouth of the Trinity as it was bringing supplies upriver for track construction, further justifying the need for the comparatively safe railroads.[23] Farmers believed river navigation could lower railroad costs through competition. However, steamboat traffic, and profits, collapsed. In 1871 the Trinity steamboat trade reached 27,942 bales; it dropped to 14,244 in 1872. On May 2, 1874, the *Galveston Daily News* reported that only 1,670 bales of cotton had been shipped to Galveston via the Trinity River since September 1 of the previous year.[24] Meanwhile, 224,125 bales had arrived via the railroad. The Trinity had lost its preeminence as a trade route. An 1881 newspaper article summed up these changes as it had become obvious, from the "blowing of the first railroad whistle," that transportation on the river was "not only uncertain, but too slow."[25]

The switch from rivers to railroads had all sorts of consequences for the lower half of the Trinity. For one, merchants were now more distant from the river. Philip Browne grew up working in his father's store in his county's centrally located town. One day, his cousin discovered that the store's supply of rice had become infested with weevils. The young boy suggested that the family avoid taking a loss on the rice by foisting the spoiled rice on their more distant patrons. Customers from farthest away, such as those living near the Trinity River, came only once or twice a month, so he "knew they weren't coming back to bring it."[26] His father used the opportunity to teach his son a moral lesson—that they would not treat their patrons with such callousness. However, this story also highlights how the lower Trinity had become a remote place, so different from when the county was first settled precisely because of the Trinity's importance as a trade route.

***After Juneteenth,*** nearly every freedperson who remained near the Trinity started out by working on plantations without the means or options to do anything else, but as the river quieted from the equivalent of a major highway to a backwoods dirt road, many took advantage of the land's devaluation to establish their independence. For example, Andy McAdams, who began by sharecropping on a plantation immediately after emancipation, came to the Trinity River and began to farm for himself.[27] Throughout the South, freedpeople were upset by having to continue to labor on plantations. Along the Trinity, disappointment was compounded by the river's repeated destruction of the crops they had worked so hard to grow. As relationships with planters and the river deteriorated, many left plantations in the late 1860s and throughout the 1870s as the federal government withdrew from enforcing the nation's citizenship laws in Texas. A few of the plantations on the Trinity continued to grow, but most ceased to exist, their prospects further worsened by a dramatic decline in cotton prices. When freedpeople moved off plantations to live independently on the river, they no longer had to focus their energy on planting cotton, whose prices were subject to the whims of the global cotton trade. Instead, they could focus more on other crops, as well as on hunting and fishing along the river.

The vast majority of Texas land had been unclaimed while it was a republic and even once it became a state. After the Civil War, however, the state worked quickly to distribute land and by 1898 had none left to give.[28] These lands went to white people, owing in part to the 1880 law that gave 1,280 acres to every disabled Confederate veteran. In contrast to white migrants, Black people found themselves denied any reasonable opportunity to obtain prime lands during Reconstruction, despite the promises of General William T. Sherman's Special Field Order No. 15 in 1865 (the order that led many freedpeople to believe they would be granted forty acres and a mule). The uneven distribution of land grants in Texas meant that more Black people remained along the state's rivers while white people found better options elsewhere for property ownership.

When Black people began to claim land for themselves, they could rarely purchase the best land for farming and selling cash crops. Instead, as W. E. B. Du Bois noted in his study of Black landownership, the land that passed into their hands was "poor, being often practically worn out or disadvantageously situated as regards a market."[29] Still, while most of the Trinity lands were increasingly distant from sites of commerce, they retained their great fertility, and crucially, the bottomlands had become an even more important refuge as federal allies like the Freedmen's Bureau left the state. By the early 1870s, as the Trinity gained a reputation as a depressed region, some of these lands came into the possession of freed slaves. This process of freedpeople and their descendants moving to the bottomlands happened in other parts of the South as well, such as in the Mississippi Delta, where Black farmers sought to "get back there among the wolves." But it lasted longer on the final frontier of plantation slavery than it did in the East.[30]

Many freedpeople who lived on the Trinity did not take a title to the land but rather squatted on it unchallenged due to its diminished value. For the next five decades, it would not matter who held the property title. Though some of these residents can be tracked using the census, others purposely lived hidden from view. Their relative invisibility served as a strength, despite the challenges it poses for historians.[31] Jane Cotton, for example, "didn't know who the land" belonged to when she settled on the Trinity. Cotton and her husband built a house out of poles. At first, they struggled to eat more than corn cracked with a hammer, hickory nuts, wild game, and fish.[32]

Like Jane Cotton, Andy McAdams's testimony reveals the practical challenges of starting out with so few possessions. "For a number of years all I had to eat was corn parched green and meat that I killed out of the woods," he said. Much of the meat he had to eat raw since he "did not have a very easy way of starting a fire," unable to afford even a box of matches.[33] What cash he had gained would have been prioritized for spending on a firearm to defend his family from panthers and Klansmen. Over time, McAdams and Cotton acquired more assets and an improved understanding of the river's environment. The Trinity was never easy, but it was possible to make a life there.

Limited cash—especially for those who lived away from the Trinity's plantations—meant that they had to diversify their food sources. They relied on fish and game in addition to a variety of crops so that if a flood destroyed their plants they could have other things to eat. William Stone moved to the Trinity shortly after Reconstruction ended and stayed there until his children grew up. Unlike most people who lived along the river, Stone found a more consistent source of cash by working in a sawmill. He credited the environment with his capacity to live independently, stating that there was so much game that his family could "eat easy."[34] Even those who continued to work on plantations relied on the Trinity to increase their independence. During the Civil War, Wayman Williams's family lived in the bottomlands and remained on the same plantation after Juneteenth. His family farmed for half the crop, but they relied on the land for much of their sustenance. The panthers that lived in the bottoms stayed there in part because of the abundant game, and these deer, squirrels, hogs, and turkeys proved crucial. "I remember times when we could go hunting and kill most anything that we wanted to," he recalled. His father could shoot a deer within sight of the house. "Living was easier then," he reasoned, because "we had all these things without having to buy them." Everything the family ate came from the bottomlands. They could not make much money from their position on the Trinity, sometimes going without flour because it was "too high to buy," but they could live off the natural bounty of the land and water.[35]

In their reflections about life on the Trinity, men and women like Andy McAdams and Jane Cotton emphasized the families they raised and the communities they belonged to. Cotton and her husband raised seven children in the bottomlands. Despite the challenges of living on the river, McAdams had been there for almost seventy years by the time his descriptions of life on the Trinity were recorded. As he put it, "[We] took us some land to farm and here I've been ever since."[36] The river was not simply a refuge; it was home.

Lost in the shift from rivers to railroads, freedom colonies have sometimes been mistaken for ghost towns in the historical record. Hall's Bluff, named after James Hall's family, ceased operating as a trading town after steamboats disappeared in the 1870s, but many of the freedpeople who lived there stayed on to start their own farms. It was a cohesive community with a school and a church in spite of the town's diminished trading fortunes.[37] One of the founding members of the post-Juneteenth community at Hall's Bluff was Joseph Houston. His father, Joshua, had been enslaved by former Texas Governor Sam Houston, after whom the city of Houston is named. Soon after Juneteenth, Joseph Houston moved from Huntsville to Hall's Bluff and used some of the money he had saved to buy two hundred acres of farmland. Even as trade dried up along the river, Houston's children prospered.

While most white planters and merchants moved away, their departure created an opportunity for people like Houston to form their own community. They could no longer load a steamboat but could haul cotton and other cash crops to the railroad hubs farther away. A descendant wrote that the Houston family had "lived happy, prosperous, and successful lives."[38] In contrast, *The State Handbook of Texas*'s 1952 entry on Hall's Bluff reads, "The town began to decline after the Houston and Great Northern Railroad came to Crockett in 1872."[39] The truth seems to be a mix of these two accounts: Hall's Bluff declined in importance for certain people, which created new opportunities for autonomy and community building for others. Freedpeople transformed Hall's Bluff from a site that supported the development of plantation slavery into a freedom colony, and if some records missed this transformation, then maybe that was the point.

Nowhere was the significance of this revolution from slavery to freedom more apparent than thirty miles south of Hall's Bluff on December 29, 1886. There the first convention of the Colored Farmers' Alliance was held at Good Hope Baptist Church a few miles east of the Trinity. Following this convention, the Colored Farmers' Alliance swept across the entire South and played a major role in the Populist movement. Despite its leaders' furtive approach to growing the organization, up to a million members joined the alliance. The original sixteen Black convention members adopted principles related to agriculture but also to "protect their individual rights," to raise "funds for the benefit of sick or disabled members, or their distressed families," and to form "a closer union among all colored people."[40] These widely popular principles were rooted in the particular context of Texas's freedom colonies and the Trinity River. During Reconstruction, freedpeople went to the bottomlands with nothing more than a hammer to crack corn with and a gun with which to defend themselves. The fact that the Colored Farmers' Alliance formed here twenty-one years after Juneteenth points to the multiple scales of community that steadily built off each other, from families to freedom colonies to a movement that swept across the nation.

## CHAPTER 8

# THE LOST CAUSE OF DALLAS STEAMBOATS

In the era when steamboats plied the Trinity, they traveled upriver from Galveston until the landscape surrounding its bottomland forests turned into prairie and the channel narrowed. Only the lower half of the river had been central to the spread of plantation slavery. However, following the Civil War, the Trinity would become a key player in the dramatic growth of Dallas and Fort Worth. On the upper river as on the lower, the story of freedpeople was intertwined with the river.

In freedom colonies like Joppa, near Dallas, the combination of independence and isolation was no less important than in the former plantation region downriver. A descendant of those who built the settlement of Joppa described it as an isolated island, since "there was a time, as a freedmen's community, when they needed those barriers."[1] Squeezed between the railroad and the river, Joppa was about six miles south of Dallas's center, close enough to commute to and far enough away for greater autonomy. The Trinity made Joppa less accessible, but it also offered opportunities for catching catfish and buffalo fish to eat and sufficient land for garden plots that reduced dependence on the markets of Dallas.

Figure 8.1. Ferries, such as the one in this photograph from around 1920 at Wallisville, near the mouth of the Trinity, played an important role on the river until bridges consistently crossed it. Courtesy of Chambers County Museum at Wallisville, Texas.

Naming their community after the biblical Joppa, the founders were clear about their hopes: In the Bible an angel of God tells a devout Christian that "your prayers and your alms have ascended as a memorial before God. And now send men to Joppa . . ."[2] This settlement on the Trinity was to be the answer to their prayers. The parallel could extend further, since biblical Joppa was a seaport town to which the cedars for building Jerusalem were brought. Perhaps the residents anticipated becoming a port in the imagined future of a fully navigable river. But in practice, it was not travel up and down the Trinity but across it that mattered in the early development of this region of North Texas.

Joppa's founder, Henry Critz Hines, was one of the tens of thousands of enslaved people brought to Texas during the Civil War. He arrived from Missouri and remained in Dallas County after Juneteenth. In 1872, the year the railroad came to Dallas, he gained ownership of the ferry, which he continued to operate into the twentieth century.[3] The increasing population and traffic to Dallas helped to sustain Hines's ferry. Ferrymen had to use their strength and energy against the river's current, whether using poles to push along the riverbed or a rope to pull the ferry across, while hauling wagons or even herds of cattle across the river.[4] High water on the Trinity offered greater pay to ferry operators but also required much more labor since the boats would need to be pushed or pulled farther.[5] County courts typically set rates for ferries; for example, in one county it was twenty-five cents for a horse and buggy, the equivalent of just over six dollars in today's inflation-adjusted values. However, the rates applied only to a nonflooding river; if it overflowed, operators were entitled to charge up to four times the regular rate.[6] In another county, ferrymen could double rates if the Trinity was high "but not over the banks"—and above that, "anything" was fair game.[7]

For men like Hines, running a ferry provided an invaluable source of cash, but this income made ferry operators into targets. Downriver from Joppa, a ferryman received an ax blow to his head before being stabbed to death and thrown into the river. Despite a confession of guilt, the murderers, who sought control of the ferry, were never convicted, because the ferryman's severely decomposed corpse could not be definitively identified.[8]

Hines was not the only person who profited from the value of crossing the upper Trinity. Its crossing points played a key role in the origins of urban North Texas. In 1841 John Neely Bryan founded Dallas on the east side of the Trinity, in what is now its downtown. Having followed the Native trails in the region, Bryan realized that these routes converged at one specific crossing on the river where the mud gave way to the hardened Austin Chalk. The Trinity would soon serve as a source of water—and a vital outlet for waste—in the early years, but Bryan chose the future city's location because of its importance as a crossing, operating a ferry there until he sold his county license to the Cockrell family.

Sarah Horton Cockrell helped to transform Dallas from a frontier town into a city. She and her husband built a wooden toll bridge across the river that collapsed in 1858. That same year her husband died in a gunfight, so she returned to operating a ferry. In 1871, Cockrell led the Dallas Bridge Company's construction of the first iron bridge across the river, despite substantial opposition. This bridge not only eased passage across the Trinity but also became a point of pride for Dallas as a significant work of engineering in Texas. Often referred to as one of Texas's original millionaires, Cockrell made much of her wealth from toll fees collected from travelers crossing the Trinity on her ferries and bridges. Cockrell's creation of the iron bridge was the first of many innovations spurred on by the Trinity, which pushed

Figure 8.2. Sarah Horton Cockrell, Dallas bridge builder. On the back of this photograph, her daughter wrote, “It was her courage and business acumen that pushed Dallas forward when water and fire had sapped its strength.” Courtesy of DeGolyer Library, Southern Methodist University, Archives of Women of the Southwest collection.

residents to envision and engineer bolder plans that reflected their growing population and ambition.

The pollution of the river served as another catalyst for planning and urban development. Much of the blood, guts, and feces from Fort Worth's stockyards and slaughterhouses ended up flowing downstream through Dallas. The use of the Trinity as a sewer was an advantage for both cities at first, but by the 1880s it had become a big problem. The summer months were especially challenging—with more evaporation on the hottest days, the sewage made up a greater proportion of the Trinity's flow. As the river became less reliable as a source of water, the Dallas city council entered into a contentious debate about where else to get the growing settlement's water. An alderman warned that Trinity water had best be avoided since it was "impure poisonous and not even fit to wash with."[9] While the debate revealed a limitation of the Trinity in its pollution, the dirty river forced Dallas leaders to look beyond city boundaries in ways that shaped the long-term development of what has become the Dallas–Fort Worth region.

Upriver from Dallas, on the Elm Fork of the Trinity, was the California Crossing, so named because of its location on the road taken by fortune seekers during the Gold Rush, including Dallas founder John Neely Bryan, in 1849. The California Crossing had been an important junction for the Comanche. They signposted key locations with marker trees by bending saplings so that the wood would grow at a distinctive angle and be easy to locate. A pecan tree bent by the Comanche earlier in the 1800s continues to mark the California Crossing to this day. The Comanche people's enduring strength directly to the north and west of Dallas and Fort Worth limited American settlement.[10]

The wet years of 1866 and 1867, which caused so much flooding and suffering for freedpeople on the lower Trinity, were a boon to the Comanche and their horses on the suddenly verdant plains. The greening of the plains allowed the Comanche to regain their strength, and they extended their raiding zone up to the edge of Fort Worth. However, their rise also coincided with Reconstruction, as the South and West were knitted (or reknitted) into the Union. Questions about the use of resources to uphold the rights of freedpeople or to control Native tribes were hotly debated. At the outset of Reconstruction, General Philip Sheridan complained that former Texas Confederates placed far too much emphasis on the Comanche and other tribes: "If a white man is killed by the Indians on an extensive frontier, the greatest excitement will take place, but over the killing of many freedmen in the settlements nothing is done."[11] By the end of Reconstruction, this debate was settled in a way that reflected the truth in Sheridan's complaint: The Comanche

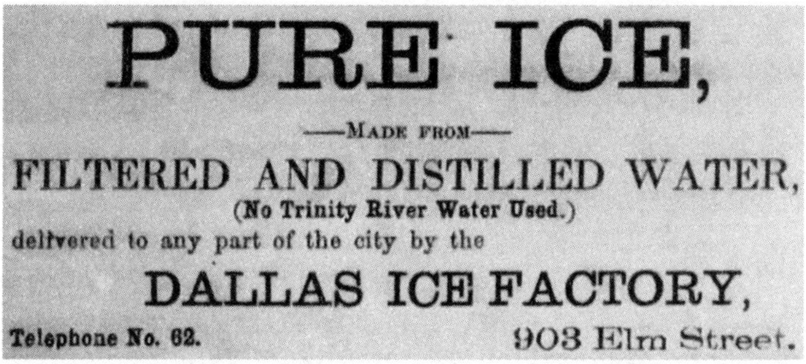


Figure 8.3. An advertisement emphasizing "Pure Ice" with "No Trinity River Water Used" that appeared in the July 29, 1887, issue of the *Dallas Herald*. Courtesy of the Portal to Texas History, University of North Texas Libraries, https://texashistory.unt.edu/ark:/67531/metapth293887/.

were decisively defeated, while the end of federal troops in the plantation region left freedpeople to focus on self-defense and their independence.

All these events conspired to make Dallas, Fort Worth, and their surrounding communities boom. Between 1870 to 1900, the population of Texas more than tripled as migrants poured in from the rest of the former Confederacy, moving in much greater numbers to the upper rather than the lower Trinity.[12] The population of Dallas increased from 3,000 people in 1870 to over 150,000 by 1920, a nearly 5,000 percent increase.

***If the practical challenge*** of building bridges and obtaining sufficient potable water pushed Dallas and Fort Worth to make regional plans and gain civic pride in their infrastructure, it was above all else the dream of navigating the Trinity that fueled city leaders' confidence in their future greatness. At no point in the development of Dallas and Fort Worth had the upper Trinity been able to support commercially feasible navigation. The head of Trinity navigation had been its midpoint, around the landing at Magnolia, from where the Confederacy had launched flatboats downriver during the Civil War. Even in these middle reaches of the Trinity, navigation was inconsistent and ended completely after the arrival of railroads in the 1870s. This history did nothing, however, to deter North Texans' hopes of turning Dallas and Fort Worth into inland port cities. And so for over a century, navigating the Trinity remained one of the main goals of North Texas politicians and business leaders.

Even as railroads began to crisscross the landscape, many North Texas leaders believed that water transport was a requirement for great cities. In

1867 Captain J. H. McGarvey made a determined effort to get his little steamboat, *The Job No. 1*, all the way to Dallas, something that had never been done before. Upon hearing of his trip, the *Dallas Herald* entreated, "Come along Captain, we want to shake hands with the first steamboatman that comes to Dallas."[13] When McGarvey arrived the following summer, he claimed, in spite of his long, grueling trip, that the river should be navigable all the way to Dallas for most of the year. Anticipating regular navigation to North Texas, the *Dallas Herald* prophesied that it would lead to dramatic wealth in real estate "before unheard of in all that region."[14] After McGarvey's auspicious journey, a town meeting was held with the aims of promoting navigation of the river, providing funds to that end, and soliciting money from the businesspeople of the city of Galveston for further river improvements.[15] Dallas even had its own steamboat constructed, the *Sallie Haynes*, named after the daughter of a prominent merchant.

But these plans never developed into actual routes that could compete with the efficiency of the railroads. Even though Dallas commerce did not rely on the river, the Trinity remained a central part of boosters' vision for the region's eventual greatness. For example, the masthead of *Norton's Union Intelligencer*, published in Dallas, boldly read, "Published at the Head of Steamboat Navigation and the Railroad Crossing of the Trinity River."[16] An 1874 article in *Scribner's* described Dallas as "set down on the banks of the Trinity River, and contributed to by the great feeders of the Texas Central and Texas Pacific. It grows like an enchanted castle in a fairy tale."[17] A later example of the enthusiasm for Trinity navigation was the arrival of the steamboat *H. A. Harvey, Jr.* on May 24, 1893. This boat was operated by a group of Dallas civic leaders who built a small dam on the river and used a snag boat to clear the river in the area around the city. When the *Harvey* arrived, a large parade and celebration was held to herald the supposed start of Trinity navigation on the upper river. Never mind that it took the *Harvey* over two months to arrive from Galveston. Meanwhile, trains crossed the entire nation from New York to San Francisco in less than a week.[18]

It was the railroads that brought Texas farmers closer to a wider economy, but that proximity came at a cost, including the actual costs of shipping via railroad. Many farmers perceived rail shipping charges as inflated due to the monopoly that railroad companies had on freight transportation. If the railroads were going to have competition and lower their rates, the Trinity offered an alternative to building another rail line. When the Populist movement was at its height in Texas, navigation of the Trinity gained a larger constituency than just the Dallas and Fort Worth business class. Populists heavily criticized the Texas Railroad Commission, created in 1891, because they believed the commission did not do enough to support their goals. The state's major Populist newspaper published a lengthy report arguing for the construction of a canal. The canal would be a public project, run by the government, and many Populists thought that it could not be monopolized like the railroads, allowing farmers to transport their crops for lower rates; in other words, a railroad would be controlled by their opponents, but the river *could* not. As one proponent put it: "If we canalize the river, they can't well get hold of it, and anybody can run boats and barges on it that wants to."[19] A public river appeared to offer farmers much greater control over their shipping costs compared with a private railroad.

One person who overlapped between public transportation advocates and the business elite was Barnett Gibbs, known as Barney. He had moved to Dallas from the Deep South in the early 1870s and married Sallie Haynes, the daughter of a prominent Dallas businessman. From there, he began his political trajectory, which led him to become lieutenant governor and a Populist spokesman. Barney's marriage made his interest in Trinity navigation personal. A February 1896 article described his outrage that Texas Democrats had left unsettled "the one great, predominant, ponderous, perpendicular and paramount issue of Trinity river navigation." The reporter concluded that the people "will have Trinity river navigation or gore."[20] At a Populist rally in August 1896, Barney argued that "the towns of Texas can't thrive without a lower freight rate" and that the federal government could afford to fund the work, benefiting both producers and consumers in the state.[21]

The platform of the Texas Populists included other issues that were much more contentious, but the possibility of Trinity River navigation was something that both the Texas Chamber of Commerce and the Texas Reform Press Association favored.[22] Because navigation appealed to a wide political base, more politicians could support funding the project. John H. Reagan, the former postmaster general of the Confederacy and the first chairman of the Texas Railroad Commission, published an open letter in December 1895 in which he expressed the commission's support of Trinity navigation. Since he had no power to start the improvements himself, he urged Congress to act.[23] Like many Texans, he believed that with a little help from the federal government, the river could be cleared of snags and, with a few locks added, made navigable all the way to North Texas.

What the boosters did not acknowledge is that the Trinity's recent history of timbering and farming made the possibility of navigation even more remote. Clear-cuts and tilling had increased the sediment load in the river, which led to more impassable sandbars. And while logjams had long existed in the river, waste cutting from the busy timber industry only made it worse down the river. The same expansion of cotton farming and land clearance that led to overproduction and low crop prices, fueling the frustration behind the Populists' rise, also made the Trinity a less feasible route to market.[24] Nevertheless, the goal of a navigable river was shared by the Dallas business elite, who would use the political momentum created by the Populists to promote their own vision of a remade river. With major lobbying efforts in the mid-1890s, and with Populist-business fusionist leaders insisting on navigation, the project found support in Congress, which approved funding for a Trinity River survey.

Not all farmers were Populists, however, and some farmers had never considered developing the Trinity to be a solution that would improve their daily lives. Though the Colored Farmers' Alliance began near the edge of the Trinity bottomlands, at no point did Trinity navigation enter any of the group's core concerns or platforms. Many of those who founded the Colored Farmers' Alliance would have remembered a time when steamboats and slaves had regularly navigated the lower Trinity, but they also would have been aware of how the river alternately flooded and nearly dried up. Controlling a river that experienced such swings seemed impractical and impossible and did not directly address inequality and exploitative practices. Soon enough, the rest of the state's farmers would realize the same.

Trinity River navigation boosters married their dreams of development with the political redemption of the former Confederacy. By the late nineteenth century, the Lost Cause had become a largely successful movement to rewrite history and to downplay the stakes of the Civil War over slavery and the cruelty of slavery itself. White Southerners wielded this myth to justify disenfranchisement and terrorism toward Black Southerners and to encourage a national reunion that blunted the war's political and social impacts. In Texas, nostalgia for the steamboat era overlapped with the Lost Cause. A 1905 newspaper article reminisced about the Magnolia landing on the Trinity, which had once been the primary endpoint for steamboats traveling upriver. The author wrote about this bustling place that shipped cotton and had a fine hotel "noted for its old-time cooking and savory dishes prepared by the old slavery time cook, which is now a lost art, unknown to the present generation." He described "farmers" rather than planters who dispatched over five hundred bales of cotton apiece, without saying who had grown and harvested it. "Those were good times," he claimed, overlooking all the evidence to the contrary, when most people who worked there were not free and would never have referred to the Trinity's plantation era as "good times." Writing in support of the new Trinity River navigation projects, the author hoped to once again be "awakened by the shrill whistle of steamboats on the Trinity."[25] The dream of navigating the entire length of the main stem of the Trinity was both a practical lost cause and an example of the Lost Cause's whitewashing of history.

***In 1899, Captain Charles Swift Riché*** led the Army Corps of Engineers survey of the Trinity River. A graduate of the United States Military Academy, Riché spent his career transforming waterways across the nation, including on the Mississippi River and the Great Lakes. Riché believed the Trinity could be made navigable to Dallas nearly year-round except during severe droughts. He wanted timber along the banks cut down and all snags removed to create a "clean river from Dallas to the mouth." He proposed installing thirty-seven locks and movable dams. During dry seasons, water would have to be either stored in the upper river or added to the river via artesian wells. The total cost for these adjustments as well as dredging and "bank protection" came to an even $4 million.[26]

Riché paid close attention to North Texas politics while ignoring those who called the lower and middle Trinity home. Riché and his men traveled the length of the river from Dallas to Trinity Bay, but neither his report nor the photos the engineers took of the lower half of the river reveal an understanding of the river's residents. Whatever families they might have encountered had no voice in their report. Instead, the surveyors photographed massive driftwood piles and their own grizzled crew floating down the river. While it is possible that people living along the river actively avoided this large group of white men, it is more likely that they simply did not fit into Riché's narrative of an undeveloped wilderness full of promise.

Riché believed that the proposed project could be paid for by the resulting increase in commerce, claiming that development "in the rich bottom lands of the river and in the territory immediately adjacent thereto will by itself justify the improvement."[27] His lack of attention to history meant no mention of either the lower Trinity's centrality to plantation slavery or the challenges that led to the end of the lower river's steamboat era. As Riché presented it, he and his men traveled through the fecund wilderness of the Trinity without encountering any of the men, women, and children who depended on the river and its bottomlands for their survival.[28]

Where others had failed to control or even develop their lands on the Trinity, federal funds and expertise would now be put to work. Captain Riché considered these changes "not only advisable, but urgently necessary." His insistence on urgency suggests that public zeal for navigation had influenced his own characterization of the project. He noted that railroad construction had "caused the river to be neglected, as its natural condition did not permit such character of navigation as could compete with rail transportation." Though the impetus for the survey had developed out of a need for competition with railroads, Riché pointed to the lack of railroads along the lower river as a factor pressing for river navigation. With one exception, the railroads did not parallel the river for any distance, which meant "its rich bottom lands are practically undeveloped." Riché's main argument for transforming the river was based on the same claim made by the Populists—namely, that a navigable Trinity would reduce freight rates throughout Texas. He contended that marine insurance would not be very high once the river was properly altered—ignoring the high rate of collisions and sunken ships that had plagued the river during the steamboat era.[29]

Figure 8.4. Two members of the 1899 Army Corps of Engineers survey party. The survey suggested an uninhabited lower half of the Trinity. Courtesy of Trinity River Authority.

Figure 8.5. This image from the 1899 Army Corps of Engineers survey captures three of the key challenges of navigation: low water, snags, and a logjam. Courtesy of Trinity River Authority.

A map made by Riché in 1899 highlights the unique emphasis placed on Trinity navigation across Texas (fig. 8.6). Riché created it for a different, smaller Texas river survey of the San Bernard River that he submitted to Congress. In the catalog description of the New York Public Library where this map is now archived, there is no mention of the Trinity, but it stands out nonetheless. The map shows all the Texas rivers that flow into the Gulf of Mexico. The rivers are color coded, with blue indicating existing opportunities to navigate and red for river sections where proposed improvements could make the river navigable. Along the coast, most waterways have a mix of red and blue. The Trinity is coded as already navigable up to Liberty, and then from there to Dallas it is colored red. Riché marked no other rivers in this manner, and the result makes the map appear as though a blood-colored gash runs across the state—as if the blood from Fort Worth's slaughterhouses dyed the Trinity.

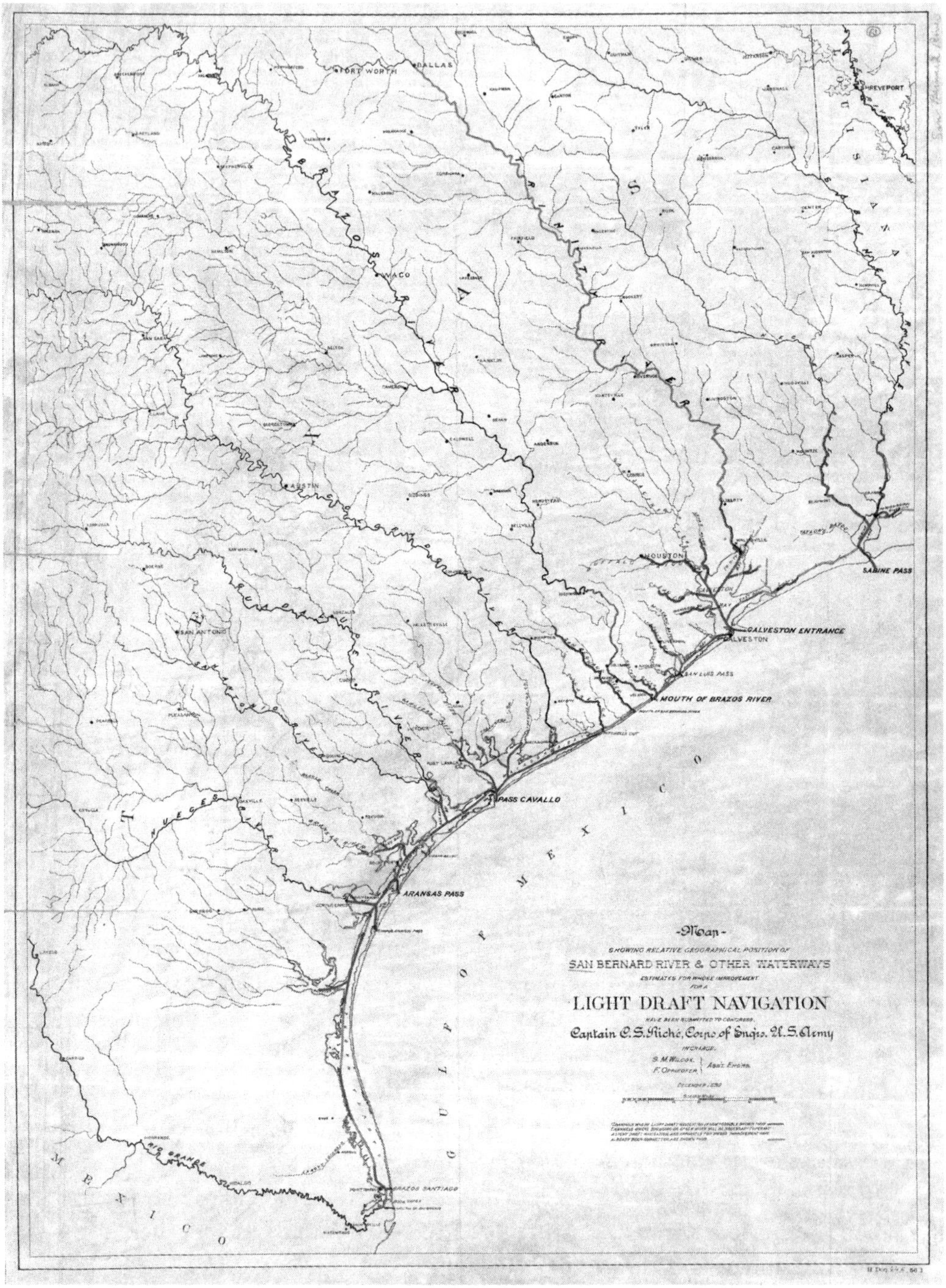


Figure 8.6. Map submitted by C. S. Riché to Congress in 1899, with much of the Trinity River highlighted to reflect its proposed improvements for navigation. Courtesy of New York Public Library Digital Collections, image ID 57488408, https://digitalcollections.nypl.org.

Because of the federal survey and continuing political support for the project, it did not take long for Congress to provide more funding. The Army Corps of Engineers had been improving river navigation across the country since the 1820s, and the Trinity was one of many promising candidates for its continued efforts. In 1902, Congress appropriated $400,000 to begin clearing the river and building locks. Though the Populists had been defeated, a widespread desire to reduce freight rates remained, and the Trinity still appeared to offer one potential solution, a prospect celebrated by national as much as local politicians. When President Theodore Roosevelt visited Dallas in 1905, he began his speech by noting how he had "signed the bill under which the Trinity river will be improved"—a statement that, according to the transcript, resulted in "continuous cheers" from the audience.[30] Enthusiasm for the project was not limited to North Texas; when a group of Dallas business leaders visited the East Texas town of Groveton, fourteen miles east of the Trinity River, "cheers for Trinity river navigation were joined in here by both the visitors and the people of Groveton."[31]

Many residents along the lower half of the Trinity may have welcomed the potential improvement of the river, but it was only in North Texas that this enthusiasm resulted in action. Politicians and lobbyists from Dallas pushed the improvement bills through Congress.[32] Capital for work on the Trinity also came from North Texas. Dallas leaders not only funded lobbying efforts but also paid out of their own pockets for the construction of locks and dams, purchasing the sites that the Corps of Engineers would use.[33] The project was ostensibly intended to benefit residents all along the river, but both the funding and the goals of the project came from Dallas, while the corps ignored potential effects on the lower river's other uses.

Work on the Trinity navigation project began shortly after it was funded by Congress in 1902. Early efforts clearing snags and building locks were intended to lay the groundwork to make the Trinity navigable. Before any locks were constructed, the Army Corps of Engineers hired crews to clear the river of obstructions. Given the corps's sense that the river represented an uninhabited wilderness, the engineers hired laborers from other parts of the state rather than from among the people who lived on or near the Trinity.[34] In addition to all this manpower, three snag boats were put into operation and dynamite was used on particularly stubborn piles of driftwood.[35] Construction of the locks began in 1906 on land purchased by the City of Dallas. Despite the fact that abundant hardwoods filled the Trinity bottomlands and Captain Riché had even suggested saving money by using the local timber, all the lumber for lock construction was shipped to the sites.[36]

Building locks and clearing the Trinity of snags was hard, dangerous work. During construction at Lock and Dam No. 2, downstream from Joppa, a worker slipped and had his foot mashed so badly in a gear that it had to be amputated. Another man lost several fingers. In the summer of 1911, a cook on the US Quarter Boat No. 1 died after he attempted to push a log away from the craft. He was pulled overboard, "and the swift current carried him under the boat." His drowning entitled his wife and twin children to compensation from the federal government.[37]

Despite the accidents, the ongoing construction along the Trinity provided useful publicity for politicians. Lobbying groups such as the Trinity River Navigation Company regularly made trips to towns near the river that stood to benefit from navigation.[38] Politicians like US Congressman A. W. Gregg took a publicity trip down the Trinity to lock construction sites in 1907. Accompanying the congressman were prominent merchants and lumbermen from the larger towns near the river. These were not the Populist farmers who had pushed for navigation. After his tour, the congressman claimed that the river "gives promise to be an easily navigable stream after the government improvements are made."[39]

In reality, the Trinity remained a long way off from being navigable on a regular basis. Given all the timber floating in the river, the snag boats would have found their work never-ending. More importantly, a handful of locks would not be enough to cope with the great variability of the water level. The ferry operators and other river residents probably could have told the engineers that they could not tame the Trinity, but even if they had, almost certainly none of the politicians and their engineers would have listened.[40]

The reputation of the flooding river and that of the people who lived within its bottomlands were intertwined. At the locks built below Dallas, the Army Corps of Engineers had repeated difficulties with river residents. Several miles downstream from Dallas at McCommas Bluff was Lock No. 1, where the lockmaster had an encounter with the "Turner Boys" in the winter of 1910. The lockmaster had previously warned these young men to keep away from the area around the lock and the river. When the Turner brothers returned, the lockmaster said, "When you come here you bring a 'Gun' and I don't want any Trouble with you so you stay off this Reservation entirely." Indeed, one of the brothers replied, "Yes, I've got my Gun and I'll use it too." After some debate, the Turners retreated, firing their pistols into the air.[41] The Trinity floodplain was one of the few remaining open lands in the area, so the brothers opposed the corps's attempt to keep them out. The lockmaster, meanwhile, framed this conflict in terms of bad characters, "the boys," who acted out of a backwoods malice.

The corps was caught in a web of competing, contradictory interests that tied its efforts to tame the Trinity with the messy reality of a booming Texas city. As Dallas grew, it depended on river water to protect property from fires. But the massive amount of pollution that had entered the river by the start of the twentieth century created an unpleasant odor. Rather than fix this stench, the corps worsened it with the impoundments it built to operate its system of locks. The impoundments kept waste sitting in pools close to Dallas rather than letting it flow downstream. The handful of locks the engineers had constructed were already causing problems by the early 1910s, but the corps would need to construct many more locks and reservoirs to potentially make the river navigable. The Dallas Commissioner of Streets wrote the corps, noting that "the Trinity Pool has become very offensive and many citizens are complaining of the odor emanating from said pool. We respectfully request you to open the dams and let the water out."[42] The noxious river crept into city residents' lives like a slow-moving flood. Dallas residents recognized that the easiest solution would be to simply allow the polluted water to flow out of Dallas rather than mount a river cleanup.[43] Yet only a few months prior, the Dallas Waterworks and Sewerage commissioner requested that the corps let the pool remain filled.[44] Insurance companies had recommended using the pool as a source of water to fight fires and to feed waterlines that were connected to the city.

Throughout the 1910s, the corps focused its efforts on remaking the Trinity into a navigable waterway despite considerable resistance from the river itself. By 1917, seven locks had been completed on the Trinity, but engineers estimated that another thirty locks would need to be constructed in order to make the river navigable up to Dallas. All the while, the corps continued clearing the river channel, a Sisyphean task along the heavily wooded bottomlands. In a single year, the corps destroyed 7,589 snags and 969 stumps and cut 4,307 shore snags and 4,421 leaning trees, in addition to other work in the river. The strong currents, eddies, and many snags in the river made the corps's work more difficult and occasionally lethal. Given the corps's experience on the river, the reality of having a navigable river seemed no closer despite the construction of seven locks. In 1921 the chief engineer reversed Riché's earlier recommendation to Congress by stating that only the lowest part of the river, from Liberty to its mouth, could be made navigable.[45] The following year Congress defunded all the work.

***While there was some pushback*** against the end of the navigation funding, the Trinity navigation dream had been paused as a more pressing battle against the river began following unprecedented flooding. Floods rarely threatened upstream communities such as Fort Worth and Dallas; they primarily affected those who lived or farmed in the bottomlands. Farmers would have to herd livestock in from the floodwaters, crops and cabins might become submerged, and ferry traffic would be more difficult; but these events were so typical as to merit limited attention from the local press.[46] In April 1908, however, a record-setting flood began along the entire river and put parts of Dallas underwater. As one river resident put it, in that moment the Trinity was navigable all the way to Dallas: "Locks and dams supposed to be 25 feet high would be out of sight as many feet." The rising waters reached homes perched on the river's highest bluffs, and all along its length, hogs could be seen "swimming for high land or floating on drift wood, seemingly contented with [their] surroundings."[47] Rabbits gathered along the treetops as the bodies of people and cows floated by. The flood of 1908 was a turning point for the entire river: It changed the way that the cities of Dallas and Fort Worth treated the Trinity.

Downstream river residents experienced the 1908 flood differently, as part of a longer history of flooding. The massive flood washed away most of the crops in the lower Trinity region. This was a regular occurrence, one that all but the newest farmers had experienced before. Farther downstream, the *Polk County Enterprise* lauded its farmers' "pluck and indomitable will power" as they set out to replant their corn and cotton crops once the land had dried enough for their plows.[48] Rural river residents understood the Trinity's history of flooding and the risks of living along its banks. Like other river folks, they were simply trying to make the most of their present situation. But with five people drowned and thousands homeless, urban Texas could not accept the Trinity's floods as stoically.

The flood of 1908 was the biggest flood in the history of the upper Trinity. Many neighborhoods were devastated. Most of downtown Dallas was covered with several feet of water, and trains could not cross the river. Farmers watched their livestock hung from the barbed wire fences that had become common in North Texas. Hundreds of homes were destroyed, while others floated down the river intact, their families still inside them.[49] Because of the strong current and many back eddies, some buildings, such as the cooperage factory, were actually carried upstream by the river.[50] The Trinity destroyed even more homes and farms downstream, while bringing evidence of the destruction from upriver. In Ennis, forty miles below Dallas, the postman

Figure 8.7. Henry Clogenson, *Trinity River at Its Height, Dallas Texas*, 1908. View of the 1908 Trinity River flood in Dallas at the Commerce Street Bridge. Courtesy of Library of Congress, https://lccn.loc.gov/2007660628.

reported that the flood had carried several houses downstream: "It is not known where the houses came from. One is a nice white cottage and probably came from Dallas."[51] Though Dallas had experienced the Trinity's floods in previous years, the scale of the damage in 1908 changed the city's relationship with the river. No longer concerned with just navigation, Dallas leaders now sought to build levees and even move the river channel to protect the city from future floods. Rather than rewrite history through the lost cause of Trinity steamboats, they would have to make history and move the river.

## CHAPTER 9

# TRINITY RIVER BLUES

Alligator gar are uniquely adapted to the Trinity, and today fishermen in search of the biggest specimens in the world travel to the river, where gar can live for more than sixty years, grow to over eight feet long, and weigh three hundred pounds. Fossils of alligator gar dating back two hundred million years have been found in Texas, and their bodies retain primitive traits found in few species other than sharks. With scales so thick that Native people once used them to create arrowheads, the alligator gar looks like a living dinosaur.

The Trinity gar have withstood many environmental changes in the past two centuries. Land clearance and farming muddied their waters in the 1800s, and later pollution from slaughterhouses and sewage reduced the river's oxygen levels. Gar were able to survive low oxygen levels because, unlike most fish that breathe exclusively through their gills, they have a unique swim bladder that allows them to inhale by gulping air at the surface. When a ferryman below Dallas reported how urban waste caused hundreds of dead bass, perch, and catfish to float to the surface in the 1920s, he noted no gar among the casualties.[1]

Gar depend on a changing river. The Trinity's miles-wide floodplains, described as an impediment by so many travelers, were nurseries for freshly hatched gar. They need the Trinity to flood in order to breed, spawning in the floodplains where their eggs (which are toxic for humans) attach to vegetation before floating back with the floodwaters into the main channel or adjacent oxbow lakes. Without flooding on the Trinity, gar would cease to exist—which is why, by the early 1900s, they faced a new threat as humans attempted to hem in the Trinity's floods with levees, limiting their access to their ancient spawning grounds.

Like the Trinity itself, the gar's reputation has undergone major shifts. Long a source of food for river residents, the gar became classified as a threat to game fish after the arrival of a new class of recreational fishermen in the early twentieth century. Gar were trapped and killed by the hundreds. Ironically, this "trash fish" was uniquely suited to survive all the trash and other pollution dumped into the river. In the 1930s, Texas wildlife officials developed a "gar machine" that used electric shocks to bring gar to the surface so that they could be scooped into the boat and destroyed.[2] But even as gar were stigmatized, many survived. They continued to be caught and eaten by longtime river residents or served to inmates in the Trinity's numerous prisons.

Figure 9.1. Fisherman with an alligator gar caught from Moon Lake on the Mississippi River in 1910. Photograph by Dwight Franklin. Courtesy of American Museum of Natural History, Gottesman Research Library, asset ID 320445.

***The 1920s and 1930s*** were a turning point for the Trinity, its fish, and its people. Pollution, levees, floods, and the Great Depression all came together to make it harder—impossible for most people—to continue calling the bottomlands home. By the time T-Bone Walker recorded "Trinity River Blues" in 1929, the Trinity had a bad reputation. Walker grew up in Dallas's Oak Cliff neighborhood, one of the places hit the hardest by the famous 1908 flood. "That dirty old Trinity River sure has done me wrong," Walker sang. "It came in my windows and doors. Now all my things are gone." Like Walker, many Texans had finally had enough. The consensus was that levees would liberate them from the flood-prone river. Walker sang, "Trinity River Blues keep me bothered all the time. . . . I believe I'm going to lose my mind." Massive levees were being erected to stop the flooding as he recorded "Trinity River Blues," but Walker left the river behind, showing the world the possibilities of the electric guitar for blues and rock and roll.[3]

Texas began pouring money into levee construction all along the Trinity after the 1908 flood. The most ambitious of these projects took place in Dallas County. City leaders trudged through twenty years of debate about how to protect Dallas from floods and how to pay for it before construction even began. Finally, leaders and engineers decided that thirty-foot-tall levees would confine the Trinity to a floodway two thousand feet wide for twenty-six miles through Dallas. It was one of the largest engineering projects in the nation at the time. Construction began in 1928 and included moving the channel of the Trinity River half a mile away from downtown Dallas.[4] Because of their scale, these levees cost over $600 per acre to construct, nearly fifty times as costly as the cheapest ones built downriver.[5] Much of the labor of clearing brush and moving earth was performed by Mexican Americans. These laborers founded their own community, La Bajada, "The Descent," next to a Trinity River bridge.[6]

The mighty Mississippi River is known for its Delta blues with famous artists such as Robert Johnson and Charley Patton, but the Trinity River produced its fair share of musicians too. When T-Bone Walker recorded "Trinity River Blues," he used the name "Oak Cliff T-Bone," reflecting the importance of his Dallas neighborhood home along the Trinity. Downriver, the Texas bluesman Sam "Lightnin'" Hopkins came from an area called Warren's Bottom in Leon County, of which he sang, "I was born on the banks of the river, that's the reason I'm a fisherman from my heart."[7] After marveling at the number of noteworthy musicians like Blind Lemon Jefferson who came from the same area, an interviewer once asked Hopkins, "All these people we've been talking about are from one rather small part of Texas?"[8] Indeed, so many Texas musicians were influenced by this place and its history.

Lightnin' Hopkins chose music as a path to get away from the unceasing labor of farming as life on the Trinity got harder and harder to scratch out. The decline began before the Great Depression but was hastened by it. Alongside a global decline in cotton prices were the Trinity's worsening pollution, flooding, and diminishing access to hunting and fishing places. By the 1930s, conditions had deteriorated even more. In one vivid example, father-and-son folklorists John and Alan Lomax visited the Smithers Farm, a Trinity River plantation, as part of a trip to record "black folk music" for the Library of Congress. At the Smithers Farm, they arranged for the forty tenants to perform and be recorded by a primitive hand-cranked cylinder Dictaphone,

Figure 9.2. The city of Dallas and the Trinity River, with its channel moved away from downtown and flanked by expensive, substantial levees in 1933. Courtesy of DeGolyer Library, Southern Methodist University, Miscellaneous Aerial Views of Dallas, 1930s–1940s, collection.

since the site lacked electricity.[9] A man called Blue sang on the record about the "tribulations of the Negro renter in the South."[10]

Perhaps the best documented eyewitness to the transformation of the Trinity was Calvin Moye. Interviewed on February 6, 1938, as part of the Works Progress Administration's Slave Narrative Collection, Moye had lived through enslavement, Reconstruction, and all that followed. Born in Georgia, Moye in the 1850s traveled as a young boy with his family and slaveholder to Rural Shade, Texas. Upriver from the core concentration of plantations on the lower Trinity, the Ingram brothers owned over twenty thousand acres and 284 human beings. Here Moye witnessed whippings and slave sales on the plantation. He recalled how they "all worked and we worked hard" and if it snowed they "would cut wood" and if it rained they "shucked corn" since Richmond Ingram "always had a job for" his slaves. After Juneteenth, Moye remained on the Trinity until the 1880s when the death of his wife, broader shifts in the economy, and a downgrading of his sharecropping contract from "on the halves"—where he received half of the crops—to the thirds all conspired to make life harder. But the Trinity itself had also become a more inhospitable place.[11]

Looking back on eight decades of the Trinity, both in slavery and freedom, Moye said the river had been altered for the worse. When he first arrived, the river "didn't overflow" like it did by the 1930s.[12] In those earlier years, he explained, the "hills had not been plowed up and washed down in the bottom of the streams and halfway filled them up." At that time Texas rivers were deeper and the banks steeper.[13] This transformation had costly consequences for Moye. Though he had moved into the nearby town of Corsicana, at the time of the interview his son was farming in the bottomlands. Just before his son began harvesting the cotton in earnest, a flood washed his crop away.[14] Like most farmers, his son had taken on substantial debt to plant, and Moye was worried he would be jailed. To protect him, Moye spent much of his savings to support his son after the flood. Making a living had become more challenging for people on the Trinity, and the situation pressured them to leave the rural sections of the river for good.

Eroded soil flowing into the river, begun by the use of slave labor to clear land for cash crops, combined with the levees to change the flow of the river. A river is defined by its bottomlands as much as by its channel. Levees cut off the ability of a river to overflow. With nowhere else to go, water that might have previously spread into the bottomlands is instead sent downstream at greater volumes and speeds. The largest levees were located on the upper section of the Trinity, which allowed for the dramatic development of nonabsorbent paved roads, parking lots, and buildings, which flushed rainwater right to it. These factors combined to worsen flooding for all the downriver people such as Calvin Moye's son.

***Pollution also pushed residents off the river.*** From the moment they became cities, Dallas and Fort Worth grappled with the challenge of waste. Since the early 1900s, city residents had filed lawsuits to demand a cleaner river; the Trinity had become so filthy it sometimes caught fire. The Trinity's degradation served as an impetus for a 1913 state law that banned the dumping of raw sewage into Texas rivers. With minimal leadership at the state level and a serious rivalry between Dallas and Fort Worth, water quality showed little sign of improvement.[15] By the 1920s, Fort Worth sent millions of gallons of raw sewage into the river daily. In Dallas, the Armstrong Packing House flushed untreated waste into the sanitary sewers. For much of the time, four-fifths of the water flowing past Dallas in the Trinity was sewage, both treated and untreated. Around the two cities, oxygen levels in the water plummeted to zero, and not for another forty miles downriver did they return to healthy levels. During floods, the Trinity carried a wall of filth that residents called "black rises" that reeked and killed many fish for hundreds of miles downstream. Where fishers had once easily caught fish, they now abandoned the site. When the Texas State Board of Health studied the Trinity in 1924, the state health officer noted that it was "evidently more grossly polluted" than any other river in the state.[16]

The Trinity's fish had been a major source of sustenance for its residents before Juneteenth; afterward, it sustained their communities when the crops failed and starvation threatened. Moye described how his favorite food had once been caught by the "wagon load."[17] One woman recalled collecting turtle and crane eggs from the riverbanks and using the eggs of the spawning buffalo fish to make "a sort of poor man's caviar." Eels also proved abundant in the lower river and made up another staple.[18] As late as 1909, a party visiting the Trinity "caught three or four hundred pounds of fish."[19] Though the increasingly polluted water did not make fish completely disappear from the Trinity, their greatly reduced numbers meant that residents could not rely on them as insurance against poor harvests or economic depressions.

Game animals that took refuge in the Trinity also became harder to find. Black bears, an important source of fatty meat, managed to hold on longer near the river than in most of East Texas. When a mother and her cubs were killed in Liberty County in 1919, they were the second to last authenticated sighting of a bear in East Texas until they began to return across state lines from Louisiana, Arkansas, and Oklahoma in more recent decades.[20] Even what Moye called the "panther's scream" could rarely be heard in the bottoms by this time. Bounties led to panthers' poisoning, shooting, and trapping, a reflection of the threat they posed to Texas's ever growing livestock industry.[21]

By the time of Moye's interview eight years into the Great Depression, it had become difficult for people to obtain sufficient fish and game for sustenance, and the same was true for hogs and cattle. Up until the early 1900s, much of the Trinity bottomlands remained as an open range without many fences, where anyone could run their animals even if they did not own the land. When Frederick Law Olmsted visited the Trinity in the 1850s, he referred to its hogs as his "dirty persecutors" and fenced them out of his camp for the night.[22] Keeping hogs out of cultivated land required sturdy fences. Southern custom and law had long dictated that the growers of the crops, rather than the owners of the livestock, were responsible for protecting their fields. Disputes involving roaming livestock regularly appeared in the courts, such as those concerning attempts to carry animals from one side of the Trinity to the other, where the theft would presumably be less noticed.[23] But in none of these legal battles was the legality of running livestock on the land ever called into question; the courts accepted the use of the Trinity as a commons.

At the start of the twentieth century, a new generation of absentee owners began to develop their properties into cattle ranches, which clashed with the custom of common grazing along the river. An increasing number of investors came from the booming cities of Dallas and Fort Worth on the upper Trinity to buy up cheap land as easy sources of investment dried up elsewhere (such as Mexico, after its revolution began).[24] A "big company" purchased a large property along the river near the former steamboat landing of Magnolia with the intention of turning the land into a cattle ranch.[25] This potential use threatened the long-standing grazing rights of nonlandowners as well as the rights of area residents to fish in the river and its oxbow lakes. But distant landowners were rarely interested in the traditional practices of the land they claimed.[26]

Open grazing customs had once existed across Texas, but they endured longer in the bottomlands because of the landscape's resistance to development. Texas counties began passing "stock laws" in the early 1900s. These laws were intended to reconfigure property rights in Texas and explicitly limit the ability of poor folks to make a living. Once again, Calvin Moye described this consequence clearly: "People use to make good money raising cattle before the stock law was passed and people had to build fences and keep their stock" confined.[27] Among the reasons that the Trinity was one of the last places to change were the practical challenges of fencing large sections of the bottomlands. To this day, floods regularly destroy fences, resulting in cattle roaming freely once more.

Land-use restrictions also began to apply to the Trinity's remaining populations of fish and game. For most of the nineteenth century, the concept of poaching did not exist in Texas. Turning poor people who hunted into criminals did not happen all at once—the bottomlands were among the last places for this to take effect. As common lands disappeared throughout Texas, the open range that endured in places like the Trinity bottomlands became even more important. Townspeople who lived ten or twenty miles away from the Trinity regularly began to travel to the river to hunt, fish, or gather pecans. As more people came to use the Trinity in this way, river residents faced greater competition for local resources. Paradoxically, the increased use helped to preserve the Trinity as a commons, a place where anyone could hunt or fish, for a little bit longer. When large landowners attempted to post their land and keep out "trespassers," middle-class townsfolk, such as a railroad boilermaker living in the central county seat, rather than poorer river residents, sued to retain access.[28]

The Trinity's pecan groves attracted many visitors in its final years as a common land. People who lived in the bottomlands harvested the nuts, which were nutrient-rich and stored well through lean winters.[29] The autumn pecan harvests regularly drew residents of both nearby and more distant towns. While some of these foragers may have been collecting pecans for their own consumption, many likely did so in order to sell the nuts to distant markets. San Antonio had been a pecan-processing hub since the 1880s, relying on cheap Mexican labor to shell the nuts before sending them to markets in the East. Texas's famous Christmas fruitcakes depended on river-bottom pecan groves, as processors received shipments of the nuts from pecan gatherers along the state's rivers.[30] In 1906, the *Palestine Daily Herald* reported that hundreds of people were gathering pecans in the woods and on the river; by 1910, the paper complained, "The nuts are hard to get. Too many people are scouring the bottoms for them, and the hogs get those that fall."[31] The combination of hungry hogs and eager townspeople sometimes meant slim pickings.

***After the timber industry*** cut the accessible upland Texas forests, the Trinity's trees became more valuable. Though small sawmills had stood on the river since the antebellum period, the exploitation of bottomland timber accelerated around 1900.[32] One man posted a notice in the newspaper indicating that any timber cutting from the Trinity River property he oversaw would be prosecuted. In keeping with the theme of absentee landownership, he made it clear that he did not own these seven thousand acres of land, only that he had been "authorized to look after it."[33]

Much like the steamboats of the past, the thousands of logs that floated down the Trinity depended on high water. If the water levels were too low, downstream mills shut down.[34] While massive log rafts would have interfered with steamboat navigation, timber was the only commodity moved in volume on the river by the 1900s. In a letter to the Army Corps of Engineers, a sawmill owner described how he depended on timber floated on the river. He wanted to know what his duties and obligations were when passing ferries downstream. His log rafts of up to a hundred thousand feet of loose logs were quite substantial and would have disrupted the operation of any ferry they passed. As the mile-long rafts traveled downstream, they interfered with competing uses of the river, such as fishing. The sawmill owner wondered whether any rules required him to limit the damage done to these users. The assistant engineer wrote back, giving him the right to dump logs in the river even if it impeded other uses. The fishermen had to protect their nets and the ferries had to "arrange for the passage of your logs."[35]

It was the arrival of the railroads that would finally enable profitable logging of the Trinity's bottomlands. The first large steam-powered sawmill on the Trinity was built in the 1870s near Liberty. While the spot had access to large and inexhaustible tracts of timber, the proprietor, an aptly named "Mr. Sawyer," built the sawmill on the promise of future railroad service.[36] Logged-out forests in other parts of Texas finally made the cost of increasing access to the Trinity's timber a prospect that could be sold to well-capitalized operations, funded by investors in Dallas or beyond the state's borders altogether.[37] While most mills in Texas focused on softwoods such as longleaf pines, the Trinity served as a major source of hardwoods for the global market. Towering sycamores and a great variety of oak trees flourished in the Trinity bottomlands. Their lumber was often exported to Europe to be made into furniture or wine barrels.[38]

As it had during the steamboat era, the unruly Trinity could stymie even the most well-backed attempts at profit. In the early 1910s, the Philip A. Ryan Lumber Company agreed to cut and purchase timber from an owner of over twelve thousand acres on the Trinity. The contract was conditional on securing a right of way for a railroad, since it was the best way for the timber to arrive at a mill. Without a way to transport the lumber over land, the forest had no value for the lumber company. Further, the contract was contingent on the railroad being built within a certain amount of time or the deal was off. But the seller could not develop this route, unsurprisingly, "on account of floods." Time elapsed, and investors could not continue to justify their investment on the Trinity when the overflows made it more costly to build the railroad than the lumber would be worth. Though the lawsuit regarding this contract took place in Texas courts and concerned the Trinity River, neither the seller nor the purchaser lived in the state; the seller came from St. Louis, Missouri, and the lumber company was in Memphis, Tennessee.[39] Distant investors' lack of familiarity with the Trinity's variable environment made their plans unattainable and further delayed development along the river.

At the same time, the relatively cheap and undeveloped Trinity lands continued to attract out-of-state speculators who then perpetuated the cycle of underinvestment by balking once they realized the costs of fighting the river. Though some areas of the Trinity were logged during the Texas logging boom from the 1880s to the 1930s, much of the region remained uncut well into the twentieth century, since it remained relatively inaccessible. Bottomland trees continued to mark the height of floods with muddy rings left by the sediment-laden river.

While widespread logging happened across the South, the more distinct Texas story is oil. In the 1920s, downstream from the Corsicana oil field, where Calvin Moye lived, oil flowed directly into the water, causing "lots of dead fish" to float to the surface. State officials noted in their 1925 sanitary report on the Trinity that Fort Worth's new oil refineries dumped sulfuric acid into the river after using it in their petrochemical plants.[40] Later that decade, when an oilman inspected his oil pipeline on a cold January day, he worried that his pipeline had cracked and would soon release oil into the river. At the river he met the Jackson brothers, who were friendly and "almost like mountain men—living right at our pipeline crossing." The river was shallow since it was a drought year, and the oilman paid the brothers in cash to wade into the freezing water to inspect the pipeline along the river bottom. The pipe was unbroken, and the brothers were "happy to earn ten dollars in this manner."[41] The eagerness of these "fishers and hunters" for cash and the polluted nature of the river show how everyone was tied into a Texas economy defined by oil and cities as much as by farms and backwoods cabins. Whatever world they belonged to, the brothers seemed to be characters out of legend rather than part of a larger community—inhabiting a place of stories about how people used to live.

The bigger urban levees on the Trinity represented the ability of the business and wealthy classes to control not only the river but the people along it as well. During construction, land was taken and condemned in neighborhoods like T-Bone Walker's Oak Cliff. The Dallas levees were remarkably effective in keeping floodwaters out, even if they appeared to have little economic effect on its most impoverished neighborhoods. These tall urban levees also made it harder to see the Trinity. It became easier to simply forget the river existed, no matter how close one lived or worked. Residents on the river side of those levees or anyone farther downstream were forgotten as well. When the Lomaxes visited Smithers Farm and Blue, a tenant farmer, sang for them, he ended by speaking directly into the Dictaphone to President Franklin Roosevelt: "You just don't know how bad they're treating us folks down here. I'm singing to you and I'm talking to you so I hope you will come down here and [do] something for us poor folks in Texas." Blue's recording was played back later that evening to all the families gathered there, which brought them "immense joy" since they "felt they had communicated their problem to the big world."[42]

In "Trinity River Blues," T-Bone Walker blamed the Trinity itself for his woes. But Calvin Moye, who had seen the Trinity change over many decades, was more specific about how the river had been transformed. He said, "People didn't use to know what had gone wrong if they had overflows every year and washed the crops away." Moye explained the history of farming and erosion that worsened flooding as well as a government that did not represent his interests. He argued that during the Great Depression, the federal government enriched planters at the expense of small farmers and tenants. He saw this as a mistake, but it was also a mistake that he believed could be undone. With the planters' subsidies gone and laws repealed, small farms would replace the government-funded transition to large, mechanized plantations. He hoped that new laws might be passed so that the wealthiest landowners had to "stop farming so much land with tractors and working poor people for 75 cents a day. . . . They are going to have to use some of this cotton to make big handkerchiefs so these men can wipe the tears out of their eyes, and I hope I can live to see that day."[43] Moye died two years after his WPA interview. Even in death, however, his actions reveal the significance of the Trinity's history. Rather than be buried in the town of Corsicana, where he had lived for the past several decades, Moye returned to the Trinity, twenty-five miles away, to be buried in a cemetery plot in Rural Shade. Despite all that had gone wrong, this was his home.[44]

## CHAPTER 10

# LEVEE DREAMS AND DISAPPOINTMENTS

Mode Ethridge, a farmer who lived near Eastham Prison in the 1920s, used inmates to clear his property, but he eventually gave up on farming because of flooding. Despite the cheap labor and the sharecropping families that worked the land, constant and worsening flooding made it hard to grow crops. His son recalled, "He finally went broke and had to leave it because we had one overflow after another." The flooding often occurred after the crops had matured. "I've seen it where the corn was ten and twelve feet high with two and three ears to the stalk," his son said, "and it set in to raining and you wake up the next morning, you could just see the top of that corn over that riverbottom, and you can't survive farming."[1] Mode Ethridge lacked the capital and government connections necessary to build levees on the lower half of the river, so he left the farm and began working as a guard at nearby Eastham Prison. Many other river residents were similarly pushed off their land as floods became more destructive; they sought jobs in nearby towns or industrial sites or moved to distant cities.

The Trinity floodplains contained some of the most fertile lands in Texas, and they held the promise of great riches if only the lands could be severed from the river that had created them. Levee construction required especially large investments of labor and capital, and thus in regions such as the rural stretches of the Trinity, they had long proved too expensive without government support. Very few planters had invested in levees before the Civil War, which made the development of the Trinity distinct when compared to plantation regions to the east.[2] On the Trinity, planters built ditches to drain excess water and split their crops between the uplands and lowlands; this had served as an insurance policy against total loss if the lowlands flooded. Once slavery ended, planters had even less capital to invest in levees, and most plantations ceased to exist in the postwar decades. Northern capital and white migrants from other parts of the former Confederacy flowed into Texas during this period, with only a trickle directed toward the former plantation region.

Having run out of new lands to claim and experiencing explosive population growth by the beginning of the twentieth century, the state turned toward reclaiming land deemed too wet or too dry. Because Texas had great variation in climate and rainfall, from its humid east to its arid west, its Reclamation Department set ambitious goals to irrigate the driest lands and drain the wetlands. Texas first authorized drainage districts with a constitutional amendment in 1903, but it was not until 1913, when the thirty-third legislature created the Office of State Reclamation Engineer, that reclamation began on a wide scale.[3] The new office held responsibility for designing, planning, and organizing local levee and improvement districts needed "to reclaim for agricultural uses the overflowed swamp lands." In addition to engineering, one of the primary jobs of the office was to coordinate funding and expertise between federal, state, and local governments.[4]

Critical funding and expertise from the state and federal governments flowed through the Reclamation Department, but these benefits were primarily extended to a small class of landowners who received the greatest benefit from reclamation. Following the creation of the Reclamation Department, levee districts were organized all along the Trinity, with landowners eager to reclaim their land by issuing bonds rather than paying major costs up front. In many counties, businessmen returned to the long-ignored Trinity to witness the construction of levees. There, they watched machines move huge quantities of dirt and then celebrated the Trinity's newfound investment potential with a fish fry.

The financial promise of the levees attracted a range of investors. The land owned by the members of a levee district in Anderson County had been nearly worthless before reclamation. Some of these investors had been based in Mexico until the Mexican Revolution.[5] When these men returned to the

United States seeking further opportunities, they decided that building levees on the Trinity with the help of the government would grant them the best return on their capital.[6] Costs varied greatly depending on the size of the levees; for example, one district in Anderson County required $32,500 to construct levees at an expense of $12.63 per acre, whereas a nearby district issued $200,000 worth of bonds and cost nearly three times as much per acre at $34.84.[7] Several districts built levees in the 1910s and had even more planned. A map of the Trinity River and the county levee districts drawn in 1920 included a note on the section where no districts had been formed, promising future development: "No levees on this sheet, yet."[8]

Initially, levees greatly increased the value of the bottomlands. Fagan Parker, a Trinity River landowner in Anderson County, wrote in 1922 that the value of his land had previously been $20 per acre but after levee construction could "conservatively" be "worth $100 per acre."[9] Unlike many of the levee investors, Parker's family had lived in the area for close to a century. His great-grandfather, a Baptist minister, arrived in the early 1830s. Parker's uncle had briefly lived on the Trinity River before heading farther west, where he was killed by the Comanche and his daughter, Cynthia Ann, was kidnapped. While living with the Comanche, Cynthia Ann Parker raised her famous son, Quanah Parker, who later led the Comanche in their final battles and continued to advocate for the tribe until his death in 1911.

Fagan Parker's roots in the region meant that he understood how the river lands had once been highly valued during the plantation era, but his deeper knowledge did not protect him from the Trinity's reputation as a refuge from law enforcement. Parker ran a levee district in Anderson County in the 1910s. His correspondence with the state reclamation engineer ended abruptly when he was shot and badly wounded in the Trinity River bottom. According to his lawyer, Parker had been in the bottom using bloodhounds to pursue the murderers of a constable across the river. When the fugitives were scented, one of them hid behind a tree, shooting Parker in the back. The lawyer predicted that the murderers would pay a high price for targeting Parker: "These two men will be shot on sight. I don't think they will ever be tried."[10] The lawyer's statement that the suspects would not be given a fair trial shows how the law didn't seem to apply in the bottoms. Only two years later, Parker found himself in court over a different matter related to the Trinity: The levees had not led to the quick profits he had imagined, and Parker was part of a group of landowners who were sued by the government and the bondholders for failing to pay the taxes that had been assessed to repay the district's bonds.[11]

From the turn of the century to the 1940s, the largest Trinity River plantation and among the biggest in Texas was the Murray Farm. Founded by the Murray family, who originally hailed from Mississippi, the plantation employed hundreds of Black, white, and Mexican tenant farmers at its peak. On weekends the community attracted musicians such as Lightnin' Hopkins to perform. The Murrays' stake in the region was such that they developed their own expensive levee system. Smaller landowners sometimes had to cede their land to facilitate the construction of these big projects. Such was the fate of Andy Patterson, who owned a farm in the nearby freedom colony of Vistula, adjacent to the Murray Farm. The 1900 census listed Patterson as a renter, but by 1910 he was a landowning farmer.[12] Patterson's rise from tenant to landowner coincided with the height of Black landownership throughout the South. But his neighbor Lloyd Murray commanded quite a bit of power as the most influential man in Houston County. The sheriff would call upon Murray before entering his property and would release his sharecroppers from jail at his request. Murray owned thousands of acres, but he needed Patterson to sell him a portion of his land in order to complete the levee, to which Patterson agreed.[13] As had been true for so many Black Trinity River residents, Patterson's land had enabled his independence. "Don't ever sell your land, the land will take care of you," he said.[14] In this case, however, Patterson had no choice but to sell some of his land in order to remain on good terms with the powerful owner of the adjacent plantation. Murray's levees became a testament to his apparent control over the landscape and its people.

Even with Murray's wealth, he could not have completed his levees without cooperation from the State Reclamation Department of Texas. Levees represented power—capital, political clout, environmental might—that furthered inequality along the river. The levee-building boom of the early twentieth century reinforced the rise of Jim Crow, a period in which Black voters were disenfranchised and new forms of segregation developed. In 1923 the Texas legislature passed the white primary law, making it illegal for Black people to vote in the primaries. Calvin Moye described this injustice clearly, saying "white folks" had wronged Black people by making them "vote for who they [white people] choose."[15] On the Trinity, the new capital-intensive levees exacerbated such injustices by reducing the ability of all but the wealthy to make a living there. Similar consequences from levee building were felt all across the South. As one historian of the Mississippi River writes, "Levees propped up Jim Crow as surely as they segregated land and water."[16]

***Historians,*** and indeed generations of Americans, have debated the consequences of the federal government's response to the Great Depression. The nation's ambition increased, but for whom? Southern Democrats were essential to any legislation that President Roosevelt passed, but they actively prevented a significant distribution of funds to the poorest Southerners. Millions of such people stopped working the land and moved to cities during the first decades of the twentieth century. Instead, federal money lined the pockets of the wealthiest landowners by funneling money to them through New Deal programs like the Agricultural Adjustment Act. Wealthy landowners used these funds to consolidate their landholdings, buy tractors, and evict sharecroppers and small farmers.[17] Calvin Moye observed that "little farmers" used to be everywhere making a living, but after the Agricultural Adjustment Act, "big tractor farmers" pushed the smaller farmers off the land.[18] On plantations like the Murray Farm, owners used funding from the federal government, funneled through local gatekeepers, to purchase tractors and work on levees.

The state government connected the Trinity River levee men with federal funding during the Great Depression. After the supervisor for one levee district wrote to the state engineer asking about how to repair the district's levees, the engineer's response included advice on how to best gain financial assistance, noting his own "special effort" to understand the most helpful federal agencies. The engineer wrote that the district could apply to either the Public Works Administration or the Works Progress Administration. He recommended applying to the WPA since it required less up-front capital on behalf of the applicant. The state engineer stated that "there is no time to lose in obtaining the aid which is available" and suggested that the board of supervisors visit him in Austin so that he could explain all the "intricate" details that went into a successful application.[19] In order to receive federal relief funding from these agencies, levee districts first had to apply to the Texas Civil Works Administration. Access to federal capital depended on local power brokers' access to state officials who controlled its distribution.

Applications for WPA funding had to describe the work that needed to be completed and the number of unemployed workers in the region to suggest the wider benefit of federal aid. The districts justified their requests by noting how much employment, labeled as "man days," would be required to complete the projects. These numbers varied greatly. For example, a district in Henderson County called for 900 man days, while a Houston County levee district called for 3,792 and an Anderson County levee district listed 11,539.[20] In addition to these estimates, applicants had to specify the "need for the proposed work and benefits to accrue to the community." They typically wrote of the necessity of improving the levees and the drainage systems behind them, claiming that such repairs would "afford relief to the entire levee district, which was erected at very large cost to the taxpayers."[21] Another application stated that the area "will be completely reclaimed, which should enable the land owner to retain their property and earn a livelihood."[22] To claim an even broader impact, applicants brought up public health and the need for remedying unhealthy living conditions.[23] Most districts on the lower Trinity included no more than ten landowners, a handful of whom owned the majority of the land. Thus, when the districts justified thousands of dollars in federal assistance, the funds primarily aided only a small fraction of county residents. Moreover, the application process ignored the ways in which levee construction worsened flooding downstream or even across the river—that is to say, in other places where residents' needs were not addressed in the grant request—and so contributed to pushing people who lacked political capital off their lands.

The Murray family had invested in miles of levees and generating plants to power pumps intended to dry out the bottomlands, but the levees could not always prevent flooding, and they still had to replant after the floodwaters departed. The "Roaring Twenties" era of levee investment coincided with a global collapse in cotton prices. Ultimately, even with all their investments and connections, making a profit proved difficult. In 1948, the half of the Murray family that owned the largest portion of the Murray Farm sold all 10,463 acres of their Trinity River holdings to the Parten family.

Rather than follow the Murrays' attempt to make money through agriculture, the Partens represented a new generation of Texans who had left farming behind to strike it rich in the oil industry. As small farms disappeared, the oil industry was one place where former farmhands could make a living outside the city. However, much more so than had ever been true in agriculture, this work was segregated. Black people were not allowed to work on the oil rigs that dotted the Texas countryside. In a 1959 interview published the following year, Lightnin' Hopkins reminisced about the performances he had given on the Murray Farm in the 1930s. "They grow cotton down in the bottoms," he said. "Now they messing up with them oil wells."[24]

***Millions of Americans*** stopped working the land and moved to cities during the first decades of the twentieth century, but this process of displacement happened at an even more dramatic rate on Southern rivers like the Trinity. As land consolidated in the wealthiest hands, urban and industrial pollution in the river worsened, and flood damage became increasingly localized in poor communities; as a result, rural Trinity residents departed in droves, almost as abruptly as railroads had replaced steamboats on the Trinity.

These sorts of dramatic changes, which ended an era of promise and independence, were chronicled not only by its musicians and individuals like Calvin Moye but also by the white novelist William Goyen. Born the son of the postmaster and sawmill employee in the river town of Trinity in 1915, Goyen moved to Houston as a young boy, though he often returned to the river in his writing. His first novel, *The House of Breath* (1950), features the Trinity as one of its main characters. Reflecting on his sexuality, Goyen wrote, "You, River, then, held like a capsule of sperm the whole seed of creation. . . . But," he continued, "even a river, River, can fall to ruin." Goyen saw the eviction of the Trinity's Black residents and the rise of the oil fields as the cause of this ruin: "In time, important men came advising the Riverbottom Nigras that the land was bought and to move; and in time the bottomlands where, it seemed, Nigras and Charity gatherers were gathered so often, like a flight of summer flies that have vanished, were cleaned smooth as [a] desert of palmettos and muscadines, and oilwells stood up over broken yellow swords." As a result of these changes, he said, the river no longer smelled the same: "Never the sweet fresh smell of the old riverbottoms. Is this the vile oil of joy, this green and yellow putrid scum over the ponds?" Goyen lamented these social and environmental changes: "Everything that used to be in East Texas is ruined, there's a terrible change in the world."[25]

Goyen might have been nostalgic, but the larger picture challenges that depiction. The Trinity's role in supporting freedom and independence in the years after Juneteenth, while vitally important, did not happen in a vacuum. It was precisely because Texas was so hostile to freedpeople that so many freedom colonies flourished on the edges of the Trinity bottomlands. The subsequent changes on the Trinity pushed people out, but they were being pulled, too, toward opportunities as they opened up, even if their former homes on the river remained a powerful memory.

A dream of a better life depended on moving to the city. The Great Migration is commonly understood as the movement of rural Black Southerners to cities beyond the South from the 1910s through the 1960s. However, this misses the story of the "Other Great Migration," when rural Black Texans moved into Texas cities.[26] As individuals settled in places like Houston, gaining housing, employment, and better educational opportunities, more of their family would come to join them, often temporarily staying in relatives' homes before finding a place of their own.

This trajectory is exactly what Ruth Simmons describes after she left East Texas for Houston, where many of her siblings already lived. She wrote of her move from the country to the city in her 2023 memoir, *Up Home: One Girl's Journey*. Simmons explains, "I was born at a crossroads: A crossroads in history, a crossroads in culture, and a geographical crossroads." The exact site of her 1945 birth was near her grandparents' homestead, purchased in 1910, close to the Trinity River border of Houston and Leon Counties. The area creeks that flow into the Trinity were used for many baptisms. Next to "this beautiful land," Simmons spent the first years of her life living in a sharecropper's cabin on the still-substantial Murray Farm, "a village unto itself."[27]

The hopelessness of any possibility beyond tenant farming at the Murray Farm contrasted with her family's church, Greater New Hope, which "represented the hope of Black farming families awaiting relief from the trials of segregation and the punishing physical labor that only enriched others." The church, founded in the 1920s, bears a resemblance to Good Hope Baptist Church, located downriver in the same county, where the inaugural convention of the Colored Farmers' Alliance had occurred in the 1880s. In contrast to her big aspirations, Simmons wondered, "How could I prevent my life and actions from being shaped forever by the Murray Farm and the poverty, isolation, and limitations it represented?"[28]

Starting her schooling in Grapeland, farther from the Murray Farm, set Ruth Simmons on her remarkable path as an educator and administrator, but it was her move to Houston the following year that made all the difference. Though the schools were segregated, her Houston teachers inspired and prepared Simmons for college and then graduate school. She became the first Black president of an Ivy League University (Brown) and also led Smith College and Prairie View A&M University. Simmons attributes her success to her teachers, her family, and her determination to learn and succeed, none of which would have been possible had she remained on the Murray Farm in its final years.

And yet to this day, Simmons owns her grandparents' land. She writes, "Though undeveloped, this land is worth my owning because it represents the strivings of the Campbells and Stubblefields and the deep and willful connections that Mama and Daddy made to each other and the region."[29] Even after the changes in East Texas meant that this land could no longer guarantee her family's independence, its connections to an inspirational history made it a powerful symbol of the dreams the family held for each other.

## CHAPTER 11

# FROM PLANTATIONS TO PRISONS

The outlaws Bonnie and Clyde, their names so consistently linked in telling their story, are divided in death. They are buried in cemeteries on opposite sides of the Trinity River in Dallas, where Clyde Barrow's oft-stolen tombstone reads, "Gone, but not forgotten." Texas's most famous fugitive couple had grown up in Dallas's Trinity River neighborhoods. When Clyde's family first arrived from rural Texas, they camped out along the river before moving a few blocks north of Oak Cliff, home of the musician T-Bone Walker. Bonnie Parker lived in Cement City, named for the Trinity Portland Cement Company, whose products covered Dallas's highways and parking lots, their concrete surfaces funneling rainfall at record rates directly into the river. Bonnie attended the Eagle Ford School, where a growing Mexican American community built the levees and worked at the cement plant. Born into poverty, both dreamed of better lives. Clyde aspired to be a musician. He played the guitar and saxophone, the latter of which was in the car when they were shot to death by the police. While running from the law, they spent time hiding in the wooded Trinity bottomlands, but it was Clyde's experience at Eastham Prison on the Trinity River, a place known locally as "Bloody Eastham," that led him toward death and destruction. At the very moment when rural Texans were leaving the country behind, there was an increasing involuntary stream of inmates into the bottomland prisons, where life became a nightmare and time felt as if it had run backward.

Eastham was part of a brutal prison system across Texas, but as one journalist has written, "This isolated prison farm was the worst of the worst."[1] While incarcerated there, Clyde Barrow suffered abuse from guards and inmates. In response to repeated sexual assaults, he killed the man who raped him. It was his first act of murder. Clyde dreamed of freeing all the inmates and killing the guards. In the winter of 1932, he cut off two of his toes so he could be relieved from a work detail and was released on bail shortly thereafter. He returned to Bloody Eastham as a free man to take revenge on the people and the system that had broken him. On January 16, 1934, having smuggled firearms to some of the prisoners, Clyde waited in the bottomlands with another accomplice. As two guards marched the prisoners out for fieldwork that morning, the outlaws opened fire, hitting both of them. Farther away, Bonnie honked the horn of the getaway car in which they made their escape, squeezing in the four freed men.[2]

While Bonnie and Clyde remain renowned for their spree of robberies and murders, the less widely known Eastham Prison Farm has been responsible for far more deaths across its history. Eastham began its long history of cruelty as an antebellum plantation. Unfree labor was reintroduced there in the 1890s, when its owner participated in Texas's convict-lease program. State officials would bring the convicts to the site, where the landowner, Mrs. Delha Eastham, provided the tools, seeds, and mules needed for planting. The state received 60 percent of the crop, while Mrs. Eastham retained 40 percent.[3] A newspaper glowingly described how the parties she hosted at "her river plantation" were a "guarantee of all sorts of pleasant things for those fortunate enough to be her guests."[4] Clearly this did not apply to the convicts laboring in her fields. In 1911, following well-publicized abuses within the convict-lease program, all the prisoners were moved to the state prison in Huntsville, thirteen miles from the Trinity. In an effort to distance it from the scandal, Mrs. Eastham renamed her property "The Free Labor Farm," thereafter renting to small farmers in the area. Finally, in 1917, the state purchased the plantation, making it an official part of the Texas prison system.[5] But even after convict-leasing officially ended, nearby farmers could still hire prisoners to work on their farms. Inmates played a key role in clearing undeveloped land along the Trinity. During the 1920s, one farmer paid the state thirty-five cents a day per man from Eastham to clear three hundred acres of land along the river. Escapees often came along the river past his farm, perhaps not only because the Trinity functioned as a natural barrier but also due to their experience working on, and consequent familiarity with, the bottoms.[6]

A penitentiary in Huntsville had been built in the late 1840s as Texas's first major public works project.[7] The site had been chosen partially due to its proximity to the navigable Trinity, which allowed it to more easily receive goods and market the products, primarily textiles, made by inmates.[8] Textile machinery was floated up the river and then carried the final thirteen miles to the prison. Huntsville had been the largest source of textiles for the Confederacy west of the Mississippi, and given its proximity to the river plantations, a major portion of its raw cotton likely came from the Trinity. The prison held both Black slaves and white men, becoming "the state's first racially integrated public institution, not by bestowing rights on bondsmen but by stripping them from citizens."[9] During Reconstruction, the local Freedmen's Bureau agent described how freedpeople were regularly sent to the penitentiary for incurring the wrath of their former enslavers.[10] This pattern of incarcerating Black men who had committed no crimes continued after Reconstruction with the rise of Jim Crow. Because of the Trinity's central role in the state's history of both plantations and prisons, federal and state authorities reflexively chose the river as a site for other unfree persons. During World War II, the first Texas prisoner of war camp sprang up next to the Trinity, just down the road from the penitentiary in Huntsville.

When the Texas prison system expanded during the twentieth century, its leaders chose sites away from the state's booming cities. As a result, prisons became a defining feature of the Trinity River. To this day, the Texas Department of Criminal Justice is the largest employer along the lower river. While plantations had developed because of the access provided by the Trinity, the prisons bet on the region's continued isolation, both to prevent escapes and to provide jobs for a region far from the economic centers that drove Texas's economy. Since many freedom colonies were adjacent to plantations, they now found themselves close to the prisons. The community of Vistula, for example, lies only ten miles upstream from Eastham. When men escaped from Eastham, they often remained along the Trinity, using the water and the woods to evade the bloodhounds. Occasionally, neighboring communities were accused of harboring fugitives.[11]

Wardens and state prison executives along the Trinity exerted power not only over inmates but also over their employees and employees' families. Louise Fulsom, whose husband was a guard at Eastham in the 1930s, recalled crossing the Trinity by ferry. Her husband asked the convict who operated the ferry whether they could buy any fish from him. "Yes sir," he replied.

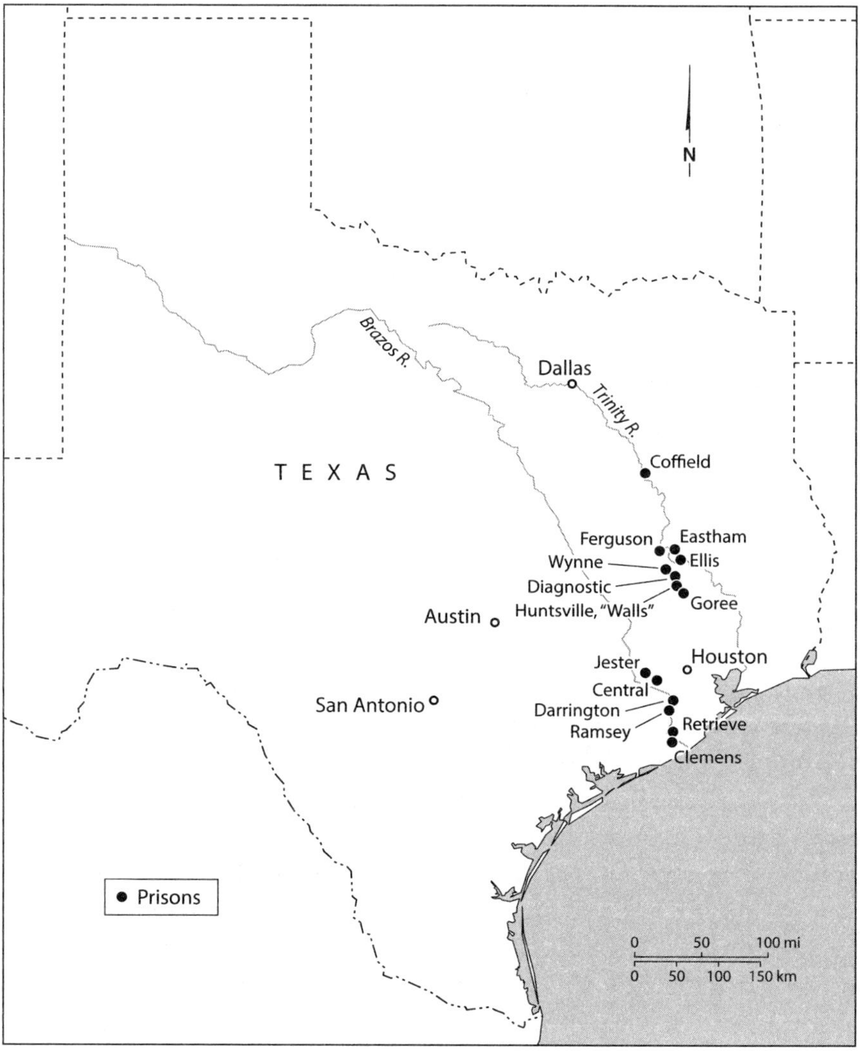


Map showing the location of Texas prisons along the Brazos and Trinity Rivers in 1978. From Robert T. Chase, *We Are Not Slaves: State Violence, Coerced Labor, and Prisoners' Rights in Postwar America* (University of North Carolina Press, 2022); used by permission.

Figure 11.1. Men hoeing cotton in the Trinity bottomlands at Ellis Prison in 1978. Courtesy of Bruce Jackson.

"I have one, and you can have it." Shortly thereafter, the general manager of the Texas prison system arrived at the ferry with his convict driver. As Fulsom remembered it, the manager acted like her family "were some of the flotsam from the river that had washed up on the ferry." He proceeded to demand the fish for himself, even though the ferryman told him it was reserved for the Fulsoms. Louise Fulsom said, "It was the principle"—if not the fish—"that would have been worth fighting for, if [we] could have had the power to fight back." The ferryman apologized after the fish-stealing manager drove off, but they let it go, as the Fulsoms recognized that he was even "more helpless."[12] Just as planters had held power over both their slaves and the poor white people who had lived on or near their plantations, so too did the leaders of Trinity prisons loom over all the people who lived and worked there.

For inmates, the power that prison officials held over them could be a matter of life or death. A decade before Clyde Barrow was first incarcerated, a group of state legislators investigated the demise of two men at Eastham. Many of the inmates refused to cooperate for fear of reprisals. One laconically stated the murdered victims were "gone and I am still here; of course I don't know how long I am going to be here." Nonetheless, some took the risk of speaking out in more detail. They had been working in the bottomlands, in a landscape that had been completely cleared and crisscrossed with drainage ditches. Two prisoners then headed toward the river, away from the main group, on a pair of old mules that would have been unable to traverse the wide ditches they were approaching, when the guards fired upon them. A guard described shooting and leaving them there while he returned to the prison building with his squad. When the lawmakers questioned why he did not shoot the mules instead of the prisoners themselves, he claimed that he had not had time to do so. Another official coldly replied, "We are not employing the men to guard mules" and noted that Eastham policy required that "if a man starts to run and you don't shoot him, don't get blood, you are fired."[13] The lawmakers made little progress in reforming the attitudes of the guards and the conditions of the prison, but their investigation revealed a world in which human life held little value.

Because of the brutal conditions and steady reports of escapes from prison farms, few area residents wanted more prisons on the Trinity River, but they lacked the influence to prevent their construction. Such opposition to the state prison system differed dramatically from opinions on the issue in the second half of the century. Local politicians lobbied for prison construction in their rural districts as a source of employment, though backing from East Texas politicians did not equate to widespread support from their

Figure 11.2. Though this image of men being marched to hoe cotton in front of a lone horseman in the Trinity bottomlands might appear to be from the era of plantation slavery, it actually depicts work at Ellis Prison in the 1960s. Courtesy of Bruce Jackson.

constituents. Many residents believed that guards received such low pay that their support of local businesses would be "insignificant."[14] Meanwhile, new prisons meant county governments would lose part of their property tax base to state control. Landowners actively lobbied against prisons, believing that their land would be devalued.

In the 1960s, Bruce Jackson, a Harvard University researcher, visited Texas's prisons to study and record their work songs. The album that Jackson made based on his recordings was later nominated for a Grammy, three years after the Trinity bluesman Lightnin' Hopkins was also nominated. The types of labor that Jackson documented, such as hoeing crops or clearing forests with axes in the bottomlands, were no longer performed on private land—it made no economic sense in a world of tractors and chainsaws. Instead, unlike in the rest of the country, a prison work song was called a "river song" in Texas because, Jackson explained, "it was down on the river bottoms where the work was done." The prisons were located along the Brazos and Trinity, often at former plantations, such as Ellis Prison, which had once been the Smithers Farm where Blue had recorded his plaintive call to President Roosevelt three decades earlier. Not only did these river songs help the imprisoned workers get through the labor, but they also allowed them to express things they could not otherwise say. As one inmate put it, "In the river songs you tell the truth about how you feel, you know, but you can't express it, see, to the boss."[15] While Black, white, and Hispanic inmates all worked in the bottomlands, only Black inmates sang the river songs.

Given the need for state funding and expertise in order to successfully build levees, Trinity prisons were leaders in levee construction. When boosters developed plans for larger engineering projects on the river, they often used the protection of the region's numerous prison farms as justification for flood control. Prison officials hired politically connected engineers and consultants to develop their own system of levees.[16] Once constructed, levees such as the one built at Ellis Prison became dramatic representations of a landscape of control. Yet as the inmates understood it, the area beyond the imposing levees lacked any oversight. Even as institutional and legal reforms attempted to make prisons into more humane spaces, prisoners and those who watched over them understood that levees hid people from view. On the far side of the levees, between the high earthen embankments and the meandering river, guards could continue to treat prisoners as they wished without fear of the consequences.

Coming from other, mostly urban parts of the state, many inmates did not know the Trinity, except by reputation, as levees hid the river and its remaining floodplain from sight. Their dislocation from an urban to a rural setting was an intentional component of their punishment. Their alienation from the Trinity coincided with the depopulation of the region, though within the boundaries of the prison farms, more people lived in those locations than at any point in history.[17] After the levee was built, the bottomlands of Ellis Prison became known as the most dangerous and unregulated area on the property. Following the activism of thousands of incarcerated Texans and the landmark 1980 *Ruiz v. Estelle* ruling, reforms limited the kind of violence that could be inflicted upon Texas inmates.[18] As a consequence, prison employees moved the beatings to the river bottoms, where they went unobserved. Inmates feared being taken to the bottoms because anything could be done to them there. According to one witness, abuse in the bottomlands was a foregone conclusion: "They take you down there to be whipped. . . . It's what's called a ride to the bottoms and everybody knows what it means."[19]

In 1981, inmate Eroy Brown drowned the Ellis warden in a drainage ditch and shot the Ellis farm manager to death because he believed they were about to take him to the river side of the levees. In court, his claim of self-defense rested on the fearsome reputation of the floodplain. Brown's lead attorney argued that the warden had threatened Brown: "We'll see if you can talk at the bottom of the Trinity River." Ultimately Texas jurors agreed that Brown was justified in killing the warden and farm boss to prevent them from taking him to the river bottoms.[20]

## CHAPTER 12

# THE MYTH OF THE WHITE HERON

There is a unique challenge in telling the history of a 710-mile-long, ever-changing river. Many stories can be shared about the Trinity and its parts. The further one zooms out in space, the more abstract it becomes and the easier to distance from reality. In Texas's transformation from a rural to an urban state, the history of the Trinity was rewritten as a well-publicized myth. The primary agent behind this rewriting of history was Amon Carter, the *Fort Worth Star-Telegram* owner and publisher. From his vantage point, he may have had little interest in knowing the true story of what happened downstream, but it is fair to consider what he also overlooked in his hometown. Within Fort Worth's bottomlands, a significant portion of the city's Greek immigrants established successful farms, selling their produce just over the levees in the city.[1] And, as elsewhere on the river, a number of freedom colonies, such as the Cheney family's Garden of Eden, hugged the banks of the branches of the Trinity River.[2] But these were not the stories Carter told. He sought to represent the river as a single political community and to rally this consciousness to support the development of the river from the Gulf of Mexico to Fort Worth. To make this grand vision a reality, Carter funded a secret public relations effort to make it appear as though rural Texans unanimously supported navigation.

Boosters had always wanted Dallas and Fort Worth to be port cities, considering that a prerequisite to join the ranks of the great world metropolises. Having seen their towns on the plains become cities, they believed the Trinity canal was an inevitable next step. From 1900 to 1950, Dallas's population increased from 42,638 to 434,462, and Fort Worth grew at an even more rapid rate, going from a population of 26,688 to 361,258. As Dallas and Fort Worth flourished, leaders in the two cities used their growing economic and political power to attempt to control the entire length of the Trinity River. Dallas had already largely contained its stretch of the Trinity with giant levees, but the next phase would be a show of force that reached beyond the borders of Texas, with the full support of the state's congressional delegation.

Veterans of the Dallas–Fort Worth canal campaign had refused to accept the Army Corps of Engineers' 1921 conclusion that navigation was hopeless. The boosters viewed themselves as white men with a duty to tame or conquer their environment, and they took the Trinity's resistance as a mockery of progress. In *Trinity River Canalization*, published in 1930 to promote this view, the author wrote, "And, just as it had done before the white man came to Texas and wrested an empire from the wilderness, the Trinity River—muddy, unclean and turtle-infested—wound sluggishly between its banks in sullen victory."[3] Labeling the Trinity as a wilderness revealed both what was true (the river was hard to tame) and what was invisible (the significant number of poor Black and white families living along the Trinity). Boosters and engineers were highly motivated to write out the existence of people downriver, as it lessened the number of stakeholders they had to convince and cajole to go along with their plans.

In 1930, boosters formed the Trinity River Canal Association (TRCA) to sustain their efforts to get the federal money they needed to turn the Trinity into a canal—a straightened and controllable waterway rather than a winding, unpredictable river. Sponsored by the Dallas and Fort Worth Chambers of Commerce, the TRCA was led by Amon Carter and John Carpenter, two of the most powerful men in the region, who intended to use all their financial and political resources to remake the Trinity. Upon the TRCA's founding, Carter proclaimed, "The battle will be backed up in a manner which will insure that retreat for any reason will never be necessary."[4] As the publisher of the *Fort Worth Star-Telegram*, Carter used his considerable influence to ensure the continued support of Texas's senators and representatives. John Carpenter, meanwhile, operated a large electric utility, founded a life insurance company, and owned thousands of acres of ranchland. The TRCA was careful to include members from East Texas, and downstream proponents received both funding and publicity from Carter. But the vast majority of the board of directors for the TRCA came from Dallas and Fort Worth.[5]

Amon Carter envisioned the project as one of the most important events in Texas history. At a 1930 TRCA meeting, he said, "I don't think there is anything confronting North Texas as big as this project will be." Carter made it clear that such a large project could be completed only with the aid of the federal government, which Dallas and Fort Worth should work together to obtain. Canal proponents believed that, like the urban levees that had already transformed the Trinity, the canal would help to counter what another TRCA member called the Trinity's bad reputation.[6] The Corps of Engineers' conclusion that the Trinity lacked sufficient rainfall had been misguided, according to the TRCA. Members argued this perception could be fixed with a simple publicity campaign that would show how the canal would take "its place as a part of the greatest inland waterway system in the world" and link Fort Worth to ports across the globe. Rather than viewing the Trinity as an engineering challenge, canal boosters framed it as a political problem they could address through media initiatives and lobbying.

The TRCA ran a persistent campaign, making use of its control of the media and influence over congressmen. US Senator Tom Connally was an early get. At the TRCA's inaugural luncheon in 1930, Connally gave a speech in which he argued that the canal project was for the good of the country. The Texas delegation had "voted as readily for waterways improvement on the Pacific Coast as on the Gulf Coast," and members were willing to call in a favor from other congressmen who had benefited from Texas's congressional votes. While "the Trinity has been a bad boy in years past . . . always either out of banks or hardly above bed level," Connally dismissed the naysayers "scoff[ing] at the idea of such inland ports as Fort Worth and Dallas" when "some of the greatest ports of the world are on inland rivers."[7] He returned three years later to give a similar speech at the TRCA's banquet, titled "Greatest Cities Follow Water Transportation." Attendees listened to Senator Connally while dining on shrimp cocktail and smoking complimentary cigars, all part of Amon Carter's charm offensive to shape state and federal water policy.[8]

Carter and his fellow businessmen readily pivoted their campaign in light of New Deal priorities in the Great Depression. The New Deal administration began an era of great engineering ambition, remaking rivers across the nation that had previously defied such efforts, such as with the Colorado

River and the completion of the Hoover Dam in 1935 (then the highest dam in the world), or with the Tennessee River and the electrification of its valley under the Tennessee Valley Authority. Carter pressed the moment by meeting with President Roosevelt and pointing to the success of the Tennessee Valley Authority as a guide to remaking the Trinity. Adapting to the moment, the TRCA claimed that a massive project on the Trinity not only would accomplish its ambition to turn Dallas and Fort Worth into port cities but also would give the region more control over flooding and the ability to reclaim land on a massive scale.[9] The lobbying was relentless.

The mission grew, and in an effort to solidify a broader political alliance, the TRCA was rebranded as the Trinity Improvement Association (TIA) in 1938. The TIA's wordy letterhead included the organization's new mandate: "Sponsoring a coordinated program of improvement for the entire Trinity Watershed, including flood control, soil and water conservation, navigation, reclamation, alleviation of stream pollution, conservation of wildlife, and storage of water for municipal, agricultural and industrial uses."[10] Many of these goals, particularly soil and water conservation, were a messaging pivot in response to the particular environmental anxieties of the Dust Bowl era, while others built on a longer historical movement for wildlife conservation.[11]

One note featuring the new letterhead, written by a TIA employee to Amon Carter, included a photograph of an exhibit in East Texas. The exhibit displayed maps of the river, a flag with the words "Trinity River Admiral" written on it, and samples of different goods from the region such as castor oil and rope fibers. The staffer reported to Carter that this exhibit had "excited much questioning" about their "comprehensive Trinity program." Its great success was "due mainly to the activities of Commodore B. M. Hatfield."[12]

***Basil Muse Hatfield*** wore many hats before he became Amon Carter's most important promoter, giving Carter an opportunity to bridge the widening rural and urban divide on the river and rewrite history. Living in a humble home in Fort Worth, Hatfield struggled to make a living at the outset of the Great Depression. He decided to make a career out of promoting navigation of the Trinity River, publicizing himself as the "Commodore" and becoming a river personality. With the support of wealthy boosters like Carter, Hatfield made several storied trips down the Trinity in order to show its potential for investment. Whether Hatfield found Carter or vice versa, sources make it clear that his publicity tours were "quietly subsidized by various backers in both Fort Worth and Dallas."[13]

When he left Fort Worth in 1933 on his first voyage down the Trinity, Hatfield vowed to never shave until the Trinity was remade, lending him an image not unlike a Texas Santa Claus. In addition to growing out his beard, Hatfield changed his appearance by donning worn clothes and of course a cowboy hat, transforming himself into an authoritative and authentic white rural Texan at the very moment Texas was becoming an urban state. Hatfield quickly came to be seen as an East Texan, and his Trinity trips became a part of folklore.[14] Reports of his progress appeared regularly in many of the state's newspapers.

Figure 12.1. The *Texas Steer* in Fort Worth. Commodore B. M. Hatfield sits in the bow while the Bluebonnet String Band plays "Over the Waves" before Hatfield's first Trinity voyage in 1933. Courtesy of the Fort Worth Star-Telegram Collection, Special Collections, The University of Texas at Arlington Libraries, https://library.uta.edu/digitalgallery/img/10021121.

Nothing could stop Hatfield from promoting himself and navigation, not even the Trinity itself. If adverse conditions on the river slowed the progress of his boat, the *Texas Steer*, and revealed the limits to navigation imposed by hazards like log jams or low water, then a truck would simply be "dispatched to pick the *Steer* up, under cover of darkness, and the next day at the bridge the Commodore aboard his refloated scow received hosannas and encomiums."[15] He was welcomed at towns near the Trinity, energizing a region hit hard by the Great Depression. He wrote directly to his supporters at the TIA about his "work" to make "people canal minded."[16] At every stop, he engaged in elaborate rituals, including the rechristening of his boat.[17] In the summer of 1934, after nearly a year of travel floating down the Trinity and back up the Mississippi River, he reached Lake Michigan, where he poured into it the water he had collected from the various rivers he had crossed.

While Hatfield's exploits were carried in newspapers across the state, he was particularly effective in galvanizing support along the lower Trinity in East Texas. White East Texans appreciated the visits of this Fort Worth resident to their region, which, except in the few boomtowns of the East Texas oil fields, had fallen behind the rest of the state's economic growth. On his excursions, Hatfield met with older men who remembered the formerly navigable lower half of the Trinity or who had even been steamboat pilots themselves in the 1860s and 1870s. He drew on the nostalgia of white residents for the antebellum era by showing how the new canal would reconnect them to an earlier idealized history of plantations and steamboats on the river, just as the previous generation of navigation proponents had relied on the power of the Lost Cause to make their case. As one correspondent reported, Hatfield's visit "brought on quite a bit of excitement and made the old-timers dream of by-gone days," when slavery made the river boom.[18]

While nostalgia for the old times certainly included a longing for the times of slavery, it increasingly included a grief over the loss of the natural environment and the subsistence it used to provide before the closing of the commons and the extinction of passenger pigeons that once blackened the skies over the Trinity's hardwood forests. Steamboat transport on the Trinity had overlapped with a moment in which white yeoman farmers had significantly more economic independence compared with their descendants' tenuous position in the Great Depression.[19] In memory, Hatfield's mission represented the uplift of "the little guy."[20] Regardless of Hatfield's receipt of funds from big city boosters like Amon Carter, he connected with white country people in a way that Carter, a wealthy urban newspaper magnate, never could have.

Hatfield's pivotal role in promoting the Trinity Canal on the lower river illustrates how North Texas boosters increased their political influence by manufacturing the appearance of consent for a canal from white rural Texans. As for Hatfield, he lived his dream of exploring the river without having to worry about making an income during the Great Depression. On Hatfield's final trip upriver, a traveling companion recalled Hatfield's appetite: "When we thought that all had had their fill, the Commodore said, 'There is a small steak left, and if no one wants it, I will eat it.' And he did." On that same trip, the party was "surprised to see a mounted, armed man ride up to the riverbank and observe us very closely." Then there were "six or eight armed horsemen riding along the riverbank." Hatfield's frightened party shouted that they meant no harm, unsure whether they had not seen a vision of "ghosts." Their boat had passed between the Ferguson and Eastham Prisons on the Trinity, where less than a decade earlier Clyde Barrow had led a daring jailbreak.[21]

Hatfield died in 1942 at the age of seventy-two, while scouting along the Trinity. He was memorialized on the front page of Carter's *Fort Worth Star-Telegram*. He had fallen, the paper reported, while climbing the Trinity's steep bank, where he was "searching for new deposits of materials he had contended will bring new wealth to that area." His funeral was paid for and organized by the state's boosters, including representatives from the Trinity Improvement Association and the Forward Trinity Valley Association (FTVA), a group Hatfield had helped form on the lower river.[22] Even in death, Hatfield remained a valuable symbol for canal proponents. His ashes were eventually spread in the Trinity River from a Fort Worth bridge in 1987, flowing downstream to East Texas in one final journey along the river.[23]

After Hatfield died, canal boosters needed new myths to sustain their project along the entire length of the river, creating the Fraternity of the White Heron. The founders claimed in their charter that a white heron they called the "Mystic Arabella" had inspired them, and ever since that time, "unselfish and spiritual values have been closely associated with the development of the Valley of the Trinity."[24] They referred back to Hatfield's "visionary prophecies" even as he had passed on to "the Rookery that lies across the Great River." The organization published its own magazine, in which it presented its "altruistic" leaders as "aiming at nothing less than America's first fully-developed watershed." In contrast to the lavish banquets attended by Dallas's and Fort Worth's elite, the Fraternity of the White Heron sponsored an annual fish fry, publicized by none other than Amon Carter, for thousands of attendees. The name chosen for this new organization, moreover, spoke to boosters' understanding of Hatfield's earlier success in promoting the canal. The use of the term "Fraternity" makes it explicit that this project was aimed at men, while the "White" in "White Heron," in the age of Jim Crow, implied that this was for white men.

As with Hatfield, both the FTVA and its publicity wing, the White Herons, depended heavily on upstream support. The general manager for the TIA wrote to Amon Carter telling him about the new organization that would be headquartered on the lower river in Liberty but primarily financed by the TIA. The manager emphasized, "My purpose is to line up the Lower Trinity folks and those of the Gulf ports solidly behind the Trinity program."[25] The FTVA sent regular reports to Carter directly, thanking him for sending journalists and for the "many helps" he gave the association over the years. In their letters members also emphasized the connections between the upper and lower Trinity, claiming that "the folks down here are imbued with the idea of building, not one or two sections, but all of the Trinity Project."[26] FTVA members were right to be grateful for the financial support from North Texas, for they would not have existed without it.

Promoters mythologized their plans for the Trinity by muddying its history. Steamboats had rarely navigated beyond the Trinity's midpoint in the heyday of river transport, and only up to that point for half the year due to seasonal changes in rainfall. However, proponents used the few exceptions to claim that the river had been navigable all the way to Fort Worth. In the book *Trinity River Canalization*, the author, a booster, described boats navigating the river while omitting how far they could travel. Instead, he used historical uncertainty to suggest that navigation up to and past Dallas had a history of nearly a century: "The records are dim and incomplete, but it appears possible that a steamboat may actually have passed the site of the city before John Neely Bryan made his home there."[27] But no plantations existed that far upriver in the 1840s, and any steamboat would have had to navigate logjams and Comanche attacks before they could even get to the landings to pick up cotton. It did not matter. Boosters rewrote the environmental history of the Trinity River in order to gain support and, ultimately, the power to remake the river for their benefit.

The Trinity Improvement Association had already succeeded in bringing major federal spending to the upper Trinity for reservoir construction. Funding from the federal government on the upper Trinity came through the 1944 Flood Control Act, which allowed for the creation of smaller reservoirs. Following the 1945 Rivers and Harbors Act, several "multipurpose" reservoirs were built as water sources and for flood control along the upper tributaries of the mainstem Trinity that could also potentially provide water for navigation.[28] In 1953 the TIA released a map showing all its actual and planned lakes and other alterations to the Trinity River. Most of the reservoirs on the map were eventually constructed to provide a mix of water supply and flood control for North Texas, promoting further urban growth. Compared with the lower river, the upper Trinity was relatively arid and needed an expanding supply of cheap water to fuel North Texas's boom.[29]

In 1954, the Fraternity of the White Heron's "principal fish fry speaker" was none other than US Senator Lyndon B. Johnson, addressing the 4,500 attendees who together ate two tons of fish. Johnson's path to power had rested on his ability to build dams on Texas's Colorado River and bring electricity to other parts of rural Texas, which he pursued with a dogged persistence that led President Roosevelt to say in regard to the then-freshman congressman, "Give the kid the dam."[30] Although the US Army Corps of Engineers had been involved in plans for the Trinity since the nineteenth century, and later for reservoir construction, Senator Johnson claimed that the federal government had little to do with the river until recently. He praised his hosts, proclaiming, "Our only real need is to tackle the water problem on a state-wide basis—with the same energy and enthusiasm that has been displayed on the Trinity."[31] In return for continued support from the Fraternity of the White Heron and the TIA, Johnson and the other congressmen at the fish fry promised to help develop the river.

Amon Carter held tremendous power over the Texas delegation in Congress—his "'rubber stamps' in Washington," as one historian put it—during the postwar years. A particularly subservient congressman wrote to Carter and apologized for once voting against Carter's interests, groveling that he had never "consciously done anything as Congressman from our District that I thought you would disapprove."[32] In 1950, when the TIA sought federal funding for flood control in the Dallas–Fort Worth region, its general manager wrote directly to Sam Rayburn, the Speaker of the House (from Texas). Addressing the Speaker by his first name, he asked whether Rayburn would "be kind enough to advise the President" to certify that a proposed flood control project related to national defense, a requirement for the appropriation of such funds.[33] Rayburn replied, "I wish to assure you that this matter will receive my best consideration."[34] Boosters believed that their relationship with some of the most powerful people in Congress would finally give them a clear path toward canalization of the Trinity.

The TIA's full-time professional staff made sure politicians, bureaucrats, and the organization's own members never lost sight of their dream of commercial navigation. Amon Carter and John Carpenter both passed away in the 1950s, but their sons, Amon Carter Jr. and Ben Carpenter, picked up where their fathers left off, lobbying politicians while raising money from their peers to support the TIA's staff and publicity campaigns. These men continued to advocate for navigation—despite the fact that the campaign for a canal had been going on long enough that it had carried into the interstate era and the height of auto travel. For them, the canal would be a symbol of their power and their ability to follow through on their fathers' dreams, even if the canal's barges carried only low-value materials like gravel.

***Amon Carter's TIA*** may have had great sway over the state's federal delegation, but in 1955 it hit on a new idea: Absorb the TIA into state government. The plan was to create the Trinity River Authority (TRA), which would develop the Trinity River and raise money through taxes and fees. There was precedent for the move; the state founded the Brazos River Authority in 1929, and most of the state's major rivers had such authorities by the 1950s. Because of this, the TIA believed it would have an easy time establishing a river authority that would allow it to canalize the Trinity. By creating their own governmental authority, canal boosters could shift their focus from lobbying to actually building the canal.

Despite their political connections, canal boosters met surprising resistance, much of it originating beyond the Trinity basin. The TRA bill was first sponsored in the Texas legislature by a Dallas legislator whose bill included provisions for taxation, flood control, irrigation, municipal water supply, conservation, and of course navigation.[35] Opposition stemmed in part from the general distaste for the TIA's existing power; giving the association its own river authority would funnel even more federal money to the Trinity that might have gone to other much-needed development projects. Another sticking point was the quixotic quest to create a navigable river. Unlike flood control or water supply, navigation did not appear to offer a widespread public good. The TIA's general manager complained of "a great deal of misunderstanding regarding the development for the canalization," but he did not deny that canalization remained the central goal of the endeavor.[36]

Finally, there was the funding. Would the TRA cover all of each county that lay along the river, or only the precincts of the county that were within the Trinity watershed? It seemed unfair to many residents that taxpayers living outside the watershed would have to pay taxes for a project that might not benefit them directly.[37] The plan to create the Trinity River Authority also raised major questions about representation and taxation. Would the TRA be able to govern and tax river residents without their consent or oversight? The plan for the governor to appoint the board of directors (from a list approved by the TIA) received pushback from river residents who believed that "the local taxpayers should elect the board" lest they have "no election where they can express their approval or disapproval of the stewardship of the board."[38] The TIA could not simply steamroll its opposition, but a democratically elected TRA would be an existential threat to its dream of a navigable river. Instead of allowing locally elected representatives, the TIA compromised by capping the tax rate in the bill to no more than two cents per hundred-dollar valuation.[39]

It was unclear to river residents and state legislators alike who exactly would benefit from a navigable Trinity, particularly for the cost. Compromise ultimately stripped the provision to provide navigation up to Dallas and Fort Worth from the final bill.[40] And so, under HR 20, the Trinity River Authority was created by the fifty-fourth legislature in the summer of 1955. A wounded TIA allowed the "badly slashed Trinity River Authority Bill" to pass, believing it could still take victory from the jaws of defeat after the bill was passed and opposition to its true goals cooled off.[41] As one reporter put it at the time, the creation of the authority "means the proponents of the navigation idea will get all the way in at a later date."[42] Ultimately, members of the association were right: Their constant work eventually restored navigation as the primary goal of the TRA. Likewise, the sponsor of the original bill took credit for backing the initial TRA legislation, publicly stating it was done "with the ultimate aim of bringing barge navigation to Dallas."[43]

As expected, the TRA did not supplant the TIA so much as expand its power. The TIA gained a direct connection to the government, and the TRA became one of the most powerful authorities in the state since it could continue to lobby and publicize efforts to reshape the Trinity through the TIA.[44] Indeed, the TIA even funded much of the consulting work proposed by the TRA while the authority developed new sources of revenue.[45] The TRA remained bound by the limitations set out in the bill that created it, but its close relationship with the TIA allowed the new authority much more flexibility to achieve its goals.

On November 3, 1955, Ben Carpenter, the first president of the TRA, held the inaugural meeting in Huntsville, since it was "centrally located within the area of the Trinity River valley."[46] The governor-appointed and senate-approved board consisted of three at-large members and one member from each county except for Dallas and Tarrant Counties. The home counties of

Dallas and Fort Worth had four and three members, respectively. Ultimately, a third of the original TRA board were former directors of the TIA.[47]

The TRA's governor-appointed directors reflected a cross section of the Trinity's urban and rural business elite: an executive of the Dr. Pepper Company in Dallas, a "prominent Fort Worth merchant," and, downriver, a petroleum executive who had recently retired to his ranch on the Trinity.[48] A TRA director who worked for a major paper company wanted to "spur both agricultural and industrial economic progress" by reclaiming the bottomlands and saw "possibilities for developing recreational facilities along the Trinity."[49] And then there was the publisher of the *Palestine Herald-Press*, who claimed a "crying need on the Trinity . . . for flood control to salvage productive acres with water impoundment through the basin for industrial and municipal development." Walker County director John T. Smither came from a Trinity plantation family—the Smithers, of the Smithers Farm—where sharecroppers had raised "cattle, cotton and feed on the banks of this controversial river" since the 1880s.[50] In 1959, most of the Smithers Farm was sold to become Ellis Prison, where, as noted, Eroy Brown would later drown the warden in a drainage ditch and shoot the farm manager in fear of what they could do to him, out of sight on the other side of the levees.

***Three years after its founding,*** the Trinity River Authority released its TIA-funded master plan. Produced under contract to the TRA by the politically connected engineering firm Forrest and Cotton, the report, informed by fifteen public hearings, called for a network of reservoirs and advanced plans to encourage barge navigation. The authors believed they could manage all the runoff within the Trinity River basin while planning for "future years of watershed development."[51] They grappled with how to balance the needs of the upstream metropolis with those of downstream rural residents.[52]

Development was centered in North Texas, which already had most of the watershed's reservoirs, but there was another city with an eye on the river: Houston, itself a rising metropolis, sought to claim the Trinity's water. That same year, the City of Houston asked the State Board of Water Engineers to grant it the Trinity's unallocated water to build a giant reservoir. Houston newspapers jumped to support their city's claims, arguing that the TRA represented the interests only of the upper Trinity. Would it be better for Dallas and Fort Worth to colonize the lower half of the river, or for Houston to do it instead? Houston was, after all, a shorter drive away from that stretch of the river. Amon Carter Jr. fought back, saying that "the cities of Dallas and Fort Worth do not control the Trinity River Authority. They have only seven of the 24 members on the board of directors, representing 17 counties."[53] Still, powerful men like Carter retained great influence over the TRA, and the closely linked TIA was unarguably a North Texas organization. For Carter and his allies, the logic of the river's downstream flow from Fort Worth meant that all its waters were rightfully theirs.

The Houston "water grab" momentarily unified the business class along the river against Houston. The *Palestine Herald-Press* editorialized that the conflict over Houston's lake plan was not between Houston and Dallas; rather, Houston was attacking the entire river, including the lower portion "that depends for its future economic growth on the proper harnessing of the Trinity River."[54] The mayor of Dallas echoed these thoughts: "I want to make it absolutely clear that the City of Dallas will stand firmly with the other people in the Trinity River Watershed to do whatever is necessary to protect our rights."[55] Invoking the "rights" of a unified watershed population, TRA allies presented Houston's plans as unjust in contrast to their own vision for the river.

In the short term, neither Dallas nor Houston needed more water from the Trinity River. Like other major cities across the Sunbelt, they wisely sought resources from their hinterlands well in advance of their actual need.[56] Houston's proposed Trinity reservoir was not a question of need so much as one of cost and ease—an abundant supply of cheap water could help to fuel a region's growth. Some people on the Trinity viewed this contest over resources as a zero-sum game. One newspaper claimed that if Houston took water from the Trinity River to fuel its growth, the city would be "eliminating the Trinity Valley, especially the lower part, as a future competitor for population and industry."[57] The economic stagnation of the lower half of the Trinity, it seemed, would only worsen if much of its water was siphoned off to fuel another metropolis's constant expansion. "The small towns and rural areas of the Trinity watershed can have some of the growth and prosperity that Houston has enjoyed for so many years if we will protect our water," said the leader of the TIA's East Texas affiliate. He claimed that Trinity water was crucial to the region's prospects: "We can't grow and prosper without plenty of water."[58]

The debate over and backlash against Houston's bid for the Trinity River revolved around the fate of rural Texas. If Houston had flourished and grown so much, East Texans asked, why should it take more resources at the expense of an economically depressed region that had already been polluted by the upstream cities of Dallas and Fort Worth? Houston leaders, in turn, argued that people from East Texas had moved to Houston, and therefore

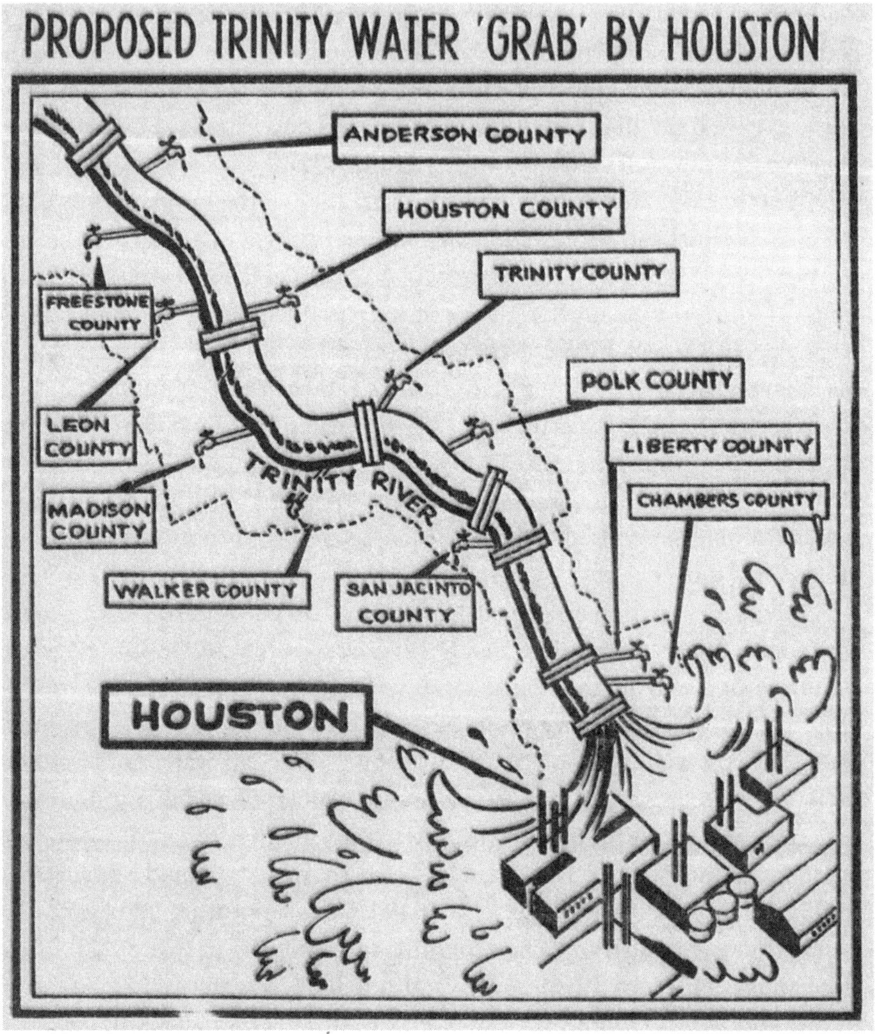


Figure 12.2. A political cartoon that was published in newspapers across the Trinity River watershed portraying Houston's reservoir plans as a huge water grab from the lower counties. From the *Carrollton (TX) Chronicle*, February 27, 1959, courtesy of Carrollton Public Library and the Portal to Texas History, University of North Texas Libraries, https://texashistory.unt.edu/ark:/67531/metapth727608.

their claim to water should not be viewed as an urban-rural conflict. At a hearing before the State Board of Water Engineers, the mayor stated, "Houston is just a grown up country town and we have men, women and children from other sections of the State."[59] Indeed, for the past forty years, there had been a ceaseless flow of rural people, like Ruth Simmons, who had moved to Texas cities to achieve their dreams. In contrast, the mayor of a town near the middle of the Trinity claimed that the remaining residents on the lower half of the river had been victims of the growing power of the state's big cities. He said, "You can bet your bottom dollar that Houston doesn't give a hoot for the welfare of the little town and the country people who must depend on the Trinity River for water—just so long as Houston gets what she wants."[60]

For their part, canal boosters were open to Houston taking water from the lower Trinity River as long as Houston went through the TRA. An editorial stated, "The key word is *control*. Behind the key word is *motive*." It continued, "If Houston does not seek Trinity *control*, and her *motive* is not almost 100 per cent selfish, why doesn't she work *with* the people of the Valley, through their own Trinity River Authority, rather than *against* the people of the Valley?"[61] Of course, the TRA represented a portion of the region's residents rather than the grand-sounding "people of the Valley," but in the debate over Houston's water grab, the organization claimed the moral high ground. Houston could take water from the Trinity so long as it reinforced rather than reduced the TRA's power.

Resistance to Houston's plans also came from its own residents, who worried that the Trinity River would not be a suitable water source. Though the water was less polluted by the time it reached the proposed site of Lake Livingston, the Trinity remained one of the most contaminated streams in Texas.[62] Indeed, some Houston residents may have moved from the Trinity in part because of its environmental degradation. Houston's plans would also have major implications for East Texas industry. If the lower Trinity became a reservoir, industry in the area would be unable to use the river as an outlet for any of its waste. While North Texans polluted and drank from the river and Houstonians drank from it, East Texans could do neither. Variations in expectations concerning the Trinity's water quality reinforced earlier inequities embedded in the river—namely, the way that Dallas's and Fort Worth's levee systems had largely precluded cost-effective levees from being built on the lower half of the river. The new reservoir would further inscribe economic inequality onto the landscape.

Once Houston and the TRA agreed to work together, concerns about East Texas's right to its own resources quickly disappeared from the press, and fewer editorials decried Houston's proposal as a water grab from country people. On September 14, 1959, the City of Houston signed a contract with the TRA for $74,500,000 to build a reservoir that would flood eighty-three thousand acres of Trinity River bottomlands; 70 percent of the water was guaranteed to Houston, with the TRA itself getting the rest. Later, as construction neared completion, Houston made a commitment to keep the Trinity's dirtier waters out of its water system for the next twenty years, highlighting the lack of a pressing need for this water.[63] While filling one's glass with Trinity water may have meant filling it with the history of Texas, Houstonians would not be prematurely subjected to tasting the treated sewage of Dallas and Fort Worth.

Construction of the reservoir began in 1966, affecting all of East Texas through the limitations it imposed on water use. Just as an earlier generation had been displaced with the building of levees and fish-killing pollution, the people who lived and worked at the site suffered the most. The loss of thousands of acres of valuable bottomlands meant less tax revenue for each county affected by the reservoir. These properties had been purchased through eminent domain, with and without the consent of owners, as the dam would flood them forever. When the Lake Livingston Dam was first closed and the reservoir began to fill up, residents remembered how the surrounding areas swarmed with cottonmouths and other snakes as they fled the water inundating the historic heart of the Trinity's plantation economy. This plague of snakes was just one more cost of development displaced from the cities onto East Texans. Thirty-one miles of the Trinity may have been permanently flooded under Lake Livingston, but the river's powerful history was not forgotten.

## CHAPTER 13

# CAN YOU TAME THE TRINITY?

In the still water of its newly built reservoirs, most Trinity fish survived, but others absolutely thrived. In the 1970s the Florida strain of the largemouth bass was introduced into Texas lakes. Bigger than the native bass, anglers broke records nearly every year.

The increasing girth of the bass paralleled the ever-growing population of Texas, and both depended on dammed rivers. Carp were also introduced to Texas reservoirs to control invasive weeds in lakes. When these carp made their way out of a reservoir into a nearby waterway, they entered the Trinity and wreaked havoc on the eelgrass beds at the mouth of the river.[1] Despite the chaotic battles for ecological niches under the surface of these Texas reservoirs, the fish quickly became naturalized, as if the lake houses and bass boats had always been there. Only the tops of dead trees sticking out above the water indicated any sign of the bottomland forests that once defined the landscape—now a home for bass rather than panthers.

These reservoirs changed the Trinity and Texas. For its part, the Trinity became more unruly. While many of the reservoirs surrounding Dallas and Fort Worth were engineered for flood control, Lake Livingston and Richland-Chambers, the two biggest reservoirs, were located well below those cities,

Figure 13.1. The author in 1991 with his father and a thirteen-pound largemouth bass he caught with a cane pole and cricket in one of the largest private lakes in Texas.

and they made flooding worse. Most of Lake Livingston's water was allocated to the city of Houston, and 95 percent of Richland-Chambers's water went to Fort Worth's Tarrant County. These two reservoirs functioned like the concrete surfaces of Dallas–Fort Worth, with little space between the top of the reservoir and the spillway. When heavy rains fell, the excess water, rather than being partially absorbed into the ground or spread into an adjacent floodplain, got flushed in its entirety downstream.

After big rains, Richland-Chambers sent water into the Trinity at much higher rates than in the past. The new floods scoured the land, washing out roads and carrying off the once fertile bottomland soil. In one case involving a downstream ranch, the Texas courts ruled that the reservoir had dire consequences. Despite the area's long history of flooding, the court found that the reservoir meant water "arrived sooner, flowed faster, and [was] more forceful, deeper, and longer-lasting."[2] The landowners, a Texas oil family, were awarded over $30 million, paid for by the ratepayers of Fort Worth's Tarrant County.[3] Urban development came at the expense of rural development, but it was less clear which people paid for and which benefited from the cost of these tradeoffs.

Between the 1930s and 1990s, Texas had a reservoir boom, resulting in over two hundred lakes. And the Trinity contains more reservoirs and stored water than any other Texas river. John Graves was prompted to write *Goodbye to a River*, about the Brazos, during this era of reservoir expansion. Published in 1959, the same year the Trinity River Authority signed a contract with the City of Houston to build Lake Livingston, *Goodbye to a River* documents Graves's final trip down a stretch of the Brazos River shortly before it lost most of its character to a series of reservoirs. A classic of Texas literature, the book has been the most widely read book about a Texas river. But Graves could just as easily have written *Goodbye to a River* about the Trinity instead of the Brazos—he grew up in Fort Worth exploring the Trinity River bottoms.[4] For many years his sister was the head librarian at the Amon Carter Museum of American Art, named after the Trinity's most influential booster. But instead Graves drew on his experiences on the seemingly wilder Brazos River, and the Trinity was overlooked even by its own children.

The Brazos and Trinity share much in common in their geology and history. Flowing through a more arid region directly to the west of the Trinity, the Brazos has a slightly higher average yearly flow and a larger drainage area. The uppermost portions of both rivers lay within the heart of Comancheria. As the site of Stephen Austin's original Anglo colony, the Brazos contained a greater number of plantations than the Trinity while being less navigable.

When the Brazos and Trinity became laden with prison farms, they became the two rivers where the term "river songs" was born.

In the opening to *Goodbye to a River*, Graves argued that the dams coming to the Brazos represented an irreplaceable loss of history. He wrote, "But if you are built like me, neither the certainty of change, nor the need for it, nor any wry philosophy will keep you from feeling a certain enraged awe when you hear that a river that you've known always, and that all men of that place have known always back into the red dawn of men, will shortly not exist. A piece of a river, anyhow, my piece."[5] By the time Graves published these words, a bigger plan was coming together on the Trinity, one that would not just alter a piece of the river with a reservoir, as on his beloved Brazos, but would transform the entire length of the Trinity from Fort Worth to its mouth. So much more history would have been lost if this proposed canal were constructed versus any single dam. But an understanding among Texans of how the Trinity had been shaped by its reservoirs, cities, and more distant past inspired them to push back against this bold plan.

Over the middle decades of the twentieth century, Trinity canal boosters laid the groundwork to receive funding from regional, state, and federal sources to finally build their canal. The population and economic booms in North Texas only increased the boosters' political power, while the economic decline of East Texas seemed to further justify a federally subsidized project. Yet precisely when canal proponents had lined up over a billion dollars in federal funding, they experienced a river-long defeat at the polls in 1973. The seemingly limitless power of boosters collided with two growing concerns that had nationwide importance: environmental destruction and fiscally responsible governance. Canal proponents rewrote laws and influenced government agencies, but Texans increasingly mistrusted government officials in general, and those who asserted the canal's benefits were doubly shunned as the canal's reputation became inextricable with corruption. As the Trinity was transformed by massive levees, reservoirs, and sprawling development in the Dallas–Fort Worth region, it became all the more unruly downstream, destroying property, crops, and lives, ultimately causing many people to move farther from the floodplain or to seek economic opportunity in Texas metropolises.

From the early nineteenth century, plantation agriculture, levee construction, urban development, and reservoir construction had transformed the Trinity, but few believed the Trinity had been tamed into a controlled pattern as a canal might be. People all along the river interpreted the river's history differently, making the climactic debate and vote over the potential canal into a debate about the past as much as about the future. Should the Trinity be tamed? Could it be? The answers to these questions differed based on a person's history not only with the river but also with the story of Texas. Was the success of Texas derived from the domination of its people and places, or from the determination of millions of people to persevere and adapt within its varied landscapes and climates?

***In 1969,*** Texas held a special election. At issue: a $3 billion bond and a change to the state constitution to support the Texas Water Plan. The plan's advocates argued that, between the growing cities and arid farmland in the southern and western parts of the state, Texas would run out of water. They proposed pumping water into these regions from the wetter eastern side of Texas as well as from outside the state altogether. The plan was not without precedent, as water from the Trinity and other East Texas rivers was already being shipped westward. Ultimately it was defeated by a small margin, with voters worried about its cost to taxpayers and the environment.[6] Texans were no longer willing to write blank checks for water development projects. Texas water politics were shifting, and the Trinity canal boosters were getting worried.

The same year the Texas Water Plan was rejected, the US Congress enacted the National Environmental Policy Act, which required federal agencies to prepare environmental impact statements for major projects. This legislation was a direct result of national concerns about the environment. For the Army Corps of Engineers and the Trinity River Authority, the act meant that the Trinity project would be subject to a comprehensive study before construction could begin. As the authors of the first National Environmental Policy Act report on the Trinity realized, "much of the Trinity Basin lacked sufficient study," so they spent much of their time learning about this region.[7] Despite a long-standing vision for a canal, the Trinity had remained significantly understudied, which illustrates the extent to which the canal had been a dream as much as a concrete plan.

The TRA portrayed the canal as a solution to many of the Trinity's challenges. The 1968 summer issue of the TRA's magazine, *Trinity Valley Progress*, had included an article headlined "Channel Only Cure for Floods," but such tactics were working against the TRA by the Nixon era, by which time Texans were apathetic at best on the canal question.[8] Dallas Congressman Earle Cabell received a letter from one of his constituents who had seen a Trinity navigation program on his television. The letter writer worried that citizens would not benefit from the project, and he questioned whether even the biggest boosters might not "need this a lot less than they (say/think) they do."[9] Alan Steelman, Cabell's 1972 Republican challenger, made the Trinity River project into a political liability for Cabell. In the spring of 1972, Steelman announced that while he had also initially supported the canal, he could not continue to do so given the project's expense. With information provided to him by the Texas Committee on Natural Resources, a state environmental group, Steelman questioned both the return on the investment and the environmental consequences.[10] Cabell had been one of the canal's biggest proponents in Congress, as had all of Texas's "rubber stamp" delegations up to this point. That November, he lost to Steelman. Cabell's incumbent loss fit a national pattern of upsets fueled by environmental issues, though the *New York Times* claimed Steelman's victory, hinging on his opposition to the particularly bold Trinity project, was one of the contests for which "conservationists were especially jubilant."[11]

Growing resistance led canal proponents to accelerate the project so that they might begin construction before it could be thwarted by the same opposition that had led to the defeat of the Texas Water Plan. In its final push for the canal, the TRA put a local bond for $150 million—roughly 10 percent of the estimated cost of the canal—on the ballot. The final total was expected to be over a billion dollars. The remainder would be paid for by the federal government. To pass, the bond needed a majority of voters and a majority of the seventeen counties along the proposed route to support the bond. The vote was to be held on March 13, 1973, shortly before the release of a final environmental impact statement.[12] Rather than wait for the results of the study and allow voters to understand the environmental and historic implications of building a canal, the TRA worked against the clock to push the canalization plan over the finish line.

Opposing the TRA was the Texas Committee on Natural Resources, one of a wave of environmental groups across the country funded and filled primarily by upper-middle-class suburbanites worried about stinking rivers and lost wilderness. Led by the relentless and charismatic (or abrasive, depending on one's perspective) lawyer Ned Fritz, the Texas Committee on Natural Resources challenged efforts to transform Texas's environment and had backed Steelman before his win over Cabell. Defeating the canal boosters became the committee's top priority, and Fritz doggedly campaigned against the canal, even traveling to Washington to testify against the project. Fritz understood that few Texans could be motivated to care about saving the dirty Trinity, but many more would care about saving public money. And so he helped to launch a mission-focused group, Citizens' Organization for a

Sound Trinity (or COST), emphasizing the group's strategic focus on financial problems.

While North Texas had been the stronghold of the canal boosters, Steelman's victory in their congressional district had left them feeling exposed and vulnerable. Outside the reach of North Texas, the lower Trinity seemed to furnish a strong base of support they could rely on. Charlie Wilson (played by Tom Hanks in the 2007 movie *Charlie Wilson's War*) had also been first elected to Congress in 1972 and was the primary US representative for East Texas. He was friends with both Amon Carter Jr. and Ben Carpenter, the two men who had taken up their fathers' mission to canalize the river. It was Wilson who, as a state senator, had quietly introduced a 1967 senate bill "at the request of the Trinity Improvement Association" that removed the original restrictions on the Trinity River Authority regarding its ability to promote navigation.[13] When Carter Jr. wrote to Wilson to describe the opposition they had faced, he referred to his opponents as "a small group of publicity-seeking college professors and self-styled ecologists."[14] Both men assumed that any money from the federal or state government would be welcomed by East Texans, in the same way that allocations for prison construction had ultimately been positively received. While prisons faced some opposition in the early years, they were now considered an important pillar of local economies and a source of jobs that the region could not do without. Thus, even as the TRA lost support in its urban base, its directors believed they could rely on politicians and residents downstream to support their plans.

Unlike in North Texas, nearly every politician in East Texas, from US Representative Charlie Wilson to local judges and county commissioners, publicly supported the canal. While they presented a united front, privately a few politicians expressed misgivings about the canal and worried that they lacked enough evidence to make an informed decision. The mayor of Palestine wrote to Representative Alan Steelman in January 1973 that the canal boosters had asked him to support their project. The mayor had heard of Steelman's opposition to the project and wanted more information so that he could make "the right decision."[15] The mayor's inquiry shows how little information politicians were given in the rush to the ballot box. Instead of evidence, proponents offered up dreams of the canal.

Voters were expected by proponents to trust advertisements framing canalization as a panacea to all the Trinity's problems. In large letters, a multipage color newspaper insert read, "The flooding Trinity has killed scores of people and wiped out many millions of dollars worth of homes and property. Isn't it about time we got the upper hand?" In boosters' telling,

Figure 13.2. Congressman Charlie Wilson showing his plaque from the Trinity River Authority on the Alabama-Coushatta Reservation, December 2, 1972. Courtesy of The History Center, Diboll, Texas, https://thehistorycenteronline.com/uploads/resources/0011_wilson-trinity-river-authority-seal-governor-for-a-day-1972.pdf.

the constraints the Trinity had imposed on the state's development were an affront to Texas pride. The advertisement claimed that by shortening the channel 213 miles and eliminating 184 severe bends, the canal would make the river less flood-prone, whereas experience has long shown that straightening rivers makes flooding much more destructive.[16] On the upper Trinity, Amon Carter Jr. pledged to donate eighty acres of Trinity River bottomlands to two schools, but only under the condition that the bond be approved. Those who wanted a park would have to vote for the canal.[17]

Canal boosters used their connections to pull the state agencies in line, though the process was not as clean as they hoped. Several months before the vote, the Texas Parks and Wildlife Department had announced that the canal would cause "wholesale devastation" to the wildlife along the river. However, the department reversed its position just a week before the vote, saying its staff had taken a closer look at the latest studies and now believed the canal would "improve" the fishing quality. Democratic Governor Dolph Briscoe claimed not to have "put any pressure on anybody," but journalists and the wider public understood the reversal to be politically motivated. Indeed, the agency admitted that its own environmental department had not even seen the latest release from its director.[18] Such abrupt, top-down directives only reinforced the impression of a forced-through project. The timing of the canal vote took place when many citizens increasingly distrusted the government to make decisions that were actually in the public interest, and blatant attempts to politicize supposedly objective and scientific agencies only proved them right.[19]

A unique Texan rural-urban partnership formed against the canal boosters, defying political and social boundaries. Citizens' Organization for a Sound Trinity was led by a professor of theology at Southern Methodist University and a Dallas lumberman. Most of the leading businessmen in North Texas supported the canal, or at least accepted its inevitability and gave hundreds of thousands of dollars to its publicity campaign. A few wealthy families contributed money toward anti-canal efforts, but overall, proponents of the canal greatly outspent their opponents. In the anti-canal activists' favor, however, was a wide coalition of voters, each of whom had their personal reasons for opposing the project.[20]

A Texas oil family led the fight to protect the river below Dallas. Oilman J. R. Parten owned one of the largest properties along the Trinity, having purchased most of the Murray Farm several decades prior. The Partens wanted to preserve the river and keep taxes low. As a wealthy and politically connected family, the Partens, led by J. R.'s son Randy, rallied other landowners and ranchers to fight the project. They ran full-page ads that countered canal proponents' efforts. People had heard about plans to canalize the river since the first decade of the century, when the Army Corps of Engineers built the first locks, and during the 1930s, when Commodore Hatfield had paraded down the river eating everything in sight. In those eras, however, the canal had been a distant possibility. Once residents had to vote on and then pay taxes for the canal, their perspectives changed. No longer a quixotic quest promoted by the charismatic Hatfield, the actual project appeared much more troubling. The federal contribution of over a billion dollars may not have been a problem, but the local bond issue could have a major effect on tax rates for a region with little to tax in the first place. While Randy Parten claimed that a few individuals may have speculated in land purchases along the proposed canal, few people were convinced that the presence of barges running through the countryside would add any value to their property.[21]

Opponents also considered the huge environmental cost of dramatically changing the river by cutting the channel off from the floodplains, removing many of its bends, and raising the water level with reservoirs and locks. The Trinity channel and bottomlands remained some of the most important fishing and hunting lands in the state. Both river residents and Texans living farther away feared losing their much-diminished access to these areas. The worsening floods were equally important, making Texans uncertain that a canal could even be created out of such an erratic and powerful stream, much less tame it. Nearly all East Texas levees built in the first half of the century, which were sold on a similar promise of domesticating the Trinity, had to be rebuilt or abandoned because they had failed to contain the river. For many Texans, the lesson to be learned was very clear: The Trinity could not be tamed.[22] Even the fact that it was a bond issue hit on raw nerves. The region's wealthiest landowners had once pushed bonds to build substantial levees to protect their own land. Lloyd Murray, who owned thousands of acres, was swallowed up by debt, despite all his investments to keep the Trinity at bay, and he eventually sold his property to the Parten family. Likewise Fagan Parker, the distant cousin to Quanah Parker, was sued in court for his inability to pay taxes on his levee district's failed investment. If these powerful men could not keep the river in check, it made little sense to many East Texans that the whole of the river could be confined by a canal and that they should share in the costs of attempting such a feat.

Because of the widespread assumption that rural Texans would fall in line, contemporary media reports portrayed the conflict as pitting the canal boosters against an urban coalition of North Texas environmentalists and

Figure 13.3. Newspaper advertisements featured images of trash in the river, claiming that voting in favor of the canal bond was the only way to clean up the river. Courtesy of Tarrant County College Northeast, Heritage Room, and the Portal to Texas History, University of North Texas Libraries, https://texashistory.unt.edu/ark:/67531/metapth28236.

fiscal conservatives. The Parten oil family was the most visible of the canal opponents, and they used their connections across the state, led a press campaign, and coordinated with canal opponents in Dallas and Fort Worth. Other less wealthy individuals also spoke up from their home counties. As one East Texas resident said of the canal, "Anyone with any judgement at all would know that it is possible but not practical."[23] The Dallas-based leader of Citizens' Organization for a Sound Trinity later reflected that his "biggest mistake" was not spending more time campaigning "down river," where many East Texans—he realized only in retrospect—opposed the project.[24]

On March 13, 1973, the majority of voters and counties along the Trinity River voted against the project. In the eleven East Texas counties where the

Tally of votes for and against the Trinity River Bond

| COUNTY | VOTES CAST | VOTES FOR | VOTES AGAINST | % FOR | % AGAINST |
|---|---|---|---|---|---|
| Anderson | 1,746 | 1,161 | 585 | 66.5 | 33.5 |
| Chambers | 1,181 | 436 | 745 | 36.9 | 63.1 |
| Dallas | 144,392 | 63,461 | 80,931 | 44.0 | 56.0 |
| Ellis | 4,198 | 1,692 | 2,506 | 40.3 | 59.7 |
| Freestone | 1,468 | 1,050 | 418 | 71.5 | 28.5 |
| Henderson | 2,874 | 1,918 | 956 | 66.7 | 33.3 |
| Houston | 1,951 | 456 | 1,495 | 23.4 | 76.6 |
| Kaufman | 2,629 | 1,508 | 1,121 | 57.4 | 42.6 |
| Liberty | 1,777 | 1,044 | 733 | 58.8 | 41.2 |
| Leon | 937 | 687 | 250 | 73.3 | 26.7 |
| Madison | 745 | 241 | 504 | 32.3 | 67.7 |
| Navarro | 4,356 | 2,764 | 1,592 | 63.5 | 36.5 |
| Polk | 915 | 285 | 630 | 31.1 | 68.9 |
| San Jacinto | 483 | 119 | 364 | 24.6 | 75.4 |
| Tarrant | 74,749 | 34,807 | 39,942 | 46.6 | 53.4 |
| Trinity | 791 | 553 | 238 | 69.9 | 30.1 |
| Walker | 1,036 | 498 | 538 | 48.1 | 51.9 |
| TOTAL | 246,228 | 112,680 | 133,548 | 45.8 | 54.2 |

Source: United States Army Corps of Engineers, Fort Worth District, *Trinity River Project, Texas, Project Memorandum No. 4*, 1979, p. 191, Edward C. Fritz Papers, Digital Collections, Special Collections and Archives, SMU Libraries, https://digitalcollections.smu.edu/digital/collection/ned/id/369.

Trinity had historically been navigable, the total added up to a tiny margin of thirty votes in favor of the canal. However, when considered individually, in several of these rural counties, the canal was soundly defeated. Madison, San Jacinto, Polk, Chambers, and Houston Counties voted against the canal anywhere from 63 to 76 percent. By way of comparison, only 56 percent of Dallas County voters opposed the project. The *New York Times* reported that the losses in East Texas came "to the surprise of proponents and opponents alike."[25]

All the East Texas counties that overwhelmingly opposed the canal had seen local organizing efforts and anti-canal newspaper advertisements. But even after the vote, there was little acknowledgment that significant opposition had come from rural Texas; instead, the rejection of the canal was consistently portrayed as a victory achieved by North Texans. No one in the press gave due attention to the extent to which several counties in East Texas had been far more opposed to the canal than the residents of Dallas and Fort Worth.

***The canal's true believers*** refused to accept a permanent defeat. Over the following month, TRA and TIA staffers performed an election autopsy. The authors never questioned the project itself, which had "a great deal of merit." Instead, they suspected the timing of the election had been against their favor or blamed "half-truths from both sides." Several employees complained that many supporters in different counties pursued the campaign half-heartedly and "were only giving lip service." Other TRA employees blamed their close ally the Army Corps of Engineers for not providing enough information. One correspondent wrote, "A large segment of the voting population never believed a project of this magnitude could be accomplished." Really, no similar grand-scale project in this era was ever completed at a cost that made economic or ecological sense, so voters' lack of faith was more evidence-based than the proponents could accept. In a moment of insight, another staff member noted that their top-down approach had backfired—though he thought such tactics were still "fine for downriver counties." A leader of the TIA argued "that the public [should] be made to feel that this is a project that 'the people' want and will fight for." He said nothing, however, about *why* average citizens would pledge themselves so fully to the cause of taming the Trinity.[26]

The canal's electoral defeat led a faction of the TRA to seek a solution that emphasized expertise over common sense.[27] With the rise of a national environmental movement, scientists and engineers felt increasingly threatened by political responses to what they claimed were strictly scientific problems.[28] Some employees believed that the enormous scale of the project made any outside criticism unjustified and that the TRA's expertise should not be questioned. "In short," they wrote, underlining for emphasis, "the River Authority, the Corps and the other agencies involved in the project *are* the experts. There are *no* other groups, institutions or individuals who are even in the same league in the field of the development of the river."[29] This trust-the-experts attitude had doomed the bond vote, but now TRA staffers argued such large-scale projects were not open to debate. The governor appointed the TRA's board; none of its officers was elected.[30] A vote had stalled the canal project, but democracy need not end the TRA's dream.

The agency regrouped and, two years later, released an internal report labeled "Highly Confidential" and titled "Alternatives for Implementing Navigation on the Trinity River." As the TRA's general manager stated, the authority's bylaws required him "to place at all times in the activities of the Authority special emphasis and the highest priority on the implementation of the improvement of the main channel into a navigable barge canal." The proposal included a continued push for the entire canal and, if that failed, a plan for a shortened canal that extended only partway to Fort Worth. Both plans still required voter approval for bond payments that would likely be even costlier than in the previous election.[31]

This secret report emphasized the TRA's political power. It highlighted the TRA's significant influence at the federal level, citing Ben Carpenter's role in leading President Nixon's campaign in Texas and describing how "almost single-handedly the Trinity interests" had prevented changes to federal cost-benefit rules for ongoing projects. Trinity canal boosters were shaping *nationwide* environmental policy, bending the federal government to their will at the same time the river and its people had thwarted their dreams. Contrary to claims that the canal rested on expertise alone, political clout rather than science governed the canal's approval. This report also singled out the support of the governor, who had "influence and indirect control" over the Texas Parks and Wildlife Department and the Texas Water Quality Board.[32]

Notwithstanding the power the TRA wielded at the state and federal level, the report urged the TRA to lead a strong "grass roots" program, and thus in the summer of 1975, the TRA began holding a series of public hearings in towns all along the river to build support for the project. Despite the close vote in much of East Texas and the several counties that voted against the canal by large margins, the organizers of the hearings claimed that any and all opposition to their project came from the cities. At one of these hearings, in Crockett, Regina Levoy, a young woman, spoke out against the canal in the lower Trinity on environmental and financial grounds only to be tarred as an outsider by the chairman: "Okay, now, just for the dickens of it, before you came to Huntsville where did you live?" When she affirmed her roots in Huntsville, 170 miles south of Dallas, the chairman asked incredulously, "Native born?" Undaunted, she responded, "I was born and raised there."[33] Decades later Regina Levoy recalled, "Dallas has always had big plans for that river. They have problems with the Trinity; they've been trying to tame it, manipulate it, and it's never worked out."[34]

One of the major selling points of the revamped project was flood control, but East Texans knew how to read a map. They had seen how reservoirs destroyed bottomland habitats and could see that the proposed reservoirs would destroy much of what was left. At the hearing in Crockett, John L. Spinks spoke out: "All right, you say flood control and the very first time you do you build more lakes, you cover 9150 acres of the best grazing land in Houston County." Drawing from his knowledge of the region's geology, Spinks stated, "When you are flooding to start with some of the best land . . . that right there is defeating its own purpose when you say we are for flood control."[35]

Because the hearings were run by the TRA, canal opponents had to develop strategies to ensure that the hearings did not become one-sided affairs. John Henry Faulk, a close friend of the Partens, was a popular radio and television personality who most famously acted on the country music television show *Hee Haw*. In the 1930s he had been an interviewer for the WPA Slave Narratives in Texas. Though Faulk had only just moved to East Texas, admiration of his show and his credentials as a country person on television made it difficult to oppose him on the boosters' favored terms of identity. Not unlike how Amon Carter had used Commodore Hatfield, a resident of Fort Worth, to appear as a champion of East Texas, canal opponents now had in Faulk their own version of a recent arrival who nonetheless appeared to be a bona fide local.

Faulk saw hypocrisy everywhere, starting with the project's reliance on federal funding from the "same men who would stand up and denounce government spending." Faulk's personal history as an FBI target for suspected communist sympathies also played a major role in motivating him to oppose the project. He was particularly sensitive, therefore, to attempts to tar genuine democratic opposition. When the TRA called opponents of the canal "extreme environmentalists," Faulk heard echoes of the Red Scare when communist labels had been "used to destroy and distort debate."[36] Faulk's experience enabled him to effectively deflect the use of the term "environmentalist" as a slur. Other canal opponents also reversed these common lines of attack. A self-described "Hungarian refugee" wrote Congressman Charlie Wilson about the threat of eminent domain in the event that the project moved forward: "The communist regime confiscated my home. . . . Do I face confiscation again? How do I explain to my children why we left Hungary?"[37]

Faulk also recognized how canal advocates attempted to intimidate female opponents. The TRA's meetings were designed to be hostile toward anyone who might be labeled an environmentalist, but they were particularly hostile toward women who opposed the canal. At one of the first hearings that took place in Huntsville, the TRA had stacked the meeting with preregistered pro-canal speakers, including businessmen from Dallas who were portrayed as public servants. Faulk, who was there himself, too, observed a woman who spoke at the meeting and then watched as proponents "really intimidated her into silence." The TRA directors knew Faulk from his role on *Hee Haw*, which was very popular across Texas, but they let him speak without knowing his position on the canal. Faulk defended the woman who had just spoken and said "that if God had wanted" a straightened Trinity, he would have done it himself. Further invoking religion, Faulk continued, "You're telling me that it's within your power to undo God's work here on earth?" The invocation of religious culture unlocked the crowd, and "the damned audience switched." When another representative from Dallas attempted to challenge Faulk, he played his final card: "Are you talking socialism to me now? So you mean that the people of this country must be taxed so that individuals can make a profit?" He had turned the tables and put canal proponents on the defensive. Finally, Faulk claimed that the project might benefit others but not East Texans: "I'm quite sure that you Dallas brethren that make a great deal of money, that's not going to make a lot of difference to these people in Crockett or here in Huntsville."[38]

After Faulk's performance, the proponents successfully barred both Faulk and Randy Parten from speaking at the next meeting, despite the fact that the Parten family's Trinity River ranch was nearby. The suppression of dissent from these prominent citizens worked only once, however, and both made their way into Parten's hometown of Madisonville for the subsequent meeting. At that meeting, several landowners spoke out, and even sixteen-year-old Ann Stroud landed a punch, stating that while she did not yet vote or pay taxes, she did not "see any sense in me paying the taxes for someone else to make the profit." Many speakers expressed frustration with the way the canal boosters had tied river cleanup to navigation. They blamed the big cities for causing the pollution and the TRA for failing to remove it. One speaker complained, "You ought to resign, get off that thing, it's been twenty years and you have done nothin'." Even claims that most of the project would be paid for with federal funds did not sit well with the hostile audience, causing another speaker to say it was "nonsense" for the TRA to claim the money would come from the federal government: "We pay income tax, we are the government." When the chairman of the hearing demanded the crowd allow him to present slides, opponents contended that they be given equal time to respond. An unidentified audience member shouted, "We defeated this in 1973 in this county 2–1."[39]

Like the flooding Trinity, the unruly audience could no longer be contained. They were not just opposed because of its environmental or financial implications; they were angry about the way the project had been pushed on them without consideration of what would be best for the people. Rural and urban river residents could work together to stop the canal and claim their rights as citizens in a democracy. As one speaker put it, "We voted this thing down 2–1, and then y'all come back here now wantin' to know what we want. We don't want nothin'. We want you to leave us alone. That's what we'd like for ya to do."[40]

By the late 1970s, the dream of a canal running all the way up to Fort Worth finally died. Its place in the legacies of both the elder and younger Amon Carter remained unfulfilled, and the vision of Dallas and Fort Worth as world-renowned port cities faded away. Their stubborn belief that ports are required for great cities was misguided and wasteful of both resources and precious time. Chastened by defeat, the TRA could now focus on its real job: ensuring water and outlets for waste to enable the growth of the region, a mission in which it has achieved impressive success. Timing mattered, as the 1972 Clean Water Act included not only new regulations but billions of dollars from the federal coffers, and the TRA was well positioned to funnel those funds into its efforts along the Trinity.[41] The TRA's focus on urban Texas from its founding has allowed it to excel at supporting urban growth more so than other Texas water authorities, such as those on rivers with competing agricultural demands.

The TRA enjoys relative jurisdictional simplicity; since the Trinity is the largest river in Texas whose watershed is exclusively within the borders of the state, it means that managing it requires no interstate negotiation, federal intervention, or international consultation for management decisions.[42] These borders are a product of history; at various points the Trinity itself could have been a border. In addition to being the eastern or western border to most of the counties or precincts that abutted it, the Trinity served as an informal border that divided eastern Texas from the rest of the republic and, later, the state. The modern TRA can also express gratitude to its predecessor for losing the war for the canal: Had it been constructed, the water level requirements would have sapped the Trinity's ability to support Dallas–Fort Worth's dramatic rise as the fourth-largest metropolitan area in the nation.

## EPILOGUE

# LIVING HISTORY

Today, more Texans live near and drink from the Trinity than any other river in the state. In terms of the human life it supports, the Trinity has become by far the most important river in Texas. So why is this book the first to tell its whole story? The ceaseless fights over the meaning of the Alamo or the role of slavery in Texas suggest that Texans value history and its lessons. Yet so much history has been erased in the course of the rapid development of Texas into a novel, sprawling environment that many newcomers and residents alike assume whole swaths of history do not exist there. In Dallas–Fort Worth, the still-flowing Trinity is one of the few places connected to a longer, fuller history, but it can be challenging to see the river.

During the final canal debates in the 1960s and 1970s, federal funding paid for highway bridges to be constructed extra high above the river to accommodate the dream of tugboats. This history of big levees and tall bridges seemingly conspires to hide the Trinity from view. But while there are many reasons to forget it, there are even more reasons to remember its importance to the past, present, and future. North Texas's population growth rates are expected to continue to significantly outpace the nation's, even as Texas's climate gets hotter. When water is pumped from other regions to meet the accompanying demand, it will eventually enter the river. The Trinity has historically had the third-highest average flow of any river in Texas, but it is possible that it will eventually have the highest flows in the state.

On the Elm Fork of the Trinity River, squeezed between highways, glass-covered buildings, and industrial parks, is the California Crossing Park. A hundred years ago, Geraldine Harris was killed here by her own fishing party, who shot out of fear of what lurked in the woods. Another seventy years before that, this place was the crossing point for migrants heading west to try their luck in the California Gold Rush. The river is still there, and so too is a Comanche marker tree, a two-centuries-old pecan tree the Comanche bent to direct their gifted riders to this crossing on the river. The tree and the Trinity are living monuments to Texas's history. Though this history has sometimes been marked by bloodshed, the growing tree and flowing river have been a constant presence and home to so many people who now run along the riverbank or stop to sit and reflect on their own lives. Unlike most of the more than sixteen thousand historical markers across Texas, many of which are tied to individual men or massacres, the Trinity is a place that offers a story of resilience, with overlapping, dueling moments of devastation and inspiration.

Figure 14.1. A Comanche marker tree in the middle of Dallas–Fort Worth at California Crossing Park, 2025. Photo by the author.

Downstream in East Texas, the Trinity offers similar connections to big Texas stories. In much of the South, many plantations have been preserved and are open to public visits. On the Trinity, however, former plantations are more likely to be hidden from sight behind the walls of river prisons or private ranches. One of these ranches includes Lake Rosewood, which had once been a bend in the river until the *Mary Conley* sank and the channel moved. Looked at from above, it would be easy to assume this oxbow lake was simply a natural formation. The story of the *Mary Conley* shows there is a need for historians as much as geologists to understand Texas rivers.

The *Mary Conley* was one of the last steamboats to navigate the Trinity, as the end of plantation slavery and the arrival of railroads made Trinity steamers obsolete. On January 10, 1873, the *Conley* sank in a bend in the river. No one attempted to raise the wreck, since by then it was a lost cause for anyone to make money moving freight on the river. After what few of its valuable pieces could be salvaged, this shipwreck was left to rot. Just over 134 feet long and almost 30 feet wide, the *Conley* changed the course of the Trinity: Lying as it did at a bend in the river, the water pushed around the wreck and carved a new course; suddenly a section of land lay on the opposite side of the river channel. Sixty-seven years later, the *Conley* surfaced again in a case before the Texas Supreme Court. In the 1940 case *Ross v. Green*, justices were asked to weigh in on a particular historical question: Had the river changed course? The court ultimately ruled that the Trinity had been changed dramatically at the close of its steamboat era. Why was the state supreme court asked to rule on the order of historical events? In a word: oil. At stake were eighty-four acres of newly valuable bottomlands, after the discovery of oil in what would become known as the Hardin Oil Field. The case was about a particular bend in the river, but a close consideration of *Ross v. Green* reveals so much more of the Trinity's history of dreams and nightmares.[1]

Texas law has long had provisions to accommodate the shifting nature of its rivers. When a river moves a little bit, it is called an accretion. If the river is a border between property lines, then the landowners on both sides of the channel must treat the accretion as the new border; otherwise, every year the courts would be choked up with claims over a few lost or gained inches. The precedent of accretion usefully maintains the middle of the river as a property boundary so that both landowners retain access to the main channel. This mattered a lot for navigable rivers like the Trinity, ensuring that property owners could access river transport and commerce, and even more so in Texas's arid west, where the survival of farms depended on access to the river for irrigation. Yet when a river acts particularly unruly and seeks a new bed, in what is called an avulsion, then the boundary remains as it was, in the center of the old channel, rather than moving with the new path of the active channel.[2] The most famous avulsion case is known as the Chamizal Dispute on the Rio Grande. The river changed course, altering the border between the United States and Mexico. After a century of negotiation, the two countries signed a 1963 treaty, marking the first time in its history that the United States ceded rather than took land from Mexico. But to this day the Trinity remains the only known river where a steamboat caused an avulsion.

*Ross v. Green* made it to the Texas Supreme Court in 1940 over a question of historical evidence. An area of land called the Hardin league had been granted by the Mexican government to A. B. Hardin, a district sheriff who had fled to Texas from Tennessee after a murder indictment, but his original

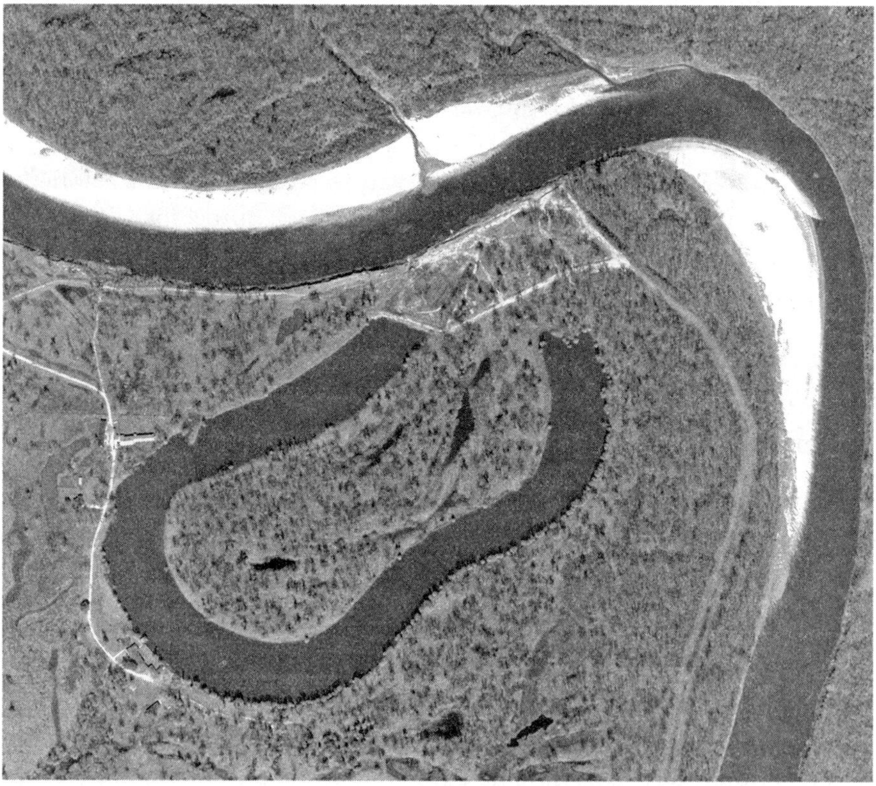

Figure 14.2. Present-day satellite image of Mary Conley Bend, with the oxbow lake, called Rosewood Lake, separated from the Trinity River's main channel by the *Mary Conley* steamboat wreck. Courtesy of the US Geological Survey, https://earthexplorer.usgs.gov/.

grant did not definitively describe its river border. The defendants argued they could claim this land based on their interpretation of another land grant. In order to win the case and regain ownership of the land between the new channel and the old course, the plaintiffs would have to rely on more than deeds and maps: They would have to call in the "old timers" as witnesses to tell their stories on the stand.

Price Daniel from Dayton was not yet thirty years old when he argued this case in front of the Texas Supreme Court. At the outset of a career that would eventually include serving as a US senator and governor of Texas, his success in this case rested on the testimony of a Black man named Henderson Day. Daniel likely knew Day because they were both from Dayton, which had fewer than a thousand residents and had been named Day's Town, after Henderson Day's father and his former enslaver.

When Price Daniel called Henderson Day, who was now in his mid-eighties, to the witness stand, he asked him to recall his experiences on the river before and after Juneteenth. Day opened his testimony by talking about historical sources, saying his expertise was not rooted in legal documents—he did not know "about the surveys at all." Instead, Day described how he had worked with cattle in that stretch "from the time he was large enough to sit on a horse." Up until after the *Conley* sank, steamboats had regularly "navigated the Trinity River around this bend." Once the boat wrecked, the river "went into" the land and "left an island there." Day learned how to navigate through the changed landscape to bring cattle to this newly formed island, noting how there was only one way in and out of the island. Day said that community members had long assumed the ownership of the land had not changed, despite the Trinity's dramatic movement after the *Conley* wrecked. He confirmed this fact by dating the existence of a fence erected by the original owners to at least his wife's death, which he could state precisely had been thirty-six years ago.[3]

Day told this history using his intertwined knowledge of this particular place and his family history. In contrast to the insufficient written survey records, Day's description proved decisive. The Texas Supreme Court concurred with the Texas Court of Civil Appeals, which found that Day's testimony "reasonably carried the existence of the fact . . . at all times from his boyhood to 1872, steamboats navigated the Trinity River around this bend. It is our conclusion, on the facts and law, that the finding of the court that the land in controversy was included within the grant of the A. B. Hardin survey in 1831 must be affirmed." Henderson Day, who would have been unable to vote in Texas's all-white primary, gave decisive testimony on the history of the Trinity River, ultimately settling a legal dispute over eighty-four acres of bottomlands that, one day, switched sides of the river.[4] Unlike in politics, where the Trinity's history and Texas's history were regularly distorted, truth mattered in the courts, even if much of this history remained consciously or unconsciously forgotten.

The case focused on the Trinity's steamboat era, but it also highlights a later turning point: It was only several decades after the river moved, once the nearby oil field was discovered, that the land was worth the expense of lawyers for the potential to get rich off the new "black gold" that replaced the old "white gold." Today, as Texas's population grows and the climate warms, another commodity shift is underway: Oil and gas drilling, still a key sector of the Texas economy, is increasingly in competition with water as the most valuable resource in Texas to be sought, drilled, and pumped into cities.

Not far from the *Mary Conley* wreck, just to the west of the floodplain, is Dayton. If you zoom out you can see how the town of Dayton is being inexorably engulfed by the rings of highways rippling out from Houston, a city once peopled by rural Trinity residents and now watered by Lake Livingston. In Dayton, Henderson Day Park is named after the man whose testimony on the history of the river and that of his own family proved crucial to a 1940 Texas Supreme Court ruling. His story is a part of the history of Dayton, of the Trinity, and all of Texas. On humid summer days you can smell the rich bottomland air, alongside grill smoke and, if it is Juneteenth, a crawfish boiling contest, a holiday born on the Trinity.

# ACKNOWLEDGMENTS

My thanks go to the many librarians and archivists who supported this research. County historical commissions in Houston, Polk, Walker, Trinity, and San Jacinto Counties not only shared sources but in some cases hosted me to share my research with members of their communities. Archivists at the Texas State Library in Austin and Liberty helped me keep up with a busy research pace. Kyle Ainsworth at the East Texas Research Library has been a great support, especially through his invaluable Texas Runaway Slave Project. The Trinity River Authority provided access to its archives in addition to reviewing my scientific claims and crafting an ecological map, with support from Glenn Clingenpeel, Kevin Ward, Jackson Fitzgerald, Mark Waters, and Webster Mangham.

I received financial support for this research from universities and libraries. This includes the William and Madeline Welder Smith Travel Award from the Briscoe Center for American History at the University of Texas, the Bonham Chapter of the Daughters of the Republic of Texas Research Travel Grant from the Clements Center for Southwest Studies at Southern Methodist University, and the Portal to Texas History Research Fellowship from the University of North Texas Libraries. The East Texas Historical Association awarded me an Ottis Lock Research Grant. Multiple grants and fellowships from the Columbia University History Department, Graduate School of Arts and Sciences, and the Heyman Center at Columbia funded this work. And the Jefferson Scholars Foundation at the University of Viriginia supported a year of research, writing, and presentations. Special thanks go to all the individuals, corporations, institutions, and tribes who have sustained my career as a historian by working with me as a client of the Oxbow History Company.

The following individuals have contributed to this project in various ways, including administrative support, research, editing, and thinking: Aaron Frith, Al Lightfoot, Alexander Neal, Angela To, Brian Balogh, Bruce Jackson, Alma Igra, Amanda Hardin, Andrew Baker, Ben Johnson, Betsy Blackmar, Bill Leach, Carl Frentress, Caroline Marris, Char Miller, Charles Halvorson, Charly Coleman, Chris Coffin, Chris Manganiello, Dan Barnes, Daniel Grant, Dick Swift, Donald Payton, Emily Murdock Baker, Gary Pinkerton, Gina Ryder, Halimat Somotan, Heath Burney, Jack Selden, James Tanzer, Jason Royal, Jay Herrington, Jeffery Darensbourg, Jeffrey Littlejohn, Jon Farr, Jorge Luis García Ruiz, Justus Hillebrand, Karen Fort, Kenna Lang Archer, Kimon Ioannides, Lawino Lurum, Linda Winecoff, Ling Zhang, Liz Bedell, Margie Crisp, Mark Philipson, Martha Desta, María González Pendás, Meg Jacobs, Meghan Scott-Chaber, Mookie Kideckel, Nat Erb-Satullo, Nataly Shahaf, Nick Linville, Owain Lawson, Patryk Babiracki, Pat Morel, Paul Sabin, Phil Blumberg, Randy Parten, Richard Chazen, Sam Epstein, Sam Rutherford, Sandra Rodgers, Sarah Ebel, Seth Kamil, Shannon Gilmore, Sharee Nash, Stephanie McCurry, Steve Houser, Ted Campbell, Thad Sitton, Timothy Seiter, Todd Kerstetter, and Zac Levine.

My agent, Chris Rogers, at Dunow, Carlson & Lerner made it possible for me to work with the University of North Carolina Press. My editor, Cate Hodorowicz, has been a consistent advocate for this project, and Tara Jordan has been a patient guide. Sonya Bonczek, Erin Granville, Julie Bush, and Madge Duffy have also been a great help.

I have learned so much from my past colleagues at the American Historical Association and Historic New England, including Alex Levy, Alissa Butler, Ben Rosenbaum, Brendan Gillis, Hannah Francis, Hope Shannon, Jake Purcell, Jim Grossman, Julia Brookins, Laura Ansley, Lauren Brand, Leo Lovermore, Lorna Condon, Nick Kryczka, Peter Gittleman, Ryan Ullrich, Sarah Weicksel, and Tricia Peone. Whit Barringer gave this manuscript special attention, making it so much more precise.

At Columbia University, the friendship of Yoav Hamdani, Barrie Blatchford, Tamar Menashe, Zeinab Azarbadegan, Brianna Nofil, Brooks Swett, Micah McElroy, and Sarina Kürsteiner has been a gift. Josh Schwartz never let me off the hook with any of my writing or thinking, this book included. Karl Jacoby helped me through each step of the PhD. Barbara Fields changed the way I think and write. Bill DeBuys was a wise mentor who helped me gain the confidence to write this book.

Loyal friends and teachers from Palestine, Concord, Aix-les-Bains, and Bowdoin have allowed me to get to this point in my life: Addy Pagano, Alain and Bernadette Diaine, Alexander Knowles, Archie Abrams, Barrett Brown, Beau Levering, Bob Levin, Carol Atwood, David Hughes, Eli Bossin, Harry Houghton, Jesse Dann, Jürgen in der Schmitten, Lisa Setrakian, Mike Huang, Nettie Houghton, Pat Pierce, Rosa Ayala, the Lilienfelds, and Tom Cote.

In Maine, Tim Ogene and Kate Olson are my writer friends. Matt Klingle has been a friend and mentor. And I have enjoyed so much fishing, history, and family fun with John Lichter, Mike Tillotson, Charlie Berdhal, Ian Stevenson, Brad Miller, Zach Bennett, the Sols, the Callahans, the Witherbys, and the Redfields.

I am thankful for the love of the women who raised me: my nana, Susanna Eszenyi Bedell, and my mom, Susanna Elizabeth Bedell. I would not be here without my twin, Anna. And of course this book is shaped by my loving father, Robert McFarlane, and the place where we are from. I am grateful for Fay and Floyd McFarlane, Lois and Byron McFarlane, and Lenese Decker. Wally and Dee Bedell have always been there for me. I appreciate the support of Charlie and Nadine Donell as well as the Seawards and Patrick and Emily. My sons Walter and Byron gave me so much joy as I wrote this book. And my wife, Molly, is my one true love.

# NOTES

## *ABBREVIATIONS*

| | |
|---|---|
| BAO | Bexar Archives Online, Dolph Briscoe Center for American History, University of Texas at Austin |
| BRFAL | Records of the Bureau of Refugees, Freedmen, and Abandoned Lands, RG 105, Texas, National Archives and Records Administration, Washington, DC |
| Carter Collection | Amon G. Carter Collection, Mary Couts Burnett Library, Texas Christian University, Fort Worth, TX |
| ETRC | East Texas Research Center, Ralph W. Steen Library, Stephen F. Austin State University, Nacogdoches, TX |
| JCWP | "A Journal of the Civil War Period by James Madison Hall, 1860–1866," manuscript, Crockett Public Library, Crockett, TX |
| RER | Texas Natural Resource Conservation Commission Reclamation Engineer Records, Archives and Manuscripts, Texas State Library and Archives Commission, Austin, TX |
| TRSP | Texas Runaway Slave Project, East Texas Research Center, Ralph W. Steen Library, Stephen F. Austin State University, Nacogdoches, TX |
| TFP | Turner Family Papers, #689, Division of Rare and Manuscript Collections, Cornell University Library, Ithaca, NY |
| WDCCR | War Department Collection of Confederate Records, RG 109, National Archives and Records Administration, Washington, DC |

## *INTRODUCTION*

1. Milosz, *Collected Poems,* 177–78.

2. The 287 bridge is located just two miles south of Wildcat Ferry; the travelers' cemetery there memorializes those who died while waiting to cross the river a century earlier.

3. Tim Rogers, "The Man Who Stopped the Pig Blood," *D Magazine*, June 23, 2014.

4. Sappington et al., *Trinity River Sanitary Survey*, 87, 86. The study was conducted from October 1924 to June 1925.

5. Sappington et al., *Trinity River Sanitary Survey*, 102, 106, 108, 145.

6. Sappington et al., *Trinity River Sanitary Survey*, 218, 7.

7. Perttula et al., "Archeological Investigations."

8. Local historians have written extensively, often in unpublished manuscripts, about the Trinity. Three women in particular—Mary Kate Hunter in Anderson County, Eliza H. Bishop in Houston County, and Vernon Fitzgerald Schuder in Walker County—have studied and uncovered this history. Other historians have published on specific eras and topics that closely follow the river, including those related to colonial Texas, steamboats, and freedom colonies. Bolton, "Spanish Activities"; Pinkerton, *Bridles and Biscuits*; Block, *Cotton Bales*; Minutaglio, *In Search of the Blues*; Sitton and Conrad, *Freedom Colonies*; Scott-Chaber, "'River of Death'"; Kerstetter, "Pipe Dreams."

9. Richard White called the Columbia River an organic machine; it is "our creation" and yet "retains a life of its own beyond our control." White, *Organic Machine*, 109.

10. Houston Wilderness, *Houston Atlas of Biodiversity*, 39.

11. Dee Cook, interview by William V. Ervin, July 1937, typescript, American Life Histories: Manuscripts from the Federal Writers' Project, 1936 to 1940, Library of Congress, Washington, DC, www.loc.gov/item/wpalh002351/.

12. Even the Trinity River's general flow patterns are relatively new, dating back about three thousand years when sea levels rose and rainfall lessened. "Geology of Texas," *Texas Almanac*, accessed April 10, 2025, www.texasalmanac.com/articles/geology-of-texas.

13. Wallace Scot McFarlane, "Fear the River: Drownings in the Trinity River," *Trinity River History* (blog), January 7, 2020, www.wsmcfarlane.com/blog/2020/1/7/fear-the-river-drownings-in-the-trinity-river.

14. "Jurors Probing Death of Woman Bullet Victim," *Dallas Times Herald*, May 21, 1923.

15. "Jurors Probing Death of Woman Bullet Victim"; "Heavy Rains May Cause Trinity to Overflow Again," *Dallas Times Herald*, May 21, 1923.

16. Sappington et al., *Trinity River Sanitary Survey*, 7.

## *CHAPTER 1*

1. Laray Polk, "The Trinity Project: The Shape of Time," *D Magazine*, October 12, 2016.

2. Michael Marks, "The Origin of the Word 'Texas' May Be Rooted in Something Other Than Friendship," *Texas Standard*, May 30, 2019, www.texasstandard.org/stories/the-origin-of-the-word-texas-may-be-rooted-in-something-other-than-friendship/; Ruiz, *Texas*; "The Yew Tree, Lexicon and Toponymy in the Area Under Research by the Life Baccatta Project," Life Baccatta, July 8, 2019, www.life-baccata.eu/en/news/yew-tree-lexicon-and-toponymy-area-under-research-life-baccata-project. As the historian Timothy Seiter put it in correspondence with me from May 2025,

> There are other theories that are equally compelling. For example, the Teja people were well known to the other Indigenous folks of Northern Mexico. Quite literally, the major trade routes from Tenochtitlan ran straight to the Caddo people. The

Spanish, when exploring new lands, asked their indigenous guides to tell them about powerful Native people and where they lived. Those early seventeenth century maps that label Texas as "Tejas" might be doing so as a way of saying "the land of the Tejas" just how the Spanish would later label a huge swath of land as Apachería and the coastal area as "the wild [Indian] coast."

3. Foster, *La Salle Expedition*, 133, 201.

4. Chapa, *Texas and Northeastern Mexico*, 243.

5. Elena Watts, "Texas A&M Conserves Prehistoric Canoe to Keep Ancient Culture Afloat," Texas A&M Stories, August 3, 2017, https://stories.tamu.edu/news/2017/08/03/texas-am-conserves-canoe-to-keep-ancient-culture-afloat/.

6. Though they would not have been as durable, in some cases canoes in colonial Texas were also made out of cottonwood trees.

7. "An Interview with Jeffery Darensbourg," Indigenous Mississippi, accessed April 11, 2025, https://indigenousmississippi.com/artists/an-interview-with-jeffery-darensbourg/.

8. The more widely used name Akokisa was modified from Orkokisak, which more clearly includes Ishāk, and Ted Campbell writes "that Orkok denoted the Trinity River on which almost all the Orkokisak peoples were located." Kimball, *Yukhíti Kóy*; Ted Campbell, "What Happened to the Native People of Southeast Texas? A Broad and Long Perspective," 2025, in the author's possession, p. 12.

9. Ellis, *Great Power of Small Nations*, 5, 8.

10. Esmaeili et al., "Rancid Rumors or Native Wisdom."

11. "E. 9/20/1754–11/20/1754, pp. 1–21," typescript, identifier e_bx_002030, box 2C18, BAO; Castañeda, *Mission Era*, 55.

12. "E. 2/19/1755–10/25/1755, pp. 1–6," typescript, identifier e_bx_002034, and "E. 2/4/1756–2/17/1756, pp. 1–24v," typescript, identifier e_bx_002039, both in box 2C19, BAO; Castañeda, *Mission Era*, 63.

13. "E. 11/30/1754, pp. 1–2v," typescript, identifier e_bx_002031, box 2C18, BAO.

14. "D., p. 1.," typescript, identifier e_bx_002089_001, box 2C19, BAO; Castañeda, *Mission Era*, 95.

15. Castañeda, *Mission Era*, 317.

16. Barr, *Peace Came*, 267.

17. Fenn, *Pox Americana*, 214.

18. Castañeda, *Mission Era*, 317.

19. Hämäläinen, *Comanche Empire*, 79.

20. Houser et al., *Comanche Marker Trees of Texas*, 103.

21. "E. 1/18/1780–1/29/1780, pp. 1–7," typescript, identifier e_bx_003199, box 2C38, BAO.

22. Hämäläinen, *Comanche Empire*, 98–99.

23. Ironically, most of these horses belonged to a French trader, Nicholas de La Mathe, who had established himself at Bucareli. Pinkerton, *Bridles and Biscuits*, 149; Castañeda, *Mission Era*, 327.

24. Castañeda, *Mission Era*, 334.

25. This rifle is now on display at the Blanche K. Werner Public Library in Trinity, Texas. Dan Barnes, conversation with author, June 1, 2025.

26. Barr, *Peace Came*, 269.

27. Hart and Hulbert, *Southwestern Journals of Zebulon Pike*, 237.

28. Bernsen, *Lost War for Texas*, 310–12; Pinkerton, *Bridles and Biscuits*, 268–69; Bob Skiles, trans., "Report of the Reduction of Trinidad de Salcedo, by Lt. Col. Ignacio Elizondo of the Royal Spanish Army, 6 September 1813," on ResearchGate, May 6, 2015, DOI: 10.13140/RG.2.1.2471.0562. The downstream Orcoquisac fort was also reestablished in some form in the early 1800s. See Bernsen, *Lost War for Texas*, 59.

29. Shuck-Hall, *Journey to the West*; Luebke, "Regionalism and the Great Plains." Or in some cases, this more open landscape could be found directly west of the floodplain.

30. Shuck-Hall, *Journey to the West*; F. Smith, *From Dominance to Disappearance*, 67; Howard N. Martin, "Indian Tribes in Polk County, Texas," unpublished manuscript in Howard Martin Papers, Archives of the Alabama-Coushatta Tribe of Texas, Livingston, TX; Rothman, *Slave Country*.

31. The Coushatta and Alabama also made alliances with the Caddo as well as with other immigrant tribes such as the Cherokee. Shuck-Hall, *Journey to the West*; Sibley, *Report from Natchitoches*, 96. One such path was named the Coushatta Trace.

32. Murph, "Search for Champ d'Asile."

33. This description, in one of the earliest Trinity River booster documents, was published in France, where the author recounted the good luck of the colonists to have the Coushatta instruct them on which plant was making them sick and on other "herbes" that could revive them. Hartmann and Millard, *Le Texas*, 34.

34. Ocampo, *Emperor's Last Campaign*, 271–74.

## *CHAPTER 2*

1. Blaufarb, *Bonapartists in the Borderlands*, 172.

2. Kent Gardien and Betje Black Klier, "Champ D'Asile," *Handbook of Texas*, updated July 6, 2017, www.tshaonline.org/handbook/online/articles/uec02.

3. Terán, *Texas by Terán*; Torget, *Seeds of Empire*; Cantrell, *Stephen F. Austin*.

4. Terán, *Texas by Terán*, 27–39.

5. Terán, *Texas by Terán*, 70.

6. Berlandier, *Journey to Mexico*, 328.

7. Terán, *Texas*, 71; Sánchez and Castañeda, "Trip to Texas in 1828," 278; Berlandier, *Journey to Mexico*, 330.

8. In the nineteenth century, naturalists and geographers played a key role in expanding empires. Edney, *Mapping an Empire*; Drayton, *Nature's Government*.

9. Terán, *Texas by Terán*, 71; Sánchez and Castañeda, "Trip to Texas in 1828," 279.

10. Terán, *Texas by Terán*, 71, 142, 91.

11. Terán, *Texas by Terán*, 132.

12. Terán, *Texas by Terán*, 133.

13. Gracy, *Moses Austin*, 202.

14. This included a dispute over land and ferry rights on the Trinity River. Pinkerton, *Trammel's Trace*.

15. Terán, *Texas by Terán*, 142.

16. Margaret Swett Henson, "Anahuac Disturbances," *Handbook of Texas*, accessed May 22, 2018, www.tshaonline.org/handbook/online/articles/jca01.

17. Henson, "Anahuac Disturbances."

18. "Battle of Velasco," *Handbook of Texas*, accessed May 22, 2018, www.tshaonline.org/handbook/online/articles/qfv01.

19. Torget, *Seeds of Empire*, 156–57, quote on 156.

20. Castañeda, *Mission Era*, 317.

21. Torget, *Seeds of Empire*, 166–67.

22. Quote from James Morgan to Unknown, March 24, 1836, in Jenkins, *Papers of the Texas Revolution*, 5:181–82. Also in James Morgan to Andrew Briscoe, March 24, 1836, in folder 6, MC055, Andrew Briscoe Papers, Albert and Ethel Herzstein Library, San Jacinto Museum of History, La Porte, TX.

23. Alan Taylor, *Internal Enemy*.

24. Morgan claimed enslaved people on the Trinity "had endeavoured to enlist the Coshatti Indians on their side and come down and murder the inhabitants & join the Mexicans." James Morgan to Unknown, March 24, 1836, 182.

25. Shuck-Hall, *Journey to the West*, 156.

26. Jenkins, *Recollections of Early Texas*, 44. Though the floodplain width varied, throughout the nineteenth century travelers consistently described the flooding Trinity as five miles wide.

27. Carson to Burnet, April 4, 1836, in Jenkins, *Papers of the Texas Revolution*, 316.

28. Jenkins, *Recollections of Early Texas*, 44.

29. Quoted in Exley, *Texas Tears*, 58.

30. H. Martin, *Myths and Folktales*, 80, 81.

31. Bollaert, *William Bollaert's Texas*, 289.

32. Quoted in Shuck-Hall, *Journey to the West*, 165.

33. F. Smith, *From Dominance to Disappearance*, 173; M. B. Lamar, "To the Citizens of Liberty County, Residing Near the Cushatta Towns and Villages," in Lamar, *Papers of Mirabeau Buonaparte Lamar*, 39–40; Franco, "Alabama-Coushatta."

34. "Act Authorizing the Survey of Land," 102–4.

35. Thomas G. Stubblefield, "Letter from Thomas G. Stubblefield to Abner L. Lipscomb, November 2, 1840," in Winfrey, *Texas Indian Papers*, 117–18.

36. F. Smith, *From Dominance to Disappearance*, 138.

37. Franco, "Alabama-Coushatta," 34–35; Shuck-Hall, *Journey to the West*, 182.

38. Howard N. Martin, "Colita's Village," *Handbook of Texas*, accessed June 1, 2018, www.tshaonline.org/handbook/online/articles/bpc08.

39. Andrew Lipman describes a similar story of water and persistence in the coastal region around present-day New York City. Lipman, *Saltwater Frontier*.

## *CHAPTER 3*

1. "John Dawson Turner [Polk County, Texas], November 1, 1862," Polk County Probate Minutes, Vol. A–C, 1847–1862, Texas, US, Wills and Probate Records, 1833–1974, Ancestry.com, www.ancestrylibrary.com/imageviewer/collections/2115/images/007574463_00049.

2. "Williamson, Turner, and Maxey," 1850 United States Federal Census, Slave Schedules, Ancestry.com, www.ancestrylibrary.com/imageviewer/collections/8055/images/TXM432_918-0137 and www.ancestrylibrary.com/imageviewer/collections/8055/images/TXM432

_918-0138; "Williamson, Turner, and Maxey," 1850 United States Agricultural Census, Ancestry .com, www.ancestrylibrary.com/imageviewer/collections/1276/images/T1134_2-00718.

3. William Williamson, William Maxey, and John D. Turner, "To the Honorable Senate and House of Representatives State of Texas," November 5, 1851, Polk County, Texas, in Race and Slavery Petitions Project, Series 2, County Court Petitions, Digital Library on American Slavery. A decade after the enslaved men's drowning, one slaveholder drafted his will, clarifying Goodwin's history of forced migration and family separation. Goodwin had been given to this slaveholder's first wife by her grandfather in Virginia. In this document he had not forgotten that Goodwin "drowned in the Trinity River while working the road." "John Dawson Turner [Polk County, Texas], November 1, 1862," Ancestry.com, 61.

4. Camp, *Closer to Freedom*, 33.

5. McFarlane, "Legacy of Plantation Slavery."

6. *Texas State Gazette*, April 4, 1854, 224, TRSP.

7. H. C. McNeil to George Aldrich, May 6, 1840, box 1, folder 3, George Aldrich Papers, ETRC.

8. *Houston Daily Telegraph*, August 19, 1864, 2, from TRSP.

9. *Texas State Gazette*, January 6, 1853, 7, from TRSP.

10. Kaye, *Joining Places*, xviii.

11. "Mintie Maria Miller," in Federal Writers' Project, *Slave Narratives*, 89.

12. S. W. Goree to Thomas J. Goree, March 20, 1853, box 1, Goree Family Papers, Thomason Room Special Collections, Sam Houston State University, Huntsville.

13. "John Dawson Turner [Polk County, Texas], November 1, 1862," Ancestry.com.

14. *Leon Pioneer* (Centerville, TX), October 6, 1852, 3, from TRSP.

15. *Northern Standard* (Clarksville, TX), June 30, 1847, 3, from TRSP.

16. Camp, *Closer to Freedom*, 54.

17. *Liberty (TX) Gazette*, September 14, 1860, 2, from TRSP.

18. *San Antonio Ledger*, August 25, 1855, 2, from TRSP.

19. Baumgartner, *South to Freedom*.

20. Bondi, *Autobiography of August Bondi*, 420.

21. Campbell, *Empire for Slavery*, 117; Litwack, *Been in the Storm So Long*, 189; Laura Cornish in Rawick, *American Slave*, vol. 4, pt. 3, 937. The editor of the published collection of the slave narratives mistakenly labeled Isaiah with an oxymoron, calling him an "abolitionist master." In Rawick, *American Slave*, vol. 1, 66.

22. Day, *Study of Some Negro-White Families*, 40.

23. Alexander, *Homelands and Waterways*, 383.

24. March 15, 1859; May 23, 1859; June 11, 1859; June 25, 1859, all in "Josephus Brooks Account of Franklin B. Sublett Plantation, 1859–1891," box 1, ETRC.

25. Dave Byrd in Rawick, *American Slave*, vol. 3, pt. 2, 563.

26. January 19, 1860, "Josephus Brooks Account of Franklin B. Sublett Plantation, 1859–1891," box 1, ETRC.

27. Bollaert, *William Bollaert's Texas*, 286. Another man echoed this paradox, calling the Trinity lands "good; first rate" but with "much of the bottom lands subject to overflow." Mirabeau B. Lamar, "Mirabeau B. Lamar Travel Journal, 1835," 121, Fondren Library, Rice University, http://hdl.handle.net/1911/21658.

28. A few Texas planters did see the value of the sediment left by flooding rivers. Jones, *Texas Roots*, 106.

29. Sam Forge in Rawick, *American Slave*, vol. 4, pt. 3, 1370.

30. Smither and Sterne, "Diary of Adolphus Sterne, III."

31. Sally Banks Chambers in Rawick, *American Slave*, vol. 3, pt. 2, 682. I have removed any caricatured language inserted by white interviewers into any of the quotes from the narratives in Rawick's collection. See Emberton, *To Walk About in Freedom*.

32. Torget, *Seeds of Empire*, 195.

33. Lamar, "Mirabeau B. Lamar Travel Journal, 1835," 124.

34. Gates and United States Public Land Law Review Commission, *History of Public Land Law Development*, 112.

35. Kittrell, *Kittrell Journal*, 15.

36. Otis Wheeler to mother, May 5, 1856, box 1, TFP.

37. Lahiri-Dutt and Samanta, *Dancing with the River*, x.

38. Aldon S. Lang and Christopher Long, "Land Grants," *Handbook of Texas*, accessed May 29, 2018, www.tshaonline.org/handbook/online/articles/mpl01. This did not mean all plantations mirrored those land grants, as they could be bigger or smaller and, as in the case of Kittrell, pieced together with no regard to prior title.

39. "Environmental Setting and Hydrologic Conditions in the Trinity River Basin," United States Geological Survey, accessed February 19, 2019, https://pubs.usgs.gov/circ/circ1171/html/envhyd.htm; E. Linacre and B. Geerts, "Rainfall and Rainfall Changes in the USA," University of Wyoming, accessed February 19, 2019, www-das.uwyo.edu/~geerts/cwx/notes/chap17/rain_usa.html.

40. August 21, 1874, "Josephus Brooks Account of Franklin B. Sublett Plantation," box 1, ETRC.

41. Leathers, "Christopher Columbus Goodman," 370n21.

42. Morris, *Big Muddy*, 117.

43. Otis Wheeler to mother, May 5, 1856, TFP.

44. Otis Wheeler to Parents and Sister, May 22, 1857, box 1, TFP. The letter describes the weather in reference to this quote.

45. Otis Wheeler to mother, May 5, 1856, TFP. On the Mississippi River, planters had enslaved laborers whose sole task was hunting. Morris, *Big Muddy*, 131.

46. Dave Byrd in Rawick, *American Slave*, vol. 3, pt. 2, 562.

47. William Byrd in Rawick, *American Slave*, vol. 3, pt. 2, 574.

48. Olmsted, *Journey Through Texas*, 91.

49. Otis Wheeler to mother, May 5, 1856, TFP.

50. Dave Byrd in Rawick, *American Slave*, vol. 3, pt. 2, 565.

51. Evans, *Diary of Elizabeth Green Gaines Smith*, December 12, 1858; March 1, 1859; October 8, 1858; April 9, 1859.

52. Evans, *Diary of Elizabeth Green Gaines Smith*, November 14, 1859.

## CHAPTER 4

1. Torget, *Seeds of Empire*, 201.

2. Campbell, *Empire for Slavery*, 58.

3. Stearns, *Empire of Commerce*.

4. "Smithfield, Texas," *Civilian and Galveston City Gazette*, January 18, 1840, 3.

5. Bonner Frizzell, "Some Early History of Palestine," Mary Kate Hunter Collection, vol. 4, 81, Palestine Public Library, Palestine, TX.

6. Block, *Cotton Bales*, 173.

7. Bondi, *Autobiography of August Bondi*, 420.

8. Petition # 21584714, November 10, 1847, San Augustine County, Texas, in Race and Slavery Petitions Project, Series 2, County Court Petitions, Digital Library on American Slavery; Otis Wheeler to dear sister, December 16, 1859, box 1, TFP.

9. Wilson, *Negro in Walker County*, 24. Shortly before the end of slavery, John Price recalled coming "by ship to Galveston up the Trinity River." John Price in Rawick, *American Slave*, vol. 8, pt. 7, 3163.

10. Evans, *Diary of Elizabeth Green Gaines Smith*, April 30, 1858.

11. Olmsted, *Journey Through Texas*, 92. See W. Johnson, *Soul by Soul*.

12. William Byrd in Rawick, *American Slave*, vol. 3, pt. 2, 576.

13. Dave Byrd in Rawick, *American Slave*, vol. 3, pt. 2, 564.

14. *Leon Pioneer* (Centerville, TX), March 16, 1853, 3, from TRSP.

15. Buchanan, *Black Life on the Mississippi*, 50.

16. Marine Fire Insurance Company v. John H. Burnett, 29 Tex. 433, 1867 Tex. Lexis 72. This particular court case describes "two negro fireman" on the steamboat *Betty Powell*, related to the burning of cotton bales that had been shipped from Elizabeth Gaines Smith's plantation.

17. Kaye, *Joining Places*.

18. Wayman Williams in Rawick, *American Slave*, vol. 10, pt. 9, 4144.

19. Evans, *Diary of Elizabeth Green Gaines Smith*, February 25, 1860.

20. Vincent, "Governor George Thomas Wood," 272.

21. John Felix Kelly diary, April 7, 1868, John F. Kelly Papers, Special Collections, Thomason Room, Newton Gresham Library, Sam Houston State University, Huntsville.

22. Crews, *Huntsville and Walker County*; Heather Hornbuckle, "Cincinnati: An Early Riverport in Walker County," *Texas Historian*, March 1978. A traveler wrote how the town "comes in for its share of" fevers. Bollaert, *William Bollaert's Texas*, 292.

23. Hogarth, *Medicalizing Blackness*.

24. Bollaert, *William Bollaert's Texas*, 110.

25. S. W. Goree to Thomas J. Goree, March 20, 1853, box 1, Goree Family Papers, Special Collections, Thomason Room, Newton Gresham Library, Sam Houston State University, Huntsville.

26. Otis Wheeler to dear mother, January 4, 1860, box 1, TFP.

27. Dave Byrd in Rawick, *American Slave*, vol. 3, pt. 2, 568.

28. Ashburn, "Slavery and Cotton Production," 267.

29. Leathers, "Christopher Columbus Goodman," 368–69.

30. Olmsted, *Journey Through Texas*, 90.

31. "Statement of Miss Fannie Gooch, Taken down by Miss Kate Hunter, Sept. 27, 1922," Mary Kate Hunter Collection, vol. 4, Palestine Public Library.

32. E. Woodward, "Internal Improvements in Texas," 165.

33. Bollaert, *William Bollaert's Texas*, 307. Today the trip can be done in an hour if there is no traffic.

34. G. Taylor, *Transportation Revolution*.

35. François et al., "Forest Cover and Watershed Hydrology," 3350.

36. September 7, 1860, "Josephus Brooks Account of Franklin B. Sublett Plantation," box 1, ETRC.

37. December 23, 1860, "Josephus Brooks Account of Franklin B. Sublett Plantation," box 1, ETRC.

38. Bondi, *Autobiography of August Bondi*, 420.

39. "Steamboat Sunk," *Galveston Weekly News*, October 23, 1855, 1.

40. "Loss of the Steamer Brownsville," *Semi-Weekly Journal* (Galveston), March 26, 1850, 3, 2.

41. Wm. H. C. Whiting, "Report from Galveston, January 23, 1853," S. Doc. No. 5, 33rd Cong., 1st Sess. (1853), at 572. Emphasis in original.

42. Twain, *Life on the Mississippi*, 302.

43. "Rates of Insurance," *Weekly Confederate* (Galveston), January 5, 1856, 3.

44. *Civilian and Galveston City Gazette*, April 15, 1843, 2.

45. "Rates of Freight on the Trinity," *Galveston Commercial, and Weekly Prices Current*, December 27, 1855, 2.

46. *Galveston News*, January 10, 1854, 2.

47. Trammell, *Seven Pines*, 123.

48. DeCordova, *Texas*, 336.

49. List of river subscriptions returned to the governor, box 301–26, folder 39, Records of the First Two Terms, Texas Governor Elisha Marshall Pease, Archives and Information Services Division, Texas State Library and Archives Commission, Austin; DeCordova, *Texas*, 336; *Civilian and Gazette Weekly*, December 15, 1857, 1.

50. Otis Wheeler to dear mother, March 10, 1860, box 1, TFP.

51. Frank Gearing to Dear Father, November 22, 1860, Unfiled Papers and Slips Belonging to Confederate Compiled Service Records database, Fold3.com, www.fold3.com, citing NARA microfilm publication M347 (Washington, DC: National Archives and Records Administration, 1962), roll 142; McCaslin, "'Curious War.'"

## CHAPTER 5

1. Fort, *Feast of Reason*.

2. Wednesday, April 25, 1860, JCWP.

3. Entry for James M. Hall, September 15, 1860, Halls Bluff, Texas, vol. 16 (Houston Co.), p. 190, R. G. Dun & Co. Credit Report volumes, Baker Library, Harvard Business School Special Collections, Cambridge, MA.

4. February 15, 1860, JCWP.

5. Donald E. Reynolds, "Texas Troubles," *Handbook of Texas*, November 1, 1995, accessed June 19, 2018, www.tshaonline.org/handbook/entries/texas-troubles; Phillips, *White Metropolis*, 30–31.

6. Hohes, *Centennial History*, 236.

7. April 6, 1861, JCWP.

8. Not just holding Texas but expanding west in places like New Mexico was a goal of the Confederacy. See Nelson, *Three-Cornered War*.

9. When Confederate officials commandeered the Gearings' steamers, they went up the Trinity to collect enslaved laborers to work on blockading the river, but planters refused these demands, willing neither to give up oversight of their property nor stop commerce on the river.

10. *Dallas Herald*, December 11, 1861, 2.

11. Lubbock, *Six Decades in Texas*, 424; letters to Governor Lubbock, March 18–20, 1862, box 2014/092-2, Texas Governor Francis Richard Lubbock Records, 1861–1904, Archives and Information Services Division, Texas State Library and Archives Commission, Austin.

12. Thomas J. Goree to Robert D. Goree, December 20, 1861, Digital Collections, Newton Gresham Library, Sam Houston State University, Huntsville, https://digital.library.shsu.edu/digital/collection/p243coll3/id/38208/rec/1.

13. "W. Hunter to General P. O. Herbert, C. S.," January 11, 1862, in *War of the Rebellion*, ser. 1, vol. 17, 157.

14. "Report of Commander Hunter, C. S. Navy, regarding the removal of the material of the schooner Dodge," October 1862, in *War of the Rebellion*, ser. 1, vol. 19, 798.

15. November 12, 1862, JCWP.

16. November 14, 1862, JCWP.

17. November 17, 1862, JCWP.

18. "Report of Commander Hunter, C. S. Navy, regarding naval operations on the coast of Texas," February 10, 1863, in *War of the Rebellion*, ser. 1, vol. 19, 837.

19. Trammell, *Seven Pines*, 175.

20. Alexander Hamilton Washington to Maj Gen JB Magruder, March 21, 1863, WDCCR.

21. "Journal of Commander W. W. Hunter, C. S. Navy," in *War of the Rebellion*, ser. 1, vol. 19, 813–14.

22. "Report of Chief Engineer Forshey, C. S. Army, referring to defenses," in *War of the Rebellion*, ser. 1, vol. 19, 847.

23. "Journal of Commander W. W. Hunter, C. S. Navy," 816. For the history of rivers and warfare, see Muscolino, *Ecology of War in China*.

24. Allan, *Allan's Lone Star Ballads*, 78.

25. Reagan and Smith correspondence, November 1862, Smith Family History, Houston County Historical Commission, Crockett, TX.

26. McCurry, *Confederate Reckoning*, 144.

27. January 15, 1863, JCWP.

28. September 23, 1861, JCWP.

29. Ural, *Soldiers and Families*.

30. March 23, 1862, JCWP.

31. Buried stumps have been found that are thousands of years old. Pearson et al., *Archaeological Investigations on the Outer Continental Shelf*.

32. August 14, 1862, JCWP.

33. January 8, 1863, JCWP.

34. December 26, 1863, JCWP.

35. February 7, 1863, JCWP.

36. June 24, 1865, JCWP.

37. "Louis Love," in Federal Writers' Project, *Slave Narratives*, 40.

38. March 27, 1861, JCWP.

39. Baum, "Slaves Taken to Texas," 74.

40. Baum, "Slaves Taken to Texas"; Massey, *Refugee Life*.

41. Baum, "Slaves Taken to Texas," 89–90.

42. *Weekly State Gazette* (Austin), February 22, 1865, 1.

43. Not that there weren't other forms of slavery that existed in the West. West, *Continental Reckoning*, 91.

44. Gerard Brandon diary, August 1863, box 2J115, Gerard C. Brandon Papers, 1823–1829, 1863–1864, Dolph Briscoe Center for American History, University of Texas at Austin. Henrietta Wood was among those traveling with Gerard Brandon. See McDaniel, *Sweet Taste of Liberty*.

45. Gerard Brandon diary, August 11, 1863, box 2J115, Gerard C. Brandon Papers, Dolph Briscoe Center for American History.

46. Massey, *Refugee Life*, 232.

47. "Louis Love," in Federal Writers' Project, *Slave Narratives*, 40.

48. Sutter, *Let Us Now Praise*; Mauldin, *Unredeemed Land*; McFarlane, "Wet Frontier of Slavery"; Duncan, *Southern Rivers*, 95–104; "Calvin Moye," Texas Slave Narrative, accessed June 9, 2025, https://freepages.rootsweb.com/~ewyatt/genealogy/_borders/Texas%20Slave%20Narratives/Texas%20M/Moye,%20Calvin.html.

49. Alexander Hamilton Washington to Captain E. P. Turner from Magnolia, May 25, 1864, WDCCR.

50. Howard N. Martin, "Indian Tribes in Polk County, Texas," unpublished manuscript in Howard Martin Papers, 18–19, Archives of the Alabama-Coushatta Tribe of Texas, Livingston, TX.

51. Alexander Hamilton Washington to Captain Turner from Magnolia, June 5, 1864, WDCCR.

52. Alexander Hamilton Washington to Major CM Mason from Magnolia, June 11, 1864, WDCCR.

53. Major Magruder Special Order on Disability for Maj. H. Washington, Galveston, 1864, WDCCR.

54. D. Smith, "Frontier Defense in Texas," 293.

55. *Weekly State Gazette*, April 6, 1864, 1

56. "Diary of William B. Duncan, Liberty County, Texas," March 7 and March 9, 1865, transcribed by Julia Duncan Welder, Albert and Ethel Herzstein Library, San Jacinto Museum of History, La Porte, TX.

57. January 26, 1865, JCWP.

58. February 5, 1865, JCWP.

59. *Henderson (TX) Times*, May 21, 1864, 1, from TRSP.

60. April 10, April 11, April 12, 1865, JCWP.

61. "Diary of William B. Duncan, Liberty County, Texas," May 24, 1865, San Jacinto Museum of History; May 23, 1865, JCWP.

62. May 23, 1865, JCWP.

63. Leathers, "Christopher Columbus Goodman," 370n21.

64. May 29, 1865, JCWP.

65. "Diary of William B. Duncan, Liberty County, Texas," June 2, 1865, San Jacinto Museum of History.

66. July 19, 1865, JCWP.

67. "Jemima Jackson [Chambers County, Texas]," 1880 United States Federal Census database, Ancestry.com, www.ancestrylibrary.comimageviewer/collections/6742/images/4244715-00559.

68. United States Court of Claims 3 Ct. Cl. 165; 1867 U.S. Ct. Cl. Lexis 140 December 1867.

## *CHAPTER 6*

1. September 19, 1865, JCWP.

2. July 28, 1865, JCWP.

3. Glymph, *Out of the House of Bondage.*

4. September 29, September 30, 1865, JCWP.

5. Border states Kentucky and Delaware did not end slavery until the Thirteenth Amendment passed on December 6, 1865.

6. Outrages, Letters of the Assistant Commissioner, roll 32, "Miscellaneous Records Relating to Murders and Other Criminal Offenses Committed in Texas 1865–1868," August 1865, BRFAL.

7. Blair, *Records of Murders and Outrages.*

8. Glasrud et al., *Blacks in East Texas History*, 59; Gregory P. Downs and Scott Nesbit, *Mapping Occupation: Force, Freedom, and the Army in Reconstruction*, March 2015, http://mappingoccupation.org.

9. Cantrell and Turner, *Lone Star Pasts*, 147.

10. US Congress, *Report of the Joint Committee on Reconstruction*, 36, 37.

11. August 5, 1865, JCWP.

12. Because Texas appeared as such a vast and ungovernable region, there were several attempts to turn the Trinity into a state border. At the Constitutional Convention of 1866, one proposed resolution was to divide Texas along the Trinity and create a new state of East Texas. Two years later, at the Constitutional Convention of 1868, representatives proposed turning Texas into three different states with the Trinity once again serving as the main border for East Texas. Neither of these proposals was realized, but they both suggest the ways that people continued to understand the Trinity as a political and ecological border. Claude Elliott, "Division of Texas," *Handbook of Texas*, accessed May 1, 2018, www.tshaonline.org/handbook/online/articles/mqd01; *Journal of the Reconstruction Convention*, 146.

13. Thomas Holliman Statement, Letters of the Assistant Commissioner, roll 7, Letters Received, M–R, February 23, 1867, BRFAL.

14. The State of Texas vs. B. F. Burroughs, Letters of the Assistant Commissioner, roll 4, Letters Received, A–C, April 1867, BRFAL.

15. John H. Potts Statement, Letters of the Assistant Commissioner, Letters Received, M–R, February 20, 1867, BRFAL.

16. Captain J. H. Bradford, Assessment of Damages Sustained by Freedmen on the Cessna plantation on the night of the 16th February AD 1867, Letters of the Assistant Commissioner, roll 4, Letters Received, A–C, April 10, 1867, BRFAL.

17. F. W. Reinhart to J. T. Kirkman, Freedmen's Bureau Field Office Records, Centerville, Letters Sent, roll 14, April 16, 1867, BRFAL.

18. Richter, "'Revolver Rules the Day!'"

19. The State of Texas vs. B. F. Burroughs, April 1867, BRFAL.

20. William Sinclair to General J. T. Kirman, Letters of the Assistant Commissioner, roll 8, Letters Received, S, April 1, 1867, BRFAL.

21. Some freedpeople did plant on upland and bottomland from the outset, though they discovered that greedy planters would take whatever the river did not. J. Carter "Confidential" letter to General Kiddoo, Letters of the Assistant Commissioner, roll 4, Letters Received, A–C, October 16, 1866, BRFAL; Daniel, *River Bottom Humor*, 55–56.

22. Records of the Field Offices for the State, Offices of Staff Officers, roll 7, Quartermaster and Disbursing Officer, Reports of Person and Articles Hired, BRFAL.

23. Elizabeth Wheeler to Parents and Sister, July 10, 1867, box 1, TFP.

24. L. S. Barnes to Colonel Sinclair, Letters of the Assistant Commissioner, roll 4, Letters Received, A–C, July 8, 1866, BRFAL.

25. A. H. Mayer to S. H. Lathrop, Letters of the Assistant Commissioner, roll 4, Letters Received, M–R, December 23, 1866, BRFAL.

26. A. H. Mayer to S. H. Lathrop, December 23, 1866, BRFAL.

27. A. H. Mayer to Major General Kiddo, Texas Field Office Records, Liberty, roll 23, January 28, 1867, BRFAL.

28. A. H. Mayer to J. T. Kirkman, Texas Field Office Records, Liberty, roll 23, June 8, 1867, BRFAL.

29. A. H. Mayer to J. T. Kirkman, Texas Field Office Records, Liberty, roll 23, June 10, 1867, BRFAL.

30. A. H. Mayer to Commanding Officer Post of Houston, Texas Field Office Records, Liberty, roll 23, June 26, 1867, BRFAL.

31. A. H. Mayer to J. T. Kirkman, Texas Field Office Records, Liberty, roll 23, July 30, 1867, BRFAL.

32. M. H. Goodin to J. T. Kirkman, Texas Field Office Records, Letters of the Assistant Commissioner, roll 5, Letters Received, D–G, June 3, 1867, BRFAL.

33. G. W. Davis to J. B. Kiddoo, Letters of the Assistant Commissioner, roll 5, Letters Received, D–G, June 15, 1867, BRFAL.

34. Armstead Barrett in Rawick, *American Slave*, vol. 2, pt. 1, 198.

35. James P. Butler to J. T. Kirkman, Assistant Commissioner, Reports, Reports of Operations and Conditions, Entered in Register 1, June–August 1867, June 30, 1867, BRFAL.

36. A. H. Mayer to J. T. Kirkman, Field Office Records, Liberty, roll 23, July 1, 1867, BRFAL.

37. A. H. Mayer to commanding officer in Galveston, Field Office Records, Liberty, roll 23, October 1, 1867, BRFAL.

38. J. Downs, *Sick from Freedom*, 7.

39. Prather and Monday, *From Slave to Statesman*, 101.

40. Bean, *Too Great a Burden*, 144.

41. Richter, *Overreached on All Sides*, 240.

42. A. H. Mayer to J. T. Kirkman, Field Office Records, Liberty, roll 23, July 30, 1867, BRFAL.

43. H. S. Johnson to J. T. Kirkman, Assistant Commissioner, Reports, Reports of Operations and Conditions, Entered in Register 1, December 1866–May 1867, June 1, 1867, BRFAL.

44. James Sharp to J. P. Richardson, Letters of the Assistant Commissioner, roll 15, Letters Received, S, November 13, 1867, BRFAL.

45. W. H. Edwards to General Reynolds, Letters of the Assistant Commissioner, roll 11, Letters Received, D–G, July 13, 1868, BRFAL; J. Downs, *Sick from Freedom*.

46. Sam Shaffer to Galveston Quartermaster, Letters of the Assistant Commissioner, roll 13, Letters Received, I–M, October 17, 1867, BRFAL.

47. A. H. Mayer to O. O. Howard, Letters of the Assistant Commissioner, roll 16, Letters Received, T–Y, February 8, 1868, BRFAL.

48. US Department of the Interior, Bureau of Pensions, Case Files of Approved Pension Applications of Widows and Other Dependents of Civil War Veterans, ca. 1861–ca. 1910, Records of the Department of Veterans Affairs, 1773–2007, RG 15, National Archives and Records Administration, Washington, DC, located via the Shapell Roster Civil War Soldier Database, accessed November 11, 1012, www.shapell.org/civil-war-soldier-database/soldier/9323.

49. A. H. Mayer to parents, February 12, 1869, US Department of the Interior, Bureau of Pensions, Case Files of Approved Pension Applications of Widows and Other Dependents of Civil War Veterans, ca. 1861–ca. 1910, Records of the Department of Veterans Affairs, 1773–2007, RG 15, National Archives and Records Administration, Washington, DC.

50. Henry Jacob Labatt statement, May 14, 1889, US Department of the Interior, Bureau of Pensions, Case Files of Approved Pension Applications of Widows and Other Dependents of Civil War Veterans, ca. 1861–ca. 1910, Records of the Department of Veterans Affairs, 1773–2007, RG 15, National Archives and Records Administration, Washington, DC.

51. Outrages, Assistant Commissioner, roll 32, Records Relating to Murders, Outrages, and Criminal Offenses, Record of Criminal Offenses, vol. 3, September 30, 1868, BRFAL.

52. "Louisa Tubbs [Walker County, Texas]," 1880 United States Federal Census database, Ancestry.com, www.ancestrylibrary.com/imageviewer/collections/6742/images/4244803-00176.

## CHAPTER 7

1. "A Vicious Panther," *Fort Worth Gazette*, February 23, 1896, 7.

2. Testimony of Aaron Sims as recorded by E. G. Betts on March 12, 1867, Assistant Commissioner, Letters Received, S, BRFAL.

3. Wayman Williams in Rawick, *American Slave*, vol. 10, pt. 9, 4143.

4. Hahn, *Nation Under Our Feet*; Hill, *Deacons for Defense*.

5. Diary, November 29, 1875, George Gordon Collection, Sam Houston Regional Library, Texas State Archives, Liberty.

6. A. H. Mayer to Galveston Office, Field Office Records, Liberty, roll 23, October 10, 1867, BRFAL.

7. Goyen, *House of Breath*, 26.

8. "Report of Crimes Committed, Polk County, by G. W. Barfield, Sheriff," 1870, box 401-864, folder 36, State Police Records, Reconstruction Records, Texas Adjutant General's Department, Archives and Information Services Division, Texas State Library and Archives Commission, Austin.

9. Mollie Kirkland in Rawick, *American Slave*, vol. 6, pt. 5, 2245.

10. Campbell, *Grass-Roots Reconstruction in Texas*.

11. G. Downs, *After Appomattox*, 233.

12. Martial law was declared in Walker County. This may be the event referred to by McAdams. Governor Edmund Davis sent the Texas State Police, not soldiers.

13. Andy McAdams in Rawick, *American Slave*, vol. 7, pt. 6, 2457.

14. *Dallas Herald*, December 18, 1869, 2.

15. *Dallas Herald*, January 19, 1867, 2.

16. Entry for Thos Stubblefield, July 1866, Texas, vol. 16 (Houston Co.), p. 194, R. G. Dun & Co. Credit Report volumes, Baker Library, Harvard Business School Special Collections, Cambridge, MA.

17. "Report from Sheriff Miller of Houston County to Gen. James Davidson," July 9, 1870, box 401-864, folder 30, State Police Records, Reconstruction Records, Texas Adjutant General's Department, Archives and Information Services Division, Texas State Library and Archives Commission, Austin.

18. "An Act to provide for the Improvement of the Navigation of the Trinity River, and to grant the Aid of the State therefor," *Special Laws of Texas*, 742.

19. As if they were geologic dentists, these snag-pulling boats were often called "toothpullers."

20. Miller, "Texas Land Grants," 140.

21. Howard C. Williams, "Texas and New Orleans Railroad," *Handbook of Texas*, accessed June 21, 2018, www.tshaonline.org/handbook/online/articles/eqt06.

22. "Report of the Chief of Engineers," 690–91.

23. "Reported Sunk," *Galveston Daily News*, May 31, 1876, 4.

24. "Sources of Galveston Receipts," *Galveston Daily News*, May 2, 1874, 3.

25. "Crockett," *Galveston Daily News*, September 8, 1881, 7.

26. Philip Dale Browne, interview by Rufus B. Spain, August 18, 1971, Interview 1, transcript, p. 9, Institute for Oral History, Baylor University, Waco.

27. Andy McAdams in Rawick, *American Slave*, vol. 7, pt. 6, 2454 and 2459.

28. T. Miller, *Public Lands of Texas*, 26.

29. Du Bois, "Negro Farmer," 84.

30. Nathans, "'Gotta Mind to Move,'" 210.

31. Holt, *Making Freedom Pay*.

32. Jane Cotton in Rawick, *American Slave*, vol. 3, pt. 2, 948.

33. Andy McAdams in Rawick, *American Slave*, vol. 7, pt. 6, 2459.

34. "William Stone," in Federal Writers' Project, *Slave Narratives*, 86.

35. Wayman Williams in Rawick, *American Slave*, vol. 10, pt. 9, 4142–48.

36. Andy McAdams in Rawick, *American Slave*, vol. 7, pt. 6, 2454.

37. Eliza H. Bishop, "Halls Bluff, TX," *Handbook of Texas*, accessed October 20, 2015, www.tshaonline.org/handbook/online/articles/hvh07.

38. Houston County Historical Commission, *History of Houston County*, 416, 608.

39. Bishop, "Halls Bluff, TX."

40. Ali, *In the Lion's Mouth*, 50, 48–49.

## *CHAPTER 8*

1. Minutaglio, *In Search of the Blues*, 60.

2. Acts 10:3–5 (English Standard Version Anglicised).

3. Donald Payton interview with author, October 7, 2015, Dallas; Minutaglio, *In Search of the Blues*, 60.

4. Pat Lum v. The State, Court of Appeals of Texas, 11 Tex. Ct. App. 483; Lexis 131 (1882).

5. White, *Organic Machine*.

6. *The Tracings* 6, no. 1 (1987) (newsletter of the Anderson County Genealogical Society).

7. "Using the Ferry Was Complicated Transaction," *Polk County Enterprise* (Livingston, TX), October 3, 1982, 1-G.

8. Jim D. Follis v. The State, Court of Criminal Appeals of Texas, 51 Tex. Crim. 186; 101 S.W. 242, Lexis 100 (1907).

9. "Water Supply," *Dallas Herald*, May 24, 1887, 1.

10. Hämäläinen, *Comanche Empire*, 316.

11. "Report of Major General Sheridan," 76.

12. Forstall, "Population of States and Counties," 3.

13. *Dallas Herald*, April 11, 1868, 2.

14. *Dallas Herald*, June 20, 1868, 2.

15. "Trinity River Meeting," *Dallas Herald*, September 5, 1868, 2.

16. *Norton's Union Intelligencer* (Dallas), June 7, 1879, 1.

17. Edward King, "Glimpses of Texas," *Scribner's Monthly* 7 (1874): 427.

18. "Dallas Swells in Glory," *Galveston Daily News*, May 25, 1893, 2.

19. J. Farley, "What I Know About Freight Rates in Texas," *Southern Mercury* (Dallas), July 2, 1896, 9.

20. "A Grave Omission," *Fort Worth Gazette*, February 11, 1896, 4.

21. "Trinity River," *Southern Mercury*, August 27, 1896, 8 and 1.

22. *Fort Worth Gazette*, May 29, 1895, 8; "To Tap the Gulf of Mexico," *Fort Worth Gazette*, June 9, 1895, 5.

23. *Southern Mercury*, January 2, 1896, 9.

24. Duncan, *Southern Rivers*, 95–104.

25. "Steamboats on Trinity River," *Palestine (TX) Daily Herald*, July 21, 1905, 3.

26. This comes out to $154 million in 2024 based on the increases in the Consumer Price Index.

27. "Survey of Trinity River," 7.

28. Jacoby, *Crimes Against Nature*.

29. "Survey of Trinity River," 2, 3, 7, 7–8.

30. *Southern Mercury*, April 13, 1905, 2.

31. "Stop at Groveton," *Southern Mercury*, May 14, 1903, 1.

32. "The Work for Trinity," *Southern Mercury*, June 26, 1902, 3.

33. "Cash Subscribed," *Palestine Daily Herald*, May 1, 1905, 5.

34. "Trinity River Improvements," *Palestine Daily Herald*, March 29, 1904, 1.

35. "Down the Trinity on a Steamer," *Palestine Daily Herald*, November 15, 1907, 3.

36. Stull, "History of Navigation," 35.

37. "Report of Death from Injury," July 26, 1911, in Corps of Engineers, Fort Worth District, Records of the Dallas Engineer Office, Southwest Division, RG 77, National Archives at Fort Worth, E.FW18, box 3.

38. *Palestine Daily Herald*, May 25, 1905, 6.

39. "Down the Trinity on a Steamer," 3.

40. The "you can't tame the Trinity" comes from an audience member at a public talk in East Texas who described what one of the "old timers" used to say about the river. July 2017, Polk County Historical Commission, Livingston, TX.

41. Geo. M. Duncan to Capt. A. E. Waldron, April 17, 1911, in Corps of Engineers, Fort Worth District, Records of the Dallas Engineer Office, Southwest Division, RG 77, National Archives at Fort Worth, E.FW18, box 11.

42. Commissioner of Streets and Public Property to Capt. A. E. Waldron, February 1, 1911, in Corps of Engineers, Fort Worth District, Records of the Dallas Engineer Office, Southwest Division, RG 77, National Archives at Fort Worth, E.FW18, box 11.

43. McFarlane, "Defining a Nuisance."

44. Waterworks and Sewerage Commissioner to Capt. A. E. Waldron, December 23, 1910, in Corps of Engineers, Fort Worth District, Records of the Dallas Engineer Office, Southwest Division, RG 77, National Archives at Fort Worth, E.FW18, box 11.

45. Stull, "History of Navigation," 39.

46. "Exciting Scenes on Trinity River," *Palestine Daily Herald,* May 17, 1905, 1.

47. "Notes from the River," *Palestine Daily Herald*, April 29, 1908, 3.

48. *Polk County Enterprise*, June 18, 1908, 4.

49. "Island Farmers Flee from Flood," *Dallas Morning News*, June 2, 1908, 1.

50. "Flood Water Crushes House on River Front," *Dallas Morning News*, June 2, 1908, 4.

51. "Owners of Houses Unknown," *Dallas Morning News*, June 3, 1908, 3.

## CHAPTER 9

1. Sappington, *Trinity River Sanitary Survey*, 145. There were other cases when the pollution was too much even for the gar.

2. "War on Gars Continued at Caddo," *East Texas Magazine*, May 1935, 15.

3. Ric Jensen, "Finding Answers to Flooding Woes," *Texas Water Resources Institute*, Fall 1990.

4. John Furlong, Greg Ajemian, and Tommie McPherson, "History of the Dallas Floodway," PowerPoint presentation, ASCE Texas Section Meeting, September 26, 2003, Dallas.

5. "The State Reclamation Department's Trinity River Reclamation Study" (1930), box 51, folder Trinity River Basin Flood Control and Navigation Study, Texas Department of Water Resources, RER.

6. Hasty, *Oak Cliff and the Missing Pieces*, 10.

7. O'Brien and Ensminger, *Mojo Hand*, 4.

8. Mack McCormick, "A Conversation with Lightnin' Hopkins," *Jazz Journal*, November 1960.

9. Alan Lomax, "Commentary on Recording with John A. Lomax," April 19, 1969, Cultural Equity, accessed April 16, 2025, https://archive.culturalequity.org/node/60386.

10. Szwed, *Alan Lomax*, 37.

11. Calvin Moye in Rawick, *American Slave*, vol. 7, pt. 6, 2843 and 2860.

12. Calvin Moye in Rawick, *American Slave*, vol. 7, pt. 6, 2824.

13. Portions of Calvin Moye's interview were deleted in the published interview transcription, but they appear here: Texas Slave Narrative, accessed June 9, 2025, https://freepages

.rootsweb.com/~ewyatt/genealogy/_borders/Texas%20Slave%20Narratives/Texas%20M/Moye,%20Calvin.html.

14. Calvin Moye in Rawick, *American Slave*, vol. 7, pt. 6, 2869.

15. Scott-Chaber, "'River of Death.'"

16. Sappington, *Trinity River Sanitary Survey*, 145.

17. Calvin Moye in Rawick, *American Slave*, vol. 7, pt. 6, 2829.

18. Sessums, *Lee-Simmons-Stephens Family*, 6–7.

19. "A Big Pair of Antlers," *Palestine Daily Herald*, November 11, 1909, 5.

20. Truett and Lay, *Land of Bears and Honey*, 54.

21. Calvin Moye in Rawick, *American Slave*, vol. 7, pt. 6, 2820.

22. Olmsted, *Journey Through Texas*, 91.

23. Sandy Robinson v. The State, Court of Appeals of Texas, 22 Tex. Ct. App. 690; 3 S.W. 736, Lexis 21 (1887).

24. *Palestine Daily Herald*, March 27, 1906, 6.

25. "Fine Stock Ranch Located," *Palestine Daily Herald*, February 9, 1906, 6.

26. Sitton, *Backwoodsmen*; Hahn, *Roots of Southern Populism*.

27. Calvin Moye in Rawick, *American Slave*, vol. 7, pt. 6, 2862.

28. "J. L. Robinson [Palestine, Texas]," 1920 United States Federal Census database, FamilySearch.com, https://familysearch.org/ark:/61903/3:1:33S7-9RFC-C23.

29. A. Adams, *Archie Adams Diary*, October 26, 1888.

30. K. Walker, "Pecan Shellers."

31. *Palestine Daily Herald*, October 29, 1906, 4; "Pecans Are Hard to Get," *Palestine Daily Herald*, October 24, 1910, 6.

32. Sitton, *Backwoodsmen*, 109.

33. "Any Timber Cutting," *Palestine Daily Herald*, September 15, 1910, 6.

34. *Palestine Daily Herald*, January 29, 1904, 4.

35. Morgan Ash Co. to U.S. Engineering Department, November 11, 1922, and R. B. Gillette Jr. to Morgan Ash Co., December 7, 1922, in Corps of Engineers, Fort Worth District, Records of the Dallas Engineer Office, Southwest Division, RG 77, National Archives at Fort Worth, E.FW18, box 10.

36. *Galveston Daily News*, April 23, 1876, 2.

37. "Sawmill at Oakwoods," *Palestine Daily Herald*, December 4, 1905, 1; "J. W. Cook Report to County Clerk of Polk County," No. 7951, July 13, 1896, Polk County Clerk Records, Sam Houston Regional Library, Texas State Archives, Liberty.

38. Block, *East Texas Mill Towns*, 328.

39. Philip A. Ryan Lumber Co. v. Ball, Court of Civil Appeals of Texas, No. 5481, 177 S.W. 226, Lexis 668 (1915).

40. Sappington, *Trinity River Sanitary Survey*, 108.

41. William Cox, interview by Thomas Charlton and Tom Parrish, November 6, 1981, transcript, Institute for Oral History, Baylor University, Waco.

42. Szwed, *Alan Lomax*, 37.

43. Calvin Moye in Rawick, *American Slave*, vol. 7, pt. 6, 2873.

44. "Calvin Moye, July 20, 1940, [Navarro County, Texas]," Texas, Death Certificates, 1903–1982, Ancestry.com, www.ancestrylibrary.com/search/collections/2272/records/22206891.

## CHAPTER 10

1. Paul Ethridge, interview by Sandra Rodgers, September 8, 2004, Trinity, Texas Prison Museum, Huntsville.

2. The term "levees" originated in eighteenth-century New Orleans from the French word meaning "to lift." Richard L. Hindle, "Levees That Might Have Been," *Places Journal*, May 2015, accessed April 18, 2025, https://doi.org/10.22269/150518.

3. Dick Smith, "Drainage Districts," *Handbook of Texas*, accessed March 6, 2019, www.tshaonline.org/handbook/online/articles/mwd01. The federal Newlands Reclamation Act of 1902 did not initially apply to Texas since it had no federal lands.

4. "H.B. No. 402," *General Laws of the State of Texas*, 292, 48.

5. Ollson, *Agrarian Crossings*.

6. "Rotary Members Inspect Big Levees," April 11, 1917, in Jack Rogers Private Collection, Palestine, TX.

7. "Map: Levee Districts in the Trinity Valley," 1930, box 51, folder Trinity River Basin Flood Control and Navigation Study, Texas Department of Water Resources, RER.

8. "Levee Improvement Districts Width of Floodways, Trinity River, Henderson, Navarro, Freestone, and Anderson Counties," December 1920, General Map Collection, General Land Office Archives, Austin.

9. Fagan Parker to Arthur A. Stiles, November 28, 1922, box 14, folder Anderson County Levee Improvement District #2, RER.

10. E. V. Swift to Arthur A. Stiles, August 15, 1918, box 14, folder Anderson County Levee Improvement District #2, RER.

11. Preston et al. v. Anderson County Levee Improvement District no. 2. Court of Appeals of Texas, No. 2891, 261 S.W. 1077, Lexis 953 (1924).

12. "Andrew Patterson [Houston County, Texas]," 1900 United States Federal Census database, Ancestry.com, www.ancestrylibrary.com/imageviewer/collections/7602/images/4118501_00266; "Andy Patterson [Houston County, Texas]," 1910 United States Federal Census database, Ancestry.com, www.ancestrylibrary.com/imageviewer/collections/7884/images/4449747_00038.

13. Correspondence and Relief files, folder Houston County Levee Improvement District #1, 1920–58, RER.

14. Quoted in Sitton and Conrad, *Freedom Colonies*, 74.

15. Calvin Moye in Rawick, *American Slave*, vol. 7, pt. 6, 2872.

16. Morris, *Big Muddy*, 168.

17. Kirby, *Rural Worlds Lost*; Daniel, *Breaking the Land*.

18. Calvin Moye in Rawick, *American Slave*, vol. 7, pt. 6, 2862.

19. Ashley Classen, State Reclamation Engineer, to P. Caprielian, Houston Levee Supervisor, August 23, 1935, folder Houston County Levee Improvement District #1, 1920–58, RER.

20. Work relief applications, folder Anderson County Levee Improvement District #1; folder Houston County Levee Improvement District #1; folder Henderson County Levee Improvement District #1, all in RER.

21. "Application Civil Works Project for Houston County Levee Improvement District #1," folder Houston County Levee Improvement District #1, 1920–58, RER.

22. "Application Work Relief Project for Anderson County Levee Improvement District #1," box 14, folder Anderson County Levee Improvement District #1, RER.

23. "Application Work Relief Project for Henderson County Levee Improvement District #1," folder Henderson County Levee Improvement District #1, RER.

24. Mack McCormick, "A Conversation with Lightnin' Hopkins," *Jazz Journal*, November 1960.

25. Goyen, *House of Breath*, 33.

26. Pruitt, *Other Great Migration*; Grossman, *Land of Hope*.

27. Simmons, *Up Home*, 3–8. Note that there were in fact two separate "Murray Farms" owned by different members of the Murray family in Houston County.

28. Simmons, *Up Home*, 38, 49.

29. Simmons, *Up Home*, 15.

## CHAPTER 11

1. Gary Cartwright, "The Whole Shootin' Match," *Texas Monthly*, February 2001.

2. Guinn, *Go Down Together*.

3. Eastham Farm contract, folder 2014.12.01–0.2, Texas Prison Museum, Huntsville.

4. *Huntsville (TX) Post-Item*, December 8, 1905, 6.

5. "Eastham Marker Application," by Louise Adams Fulsom, Texas Prison Museum, Huntsville.

6. Paul Ethridge, interview by Sandra Rodgers, September 8, 2004, Trinity, Texas Prison Museum, Huntsville.

7. Perkinson, *Texas Tough*, 75.

8. Donald R. Walker, "Texas State Penitentiary at Huntsville," *Handbook of Texas*, accessed October 19, 2015, www.tshaonline.org/handbook/online/articles/jjt01.

9. Perkinson, *Texas Tough*, 79, 81.

10. Report of Jack Devine for year ending December 1866, Letters of the Assistant Commissioner, roll 20, Reports on Operations and Conditions, January 12, 1867, BRFAL.

11. "Six Convicts Escaped," *Palestine Daily Herald*, June 30, 1909, 1.

12. Fulsom, *Prison Stories*, 10, 11.

13. Transcript of testimony, 1921: Eastham and Ferguson Farms, February 16–17, 1921, box 1988/068–1, pp. 7, 80, 59, Joint Penitentiary Investigating Committee Records, Texas Legislature, Archives and Information Services Division, Texas State Library and Archives Commission.

14. *Polk County Enterprise*, July 14, 1955, 1.

15. Jackson, *Wake Up Dead Man*, 314, 18.

16. Forrest and Cotton, Consulting Engineers, "Report on Eastham and Ferguson Prison Farm Levee Study, Prepared for Texas Department of Corrections," May 1970, Environmental Research Library, Texas Commission on Environmental Quality, Austin.

17. For example, Coffield Prison has a capacity of over four thousand inmates.

18. Ruiz v. Estelle, 503 F. Supp. 1265 (S.D. Tex. 1980).

19. Berryhill, *Trials of Eroy Brown*, 85. These river prisons had been referred to as "the bottom" since the 1930s. O'Brien and Ensminger, *Mojo Hand*, 31.

20. Berryhill, *Trials of Eroy Brown*, 109, 65.

## *CHAPTER 12*

1. Pate, *North of the River*, 60.

2. Saunders, *Garden of Eden*, 88.

3. E. Brown, *Trinity River Canalization*, 54.

4. Quoted in E. Brown, *Trinity River Canalization*, 55.

5. M. A. Glasscock, Forward Trinity Valley Association secretary, to Amon Carter, January 26, 1942, box 211, Carter Collection; Schiller, "Nature's Entrepreneur," 48.

6. Minutes of the meeting of the Trinity River Canal Association, August 28, 1930, pp. 6, 18, box 213, Carter Collection.

7. Minutes of the meeting of the Trinity River Canal Association, August 28, 1930, p. 33, box 213, Carter Collection.

8. "Third Annual Dinner, Trinity Canal Association, 1933," box 213, Carter Collection.

9. Cervantez, "'For the Exclusive Benefit,'" 137, 138.

10. Forrest L. Park to Amon Carter, March 29, 1940, box 211, Carter Collection.

11. Sutter, *Let Us Now Praise*; Karl Jacoby, *Crimes Against Nature*.

12. Park to Carter, March 29, 1940.

13. Boyle et al., *Water Hustlers*, 48.

14. K. Miller, *Segregating Sound*.

15. Boyle et al., *Water Hustlers*, 49.

16. Col. B. M. Hatfield to John W. Carpenter, November 15, 1933, box 213, Carter Collection.

17. Michael J. Vaughn, "The History of Cayuga," p. 17, unpublished manuscript, 1960, Palestine Public Library, Palestine, TX.

18. Vaughn, "History of Cayuga," 17.

19. Hahn, *Roots of Southern Populism*.

20. At a research presentation in the town of Cold Springs near the Trinity River in the summer of 2017, one attendee shared his memories of Hatfield, who had visited his school in the 1930s.

21. John H. Walker, "Adventure on the Trinity," *Texas Highways*, July 1993, 34–36.

22. "Hatfield, of Trinity River Fame, Dies," *Fort Worth Star-Telegram*, March 24, 1942, 1.

23. Wanda Bobinger, "Commodore Makes Waves," January 2013, Stephen F. Austin State University, Center for Regional Heritage Research, Local Writers' Columns, accessed November 11, 2025, www.sfasu.edu/heritagecenter/6992.asp.

24. Lower Trinity Valley Association Editors, "Mystic Arabella . . . Her Influence Yesterday, Today and Tomorrow," *Trinity Project*, June 1960, 1.

25. John Fouts, General Manager, to Amon Carter, June 28, 1944, box 211, Carter Collection.

26. Dean Tevis, Secretary Manager of FTVA, to Amon Carter, June 26, 1947, box 211, Carter Collection.

27. E. Brown, *Trinity River Canalization*, 34.

28. Sparkman, *North Texas Region*, chapter 6.

29. "1952–1955 Progress Report of Trinity Improvement Association," box SRH 3R-333, Sam Rayburn Papers, Dolph Briscoe Center for American History, University of Texas at Austin.

30. Caro, *Path to Power*, 460.

31. "Johnson Promises Lake Liberty Survey to Be Resumed," *Anahuac (TX) Progress*, June 24, 1954, 1.

32. Cervantez, "Lone Star Booster," 250, 251.

33. John Fouts, TRA General Manager, to Sam Rayburn, November 27, 1950, box SRH 3R-333, Sam Rayburn Papers, Dolph Briscoe Center for American History.

34. Sam Rayburn to John Fouts, December 16, 1950, box SRH 3R-333, Sam Rayburn Papers, Dolph Briscoe Center for American History.

35. Original draft of bill is included in the final bill that passed: Texas State Legislature, An Act to Create the Trinity River Authority of Texas, H.B. 20, 54th Regular Session, 1955.

36. Letters to the editor, *Polk County Enterprise*, February 10, 1955, 13.

37. *Ennis (TX) Daily News*, June 4, 1955, 1.

38. Letters to the editor, *Polk County Enterprise*, February 24, 1955, 2.

39. "Trinity R. Bill Passes in House," *Ennis Daily News*, June 7, 1955, 1.

40. *Ennis Daily News*, June 4, 1955, 1.

41. *Polk County Enterprise*, June 2, 1955, 1; "Trinity R. Bill Passes in House," 1.

42. "Even the Trinity," *Denison (TX) Press*, June 24, 1955, 2.

43. "Barefoot Sanders Seeking Re-Election," *Weekly Chronicle* (Duncanville, TX), July 12, 1956.

44. Baker, "Southern Landscapes."

45. E. Davis, "Movement for Trinity River Development," 95.

46. "Trinity River Authority to Meet in Huntsville," *Carrollton (TX) Chronicle*, October 28, 1955, 2.

47. E. Davis, "Movement for Trinity River Development," 86.

48. "Know Your TRA Directors," *Carrollton Chronicle,* July 24, 1959, 2; "Know Your TRA Directors," *Carrollton Chronicle*, July 17, 1959, 3; "Know Your TRA Directors," *Carrollton Chronicle*, June 12, 1959, 1.

49. "Know Your TRA Directors," *Carrollton Chronicle*, July 10, 1959, 3.

50. "Know Your TRA Directors," *Carrollton Chronicle*, July 3, 1959, 4.

51. "Trinity River Basin Master Plan," 1958, p. 53, Trinity River Authority Archives, Arlington, TX.

52. Williams and Sansom, *Untold Story of the Lower Colorado River Authority*, 239.

53. *Fort Worth Star-Telegram*, February 4, 1959.

54. *Palestine Herald-Press*, February 9, 1959.

55. *Carrollton Chronicle*, February 27, 1959, 2.

56. Hundley, *Great Thirst*; Manganiello, *Southern Water*.

57. "'Home Base' Water Threatened," *Carrollton Chronicle*, February 27, 1959, 6.

58. "Area Water Threatened by Houston," *Carrollton Chronicle*, February 27, 1959, 1.

59. State Board of Water Engineers Minutes, "Hearing on Trinity River and Tributaries Master Plan," November 6, 1958, Huntsville, TX, Texas Department of Water Resources, Austin.

60. "'Big City' Plan," *Carrollton Chronicle*, February 27, 1959, 2.

61. "Houston's Amazing New Interest," *Liberty (TX) Vindicator*, February 12, 1959 (emphasis in original).

62. Baker, *Southern Landscapes*, 204.

63. Baker, *Southern Landscapes*, 218, 220.

## *CHAPTER 13*

1. Baker, "Risk, Doubt."

2. Tarrant Regional Water Dist. v. Gragg, 151 S.W.3d 546 (Tex. 2004).

3. "Ranch Flooded by Lake," January 30, 2015, Dawson & Sodd, accessed on April 18, 2025, www.dawsonsodd.com/case_results/ranch-flooded-lake/.

4. "John Graves, Contributor," *Texas Monthly*, accessed April 18, 2025, www.texasmonthly.com/contributors/john-graves/.

5. Graves, *Goodbye to a River*, 8–9.

6. Kramer, "Texas Water Politics," 121.

7. *Environmental and Cultural Resources*, ii.

8. Editors, "Channel Only Cure for Floods," *Trinity Valley Progress*, May–June 1968, 3.

9. R. D. Christal to Earle Cabell, March 13, 1968, box 92, Earle Cabell Papers, DeGolyer Library, Southern Methodist University, Dallas.

10. *Dallas Times Herald*, April 28, 1972; James White, interview by J. B. Smallwood, November 10, 1977, transcript, Oral History Collection, Special Collections, University of North Texas, Denton.

11. Gladwin Hill, "Environment Vote a Factor in 50 Congress Contests," *New York Times*, November 12, 1972.

12. Dave McNeely and Luke Thompson, "The Unholy Trinity Incident," *Texas Monthly*, June 1973.

13. "Newsletter from State Senator Charles Wilson," *Polk County Enterprise*, March 30, 1967, 4.

14. Amon Carter to Congressman Wilson, January 30, 1973, box 10, folder 20, Charles Wilson Congressional Papers, ETRC.

15. Jack Rogers, Palestine Mayor, to Congressman Steelman, January 17, 1973, box 170, folder 1, Baylor Collections of Political Materials, W. R. Poage Legislative Library, Baylor University, Waco.

16. Munoz et al., "Climatic Control."

17. "Voters to Decide March 13," *Rambler* (Fort Worth), March 9, 1973, 6.

18. Harold Scarett, *Houston Post*, March 7, 1973, 1.

19. Jacobs, *Panic at the Pump*.

20. White interview by Smallwood, Special Collections at University of North Texas.

21. White interview by Smallwood, Special Collections at University of North Texas, 25; Randy Parten, "Conflict of Interest Within the Trinity River Authority of Texas: Proposals for Reform," unpublished paper, May 1, 1973, 7, in author's possession.

22. Public comments, invited talk on Trinity River, July 18, 2017, Livingston Public Library, Livingston, TX.

23. "To the Editor," *Houston County Courier*, March 1, 1973, 2.

24. White interview by Smallwood, Special Collections at University of North Texas, 22.

25. "Texas Voters Reject Bond Issue for Trinity River Canal Project," *New York Times*, March 15, 1973.

26. "The Trinity River Authority of Texas: Tax and Bond Election, March 13, 1973," March 1973, Trinity River Authority Archives, Arlington, TX.

27. After all, river control and water management projects had a long history of centralizing power. See, for example, Worster, *Rivers of Empire*.

28. McFarlane, "Defining a Nuisance."

29. "The Trinity River Authority of Texas: Tax and Bond Election, March 13, 1973," Trinity River Authority Archives.

30. My father, appointed by Governor Greg Abbott, currently serves on the board of the Trinity River Authority.

31. "Alternatives for Implementing Navigation on the Trinity River, labeled Highly Confidential," July 28, 1975, Trinity River Authority Archives, Arlington.

32. "Alternatives for Implementing Navigation."

33. "Trinity River Authority of Texas Public Hearing on Trinity Master Plan," Crockett, TX, August 25, 1975, transcript, p. 81, Trinity River Authority Archives, Arlington.

34. Regina Levoy phone call with author, October 10, 2019.

35. "Trinity River Authority of Texas Public Hearing on Trinity Master Plan," 46, Trinity River Authority Archives.

36. John Henry Faulk, interview by J. B. Smallwood, June 9, 1981, transcript, Oral History Collection, Special Collections, University of North Texas, Denton, 53, 56.

37. George Vetek to Charlie Wilson, box 11, folder 24, Charles Wilson Congressional Papers, ETRC.

38. Faulk, interview by Smallwood, Special Collections at University of North Texas, 58, 60, 61, 61–62.

39. "Trinity River Authority of Texas Public Hearing on Trinity Master Plan," October 21, 1975, Madisonville, TX, transcript, box 8, folder 23, Charles Wilson Congressional Papers, ETRC, 103, 19, 96, 16.

40. "Trinity River Authority of Texas Public Hearing on Trinity Master Plan," ETRC, 18.

41. Scott-Chaber, "'River of Death.'"

42. In debates over internal improvement in Texas, politicians frequently referred to the east/west division of the state "with the Trinity River dividing the two great sections." Even coming from Houston, less than fifty miles from the Trinity, could lead to a politician being labeled as "western." Though not enacted, in Reconstruction a resolution at the 1866 Constitutional Convention proposed dividing Texas in two with the Trinity River marking the border with East Texas. Griffin, "Intrastate Sectionalism," 159; Baum, *Shattering of Texas Unionism*, 93.

## *EPILOGUE*

1. Alexander, *Homelands and Waterways*, 11. The historian Adele Logan Alexander, whose aunt married Aaron Day, Henderson Day's nephew, described how family history, containing both dreams and nightmares, can be particularly useful for understanding American history. She writes, "Here is a quintessentially American story about legacies and traditions, gains and losses, blissful reveries and hair-raising nightmares, obligations, allegiances, devotion to and sacrifices for country, community, and family."

2. W. W. Ross et al. v. W. J. Green, No. 7653, Supreme Court of Texas, 135 Tex. 103, 139 S.W.2d 565, 1940 Tex. April 17, 1940.

3. Ross v. Green (1940).

4. Ross et al. v. Green et al., No. 3383, Court of Civil Appeals of Texas, Beaumont, 128 S.W.2d 477, 1939 Tex. App. Lexis 1121, May 12, 1939, Decided.

# BIBLIOGRAPHY

## *PRIMARY SOURCES*

### Archives

Archives of the Alabama-Coushatta Tribe of Texas, Livingston, TX
  Howard Martin Papers
Baylor University, Waco, TX
  Institute for Oral History
  Texas Collection
  W. R. Poage Legislative Library
    Baylor Collections of Political Materials
Cornell University Library, Ithaca, NY
  Division of Rare and Manuscript Collections
    Turner Family Papers
Crockett Public Library, Crockett, TX
Dallas Public Library, Dallas, TX
  Dallas History and Archives Division
General Land Office Archives, Austin, TX
  General Map Collection
Harvard Business School, Cambridge, MA
  Special Collections and Archives, Baker Library
    R. G. Dun & Co. Credit Report volumes
The History Center, Diboll, TX
Houston County Historical Commission, Crockett, TX
  Smith Family History
Houston Public Library, Houston, TX
  Houston Metropolitan Research Center
Leon County Genealogical Society, Centerville, TX
Library of Congress, Washington, DC
  American Life Histories: Manuscripts from the Federal Writers' Project, 1936 to 1940

National Archives and Records Administration, Washington, DC
RG 105: Records of the Bureau of Refugees, Freedmen, and Abandoned Lands
RG 15: Records of the Department of Veterans Affairs, 1773–2007
RG 109: War Department Collection of Confederate Records
National Archives at Fort Worth, TX
RG 77: Records of the Office of the Chief of Engineers
Southwestern Division, Fort Worth District
New York Public Library
Schomburg Center for Research in Black Culture
Palestine Public Library, Palestine, TX
Mary Kate Hunter Collection
Polk County Historical Commission, Livingston, TX
Rosenberg Library, Galveston, TX
San Jacinto County Historical Commission, Coldspring, TX
San Jacinto Museum of History, La Porte, TX
Albert and Ethel Herzstein Library
Andrew Briscoe Papers
Southern Methodist University, Dallas, TX
Bridwell Library
DeGolyer Library
Earle Cabell Papers
Stephen F. Austin State University, Nacogdoches, TX
East Texas Research Center, Ralph W. Steen Library
Charles Wilson Congressional Papers
George Aldrich Papers
Texas Runaway Slave Project
Texas Baptist Historical Collection, Waco, TX
Texas Christian University, Fort Worth, TX
Mary Couts Burnett Library
Amon G. Carter Collection
Texas Commission on Environmental Quality, Austin, TX
Environmental Research Library
Texas Prison Museum, Huntsville, TX
Texas State Archives, Liberty, TX
Sam Houston Regional Library
George Gordon Collection
Polk County Clerk Records
Texas State Library and Archives Commission, Austin, TX
Archives and Information Services Division
Joint Penitentiary Investigating Committee Records, Texas Legislature
Records of the First Two Terms, Texas Governor Elisha Marshall Pease
State Board of Water Engineers Minutes
State Police Records, Reconstruction Records, Texas Adjutant General's Department
Texas Governor Francis Richard Lubbock Records, 1861–1904
Texas Natural Resource Conservation Commission Reclamation Engineer Records

Sam Houston State University, Huntsville, TX
Special Collections, Thomason Room, Newton Gresham Library
Goree Family Papers
John F. Kelly Papers
Trinity County Historical Commission, Groveton, TX
Trinity River Authority Archives, Arlington, TX
Trinity River Authority Lake Livingston Archives, Livingston, TX
University of North Texas, Denton, TX
Special Collections
Oral History Collection
University of Texas at Austin
Dolph Briscoe Center for American History
Bexar Archives Online
Gerard C. Brandon Papers
Sam Rayburn Papers
Perry-Castañeda Library
Walker County Historical Commission, Huntsville, TX

## Digital Databases

Ancestry.com
1850 United States Federal Census, Slave Schedules
1850 United States Agricultural Census
1880 United States Federal Census
1900 United States Federal Census
1910 United States Federal Census
Navarro County, Texas Department of State Health Services, Texas, Death Certificates, 1903–1982
Polk County Probate Minutes, Vol. A–C, 1847–1862, Texas, US, Wills and Probate Records, 1833–1974
Digital Collections, Newton Gresham Library, Sam Houston State University, https://digital.library.shsu.edu/
Digital Library on American Slavery, dlas.uncg.edu
Race and Slavery Petitions Project, Series 2, County Court Petitions
FamilySearch.org
1920 United States Federal Census
Fold3.com
Unfiled Papers and Slips Belonging to Confederate Compiled Service Records
LexisNexis.com
Texas Court Cases
Portal to Texas History, University of North Texas Libraries, https://texashistory.unt.edu/
Texas State Historical Association
*Handbook of Texas*, tshaonline.org/handbook

## Periodicals

*Anahuac (TX) Progress*
*Carrollton (TX) Chronicle*
*Civilian and Galveston City Gazette / Civilian and Gazette Weekly*
*Crockett (TX) Courier*
*Dallas Herald*
*Dallas Morning News*
*Dallas Observer*
*Dallas Times Herald*
*Denison (TX) Press*
*D Magazine*
*East Texas Magazine*
*Ennis (TX) Daily News*
*Fort Worth Gazette*
*Fort Worth Star-Telegram*
*Galveston Commercial, and Weekly Prices Current*
*Galveston Daily News / Galveston News*
*Galveston Weekly News*
*Henderson (TX) Times*
*Houston County Courier*
*Houston Daily Telegraph*
*Houston Post*
*Huntsville (TX) Post-Item*
*Jazz Journal*
*Leon Pioneer* (Centerville, TX)
*Liberty (TX) Gazette*
*Liberty (TX) Vindicator*
*New York Times*
*Northern Standard* (Clarksville, TX)
*Norton's Union Intelligencer* (Dallas)
*Palestine (TX) Daily Herald / Palestine (TX) Herald-Press*
*Polk County Enterprise* (Livingston, TX)
*Rambler* (Fort Worth)
*San Antonio Ledger*
*Scribner's Monthly*
*Semi-Weekly Journal* (Galveston)
*Southern Mercury* (Dallas)
*Texas Highways*
*Texas Historian*
*Texas Monthly*
*Texas State Gazette*
*Trinity Project*
*Trinity Valley Progress*
*Weekly Chronicle* (Duncanville, TX)
*Weekly Confederate* (Galveston)
*Weekly State Gazette* (Austin)
*Wylie (TX) News*

## Books and Articles

"An Act Authorizing the Survey of Land for the Coushatta and Alabama Indians, January 14, 1840." In *Texas Indian Papers, 1825–1843*, edited by Dorman H. Winfrey. Austin: Texas State Library, 1959.

Adams, Archie. *The Archie Adams Diary*. Crockett, TX: Houston County Historical Commission, 1990.

Allan, Francis D. *Allan's Lone Star Ballads: A Collection of Southern Patriotic Songs: Made During Confederate Times*. Galveston: J. D. Sawyer, 1874.

Berlandier, Jean Louis. *Journey to Mexico During the Years 1826 to 1834*. Austin: Texas State Historical Association in cooperation with the Center for Studies in Texas History, University of Texas at Austin, 1980.

Bollaert, William. *William Bollaert's Texas*. Norman: Published in cooperation with the Newberry Library, Chicago, by the University of Oklahoma Press, 1956.

Bondi, August M. *Autobiography of August Bondi, 1833–1907*. Galesburg, IL: Wagoner Print Co., 1910.

Brown, Edgar Herbert. *Trinity River Canalization*. Dallas: Published under the auspices of the Trinity River Canal Association, 1930.

Daniel, Theo S. *River Bottom Humor*. San Antonio: Naylor Co., 1968.

Day, Caroline Bond. *A Study of Some Negro-White Families in the United States*. Cambridge, MA: Peabody Museum of Harvard University, 1932.

DeCordova, Jacob. *Texas: Her Resources and Her Public Men*. Philadelphia: E. Crozet, 1858.

*Environmental and Cultural Resources Within the Trinity River Basin*. Assembled by James V. Sciscenti. Dallas, 1971. https://apps.dtic.mil/sti/tr/pdf/ADA096191.pdf.

Evans, James B., ed. *Diary of Elizabeth Green Gaines Smith and the John Titus and Elizabeth Gaines Smith Family*. Crockett, TX: Houston County Historical Commission, 1988.

Exley, Jo Ella Powell, ed. *Texas Tears and Texas Sunshine: Voices of Frontier Women*. College Station: Texas A&M University Press, 1985.

Federal Writers' Project. *Slave Narratives: A Folk History of Slavery in the United States from Interviews with Former Slaves*. Vol. 16, Texas, part 3, Lewis–Ryles. Washington, DC: Works Project Administration, 1941. www.loc.gov/item/mesn163/.

Forstall, Richard L. "Population of States and Counties of the United States: 1790–1990." US Bureau of the Census. Washington, DC: Government Printing Office, 1996.

Foster, William, ed. *The La Salle Expedition to Texas: The Journal of Henri Joutel, 1684–1687*. Translated by Johanna S. Warren. Austin: Texas State Historical Association, 1998.

Frances Jane Leathers, "Christopher Columbus Goodman: Soldier, Indian Fighter, Farmer, 1818–1861." *Southwestern Historical Quarterly* 69, no. 3 (1966): 353–76.

Fulsom, Louise Adams. *Prison Stories: The Old Days*. Huntsville, TX: privately printed, 1998.

*General Laws of the State of Texas Passed by the Thirty-Third Legislature*. Austin: Von Boeckmann-Jones, 1913.

Hart, Stephen Harding, and Archer Butler Hulbert, eds. *Southwestern Journals of Zebulon Pike, 1806–1807*. Albuquerque: University of New Mexico Press, 2006.

Hartmann, Louis, and Jean-Baptiste Millard. Le Texas, ou Notice historique sur le Champ-d'asile [. . .]. Paris: Beguin, 1819.

Houston County Historical Commission. *History of Houston County, Texas, 1687–1979*. Houston County, TX: Heritage, 1979.

Humphrey, R. M. "History of the Colored Farmers' National Alliance and Co-operative Union." In *The Farmers' Alliance History and Agricultural Digest*, edited by N. A. Humphrey. Washington, DC: Alliance, 1891.

Jenkins, John Holland. *Recollections of Early Texas: The Memoirs of John Holland Jenkins*. Austin: University of Texas Press, 1958.

Jenkins, John Holmes. *Papers of the Texas Revolution, 1835–1836*. Vol. 5. Austin: Presidial Press, 1973.

*Journal of the Reconstruction Convention, Which Met at Austin, Texas, June 1, A.D., 1868*. Austin: Tracy, Siemering & Co., 1870.

Kittrell, Pleasant Williams. *The Kittrell Journal, 1853–1867*. Bryan, TX: Family History Foundation, 1980.

Lamar, Mirabeau Buonaparte. *The Papers of Mirabeau Buonaparte Lamar, Volume III*. Edited from the original papers in the Texas State Library by Charles Adams and Katherine Elliott. Austin: Von Boeckmann, 1923.

Lubbock, Francis Richard. *Six Decades in Texas; or, Memoirs of Francis Richard Lubbock, Governor of Texas in War Time, 1861–63. A Personal Experience in Business, War, and Politics.* Austin: B. C. Jones & Co., 1900.

Olmsted, Frederick Law. *A Journey Through Texas: or, A Saddle-Trip on the Southwestern Frontier.* Austin: University of Texas Press, 1978.

Rawick, George P., ed. *The American Slave: A Composite Autobiography.* Supplement, Series 2. 10 vols. Westport, CT: Greenwood Press, 1979.

"Report of Major General Sheridan." In *Supplemental Report of the Joint Committee on the Conduct of the War, 38th Congress, 2nd Session.* Vol. 2. Washington, DC: Government Printing Office, 1866.

"Report of the Chief of Engineers." In *Report of the Secretary of War, [. . .] First Session of the Forty-Third Congress.* Vol. 2. Washington, DC: Government Printing Office, 1873.

Sappington, H. O., et al. *Trinity River Sanitary Survey.* Austin: State Health Department of Texas, 1925.

Seaton, Benjamin M., and Harold E. Simpson. *The Bugle Softly Blows: The Confederate Diary of Benjamin M. Seaton.* Waco, TX: Texian Press, 1965.

Sessums, Charles V. *The Lee-Simmons-Stephens Family of the Lower Trinity River Valley.* Knoxville, TN: self-published, 1997.

Sibley, John. *A Report from Natchitoches in 1807.* Edited by Annie Heloise Abel. New York: Museum of the American Indian, 1922.

Smither, Harriet, and Adolphus Sterne. "Diary of Adolphus Sterne, III." *Southwestern Historical Quarterly* 30, no. 4 (1927): 305–24.

*Special Laws of the State of Texas Passed at the Thirteenth Legislature.* Austin: John Cardwell, 1873.

"Survey of Trinity River, Texas." In *Letter from the Secretary of War, Transmitting, with a Letter from the Chief of Engineers, Report of a Survey of Trinity River, Texas.* 56th Cong., 1st Sess., Doc. No. 409. Washington, DC: Government Printing Office, 1900.

Terán, Manuel de Mier y. *Texas by Terán: The Diary Kept by General Manuel de Mier y Terán on His 1828 Inspection of Texas.* Edited by Jack Jackson. Austin: University of Texas Press, 2000.

Trammell, Camilla Davis. *Seven Pines: Its Occupants and Their Letters, 1825–1872.* Dallas: Southern Methodist University Press, 1987.

Twain, Mark. *Life on the Mississippi.* Boston: James R. Osgood, 1883.

US Congress. *Report of the Joint Committee on Reconstruction: Florida, Louisiana, Texas.* Washington, DC: Government Printing Office, 1866.

*The War of the Rebellion: A Compilation of the Official Records of the Union and Confederate Armies.* Series 1, vol. 17. Washington, DC: Government Printing Office, 1903.

*The War of the Rebellion: A Compilation of the Official Records of the Union and Confederate Armies.* Series 1, vol. 19. Washington, DC: Government Printing Office, 1905.

Watson, William. *The Adventures of a Blockade Runner; or, Trade in Time of War.* London: T. F. Unwin, 1892.

Winfrey, Dorman H., ed. *Texas Indian Papers, 1825–1843.* Austin: Texas State Library, 1959.

Wright, Jim. *Balance of Power: Presidents and Congress from the Era of McCarthy to the Age of Gingrich.* Atlanta: Turner Publishing, 1996.

Wright, Solomon Alexander. *My Rambles as East Texas Cowboy, Hunter, Fisherman, Tie-Cutter*. Range Life Series. Austin: Texas Folklore Society, 1942.

## *SECONDARY SOURCES*

### Books

Alexander, Adele Logan. *Homelands and Waterways: The American Journey of the Bond Family, 1846–1926*. New York: Pantheon Books, 1999.

Ali, Omar H. *In the Lion's Mouth: Black Populism in the New South, 1886–1900*. Jackson: University Press of Mississippi, 2010.

Alonzo, Armando C. *Tejano Legacy: Rancheros and Settlers in South Texas, 1734–1900*. Albuquerque: University of New Mexico Press, 1998.

Archer, Kenna Lang. *Unruly Waters: A Social and Environmental History of the Brazos River*. Albuquerque: University of New Mexico Press, 2015.

Ayers, Edward L. *The Promise of the New South: Life After Reconstruction*. New York: Oxford University Press, 1992.

Baker, Andrew C. *Bulldozer Revolutions: A Rural History of the Metropolitan South*. Athens: University of Georgia Press, 2018.

Barr, Julianna. *Peace Came in the Form of a Woman: Indians and Spaniards in the Texas Borderlands*. Chapel Hill: University of North Carolina Press, 2007.

Baum, Dale. *The Shattering of Texas Unionism: Politics in the Lone Star State During the Civil War Era*. Baton Rouge: Louisiana State University Press, 1998.

Baum, Dale. "Slaves Taken to Texas for Safekeeping During the Civil War." In *The Fate of Texas: The Civil War and the Lone Star State*, edited by Charles D. Grear. Fayetteville: University of Arkansas Press, 2008.

Baumgartner, Alice. *South to Freedom: Runaway Slaves to Mexico and the Road to the Civil War*. New York: Basic Books, 2020.

Bean, Christopher B. *Too Great a Burden to Bear: The Struggle and Failure of the Freedmen's Bureau in Texas*. New York: Fordham University Press, 2016.

Berlin, Ira. *Many Thousands Gone: The First Two Centuries of Slavery in North America*. Cambridge, MA: Harvard University Press, 2009.

Bernsen, James Alan. *The Lost War for Texas: Mexican Rebels, American Burrites, and the Texas Revolution of 1811*. College Station: Texas A&M University Press, 2024.

Berryhill, Michael. *The Trials of Eroy Brown: The Murder Case That Shook the Texas Prison System*. Austin: University of Texas Press, 2011.

Blair, William A. *The Records of Murders and Outrages: Racial Violence and the Fight over Truth at the Dawn of Reconstruction*. Chapel Hill: University of North Carolina Press, 2021.

Blaufarb, Rafe. *Bonapartists in the Borderlands: French Exiles and Refugees on the Gulf Coast, 1815–1835*. Tuscaloosa: University of Alabama Press, 2005.

Block, W. T. *Cotton Bales, Keelboats and Sternwheelers: A History of the Sabine River and Trinity River Cotton Trades, 1837–1900*. Woodville, TX: Dogwood Press, 1995.

Block, W. T. *East Texas Mill Towns and Ghost Towns*. Lufkin, TX: Best of East Texas Publishers, 1994.

Boyle, Robert, John Graves, and T. H. Watkins. *The Water Hustlers*. San Francisco: Sierra Club, 1971.

Brady, Lisa M. *War upon the Land: Military Strategy and the Transformation of Southern Landscapes During the American Civil War*. Athens: University of Georgia Press, 2012.

Brosnan, Kathleen A. *Uniting Mountain and Plain: Cities, Law, and Environmental Change Along the Front Range*. Albuquerque: University of New Mexico Press, 2002.

Brown, Deward. *Rivers, Rockets, and Readiness: Army Engineers in the Sunbelt*. Fort Worth: Fort Worth District, US Army Corps of Engineers, 1979.

Buchanan, Thomas C. *Black Life on the Mississippi: Slaves, Free Blacks, and the Western Steamboat World*. Chapel Hill: University of North Carolina Press, 2004.

Buenger, Walter L. *The Path to a Modern South: Northeast Texas Between Reconstruction and the Great Depression*. Austin: University of Texas Press, 2001.

Bullard, Robert D. *Dumping in Dixie: Race, Class, and Environmental Quality*. Boulder: Westview Press, 1990.

Camp, Stephanie M. H. *Closer to Freedom: Enslaved Women and Everyday Resistance in the Plantation South*. Chapel Hill: University of North Carolina Press, 2004.

Campbell, Randolph B. *An Empire for Slavery: The Peculiar Institution in Texas, 1821–1865*. Baton Rouge: Louisiana State University Press, 1989.

Campbell, Randolph B. *Grass-Roots Reconstruction in Texas, 1865–1880*. Baton Rouge: Louisiana State University Press, 1997.

Cantrell, Gregg. *Stephen F. Austin: Empresario of Texas*. New Haven: Yale University Press, 1999.

Cantrell, Gregg, and Elizabeth Hayes Turner, eds. *Lone Star Pasts: Memory and History in Texas*. College Station: Texas A&M University Press, 2007.

Caro, Robert. *The Path to Power: The Years of Lyndon Johnson, Volume 1*. New York: Knopf, 1982.

Carrigan, William D. *The Making of a Lynching Culture: Violence and Vigilantism in Central Texas, 1836–1916*. Urbana: University of Illinois Press, 2004.

Castañeda, Carlos E. *The Mission Era: The Passing of the Missions, 1762–1782*. Vol. 4 of *Our Catholic Heritage in Texas, 1519–1936*. Austin: Von Boeckman-Jones, 1939.

Caudill, Philip. *Moss Bluff Rebel: A Texas Pioneer in the Civil War*. College Station: Texas A&M University Press, 2009.

Chang, David A. *The Color of the Land: Race, Nation, and the Politics of Landownership in Oklahoma, 1832–1929*. Chapel Hill: University of North Carolina Press, 2010.

Chapa, Juan Bautista. *Texas and Northeastern Mexico, 1630–1690*. Austin: University of Texas Press, 2010.

Chase, Robert T. *We Are Not Slaves: State Violence, Coerced Labor, and Prisoners' Rights in Postwar America*. Chapel Hill: University of North Carolina Press, 2020.

Cobb, James. *The Selling of the South: The Southern Crusade for Industrial Development, 1936–1990*. Urbana: University of Illinois Press, 1993.

Crews, D'Anne McAdams, ed. *Huntsville and Walker County, Texas: A Bicentennial History*. Huntsville: Sam Houston State University Press, 1976.

Cronon, William. *Nature's Metropolis: Chicago and the Great West*. New York: W. W. Norton, 1991.

Cunha, Dilip da. *The Invention of Rivers: Alexander's Eye and Ganga's Descent*. Philadelphia: University of Pennsylvania Press, 2019.

Daniel, Pete. *Breaking the Land: The Transformation of Cotton, Tobacco, and Rice Cultures Since 1880*. Urbana: University of Illinois Press, 1986.

Davis, Clark. *It Starts with Trouble: William Goyen and the Life of Writing*. Austin: University of Texas Press, 2015.

Davis, Steven L., and Sam L. Pfiester, eds. *Viva Texas Rivers! Adventures, Misadventures, and Glimpses of Nirvana Along Our Storied Waterways*. College Station: Texas A&M University Press, 2021.

deBuys, William, and Alex Harris. *River of Traps: A Village Life*. Albuquerque: University of New Mexico Press, 1990.

Downs, Gregory P. *After Appomattox: Military Occupation and the Ends of War*. Cambridge, MA: Harvard University Press, 2015.

Downs, Jim. *Sick from Freedom: African-American Illness and Suffering During the Civil War and Reconstruction*. New York: Oxford University Press, 2012.

Drayton, Richard Harry. *Nature's Government: Science, Imperial Britain, and the "Improvement" of the World*. New Haven: Yale University Press, 2000.

Du Bois, W. E. B. *Black Reconstruction in America, 1860–1880*. New York: Free Press, 1935.

Duncan, R. Scot. *Southern Rivers: Restoring America's Freshwater Biodiversity*. Tuscaloosa: University of Alabama Press, 2024.

Edney, Matthew H. *Mapping an Empire: The Geographical Construction of British India, 1765–1843*. Chicago: University of Chicago Press, 1997.

Ellis, Elizabeth. *The Great Power of Small Nations: Indigenous Diplomacy in the Gulf South*. Philadelphia: University of Pennsylvania Press, 2022.

Emberton, Carole. *To Walk About in Freedom: The Long Emancipation of Priscilla Joyner*. New York: W. W. Norton, 2022.

Fenn, Elizabeth. *Pox Americana: The Great Smallpox Epidemic of 1775–82*. New York: Hill and Wang, 2001.

Fiege, Mark. *Irrigated Eden: The Making of an Agricultural Landscape in the American West*. Seattle: University of Washington Press, 1999.

Foley, Neil. *The White Scourge: Mexicans, Blacks, and Poor Whites in Texas Cotton Culture*. Berkeley: University of California Press, 1997.

Fort, Karen Gerhardt Britton. *A Feast of Reason: The Civil War Journal of James Madison Hall*. Abilene: State House Press, 2016.

Frantz, Joe Bertram, Mike Cox, Roger A. Griffin, and Texas General Land Office. *Lure of the Land: Texas County Maps and the History of Settlement*. College Station: Published for the Texas General Land Office by Texas A&M University Press, 1988.

Gates, Paul W., United States Public Land Law Review Commission. *History of Public Land Law Development*. Washington, DC: Government Printing Office, 1968.

Genovese, Eugene D. *The Political Economy of Slavery: Studies in the Economy and Society of the Slave South*. New York: Pantheon Books, 1965.

Giesen, James C. *Boll Weevil Blues: Cotton, Myth, and Power in the American South*. Chicago: University of Chicago Press, 2011.

Glasrud, Bruce A., Archie P. McDonald, and Alwyn Barr. *Blacks in East Texas History: Selections from the East Texas Historical Journal*. College Station: Texas A&M University Press, 2008.

Glymph, Thavolia. *Out of the House of Bondage: The Transformation of the Plantation Household.* New York: Cambridge University Press, 2008.

Goodwyn, Lawrence. *The Populist Moment: A Short History of the Agrarian Revolt in America.* New York: Oxford University Press, 1978.

Governar, Alan. *Lightnin' Hopkins: His Life and Blues.* Chicago: Chicago Review Press, 2010.

Goyen, William. *The House of Breath.* New York: Random House, 1950.

Gracy, David B. *Moses Austin: His Life.* San Antonio: Trinity University Press, 1987.

Graff, Harvey J. *The Dallas Myth: The Making and Unmaking of an American City.* Minneapolis: University of Minnesota Press, 2008.

Graves, John. *Goodbye to a River: A Narrative.* New York: Knopf, 1959.

Grossman, James R. *Land of Hope: Chicago, Black Southerners, and the Great Migration.* Chicago: University of Chicago Press, 1989.

Guinn, Jeff. *Go Down Together: The True, Untold Story of Bonnie and Clyde.* New York: Simon and Schuster, 2009.

Hahn, Steven. *A Nation Under Our Feet: Black Political Struggles in the Rural South, from Slavery to the Great Migration.* Cambridge, MA: Harvard University Press, 2003.

Hahn, Steven. *The Roots of Southern Populism: Yeoman Farmers and the Transformation of the Georgia Upcountry, 1850–1890.* New York: Oxford University Press, 2006.

Hämäläinen, Pekka. *The Comanche Empire.* New Haven: Yale University Press, 2008.

Hardin, Stephen L. *Texian Exodus: The Runaway Scrape and Its Enduring Legacy.* Austin: University of Texas Press, 2024.

Hasty, Gregory M. *Oak Cliff and the Missing Pieces.* Bloomington: Archway, 2023.

Hays, Samuel P., and Barbara D. Hays. *Beauty, Health, and Permanence: Environmental Politics in the United States, 1955–1985.* Studies in Environment and History. New York: Cambridge University Press, 1987.

Hill, Lance. *The Deacons for Defense: Armed Resistance and the Civil Rights Movement.* Chapel Hill: University of North Carolina Press, 2004.

Hogarth, Rana A. *Medicalizing Blackness: Making Racial Difference in the Atlantic World, 1780–1840.* Chapel Hill: University of North Carolina Press, 2017.

Hohes, Pauline Buck. *A Centennial History of Anderson County, Texas.* San Antonio: Naylor, 1936.

Holt, Sharon Ann. *Making Freedom Pay: North Carolina Freedpeople Working for Themselves, 1865–1900.* Athens: University of Georgia Press, 2003.

Horowitz, Andy. *Katrina: A History, 1915–2015.* Cambridge, MA: Harvard University Press, 2020.

Houser, Steve, et al. *Comanche Marker Trees of Texas.* College Station: Texas A&M University Press, 2016.

Houston Wilderness. *Houston Atlas of Biodiversity.* College Station: Texas A&M University Press, 2007.

Howell, Kenneth, ed. *Still the Arena of Civil War: Violence and Turmoil in Reconstruction Texas, 1865–1874.* Denton: University of North Texas Press, 2012.

Hudson, Angela Pulley. *Creek Paths and Federal Roads: Indians, Settlers, and Slaves and the Making of the American South.* Chapel Hill: University of North Carolina Press, 2010.

Hundley, Norris. *The Great Thirst: Californians and Water, 1770s–1990s.* Berkeley: University of California Press, 1992.

Huser, Verne. *Rivers of Texas*. College Station: Texas A&M University Press, 2000.

Jackson, Bruce. *Inside the Wire: Photographs from Texas and Arkansas Prisons*. Austin: University of Texas Press, 2013.

Jackson, Bruce. *Wake Up Dead Man: Hard Labor and Southern Blues*. Athens: University of Georgia Press, 1999.

Jacobs, Meg. *Panic at the Pump: The Energy Crisis and the Transformation of American Politics in the 1970s*. New York: Hill and Wang, 2016.

Jacoby, Karl. *Crimes Against Nature: Squatters, Poachers, Thieves, and the Hidden History of American Conservation*. Berkeley: University of California Press, 2003.

Johnson, Ben. *Texas: An American History*. New Haven: Yale University Press, 2025.

Johnson, Walter. *Soul by Soul: Life Inside the Antebellum Slave Market*. Cambridge, MA: Havard University Press, 1999.

Jones, C. Allan. *Texas Roots: Agriculture and Rural Life Before the Civil War*. College Station: Texas A&M University Press, 2005.

Jordan-Bychkov, Terry G. *Texas: A Geography*. Boulder: Westview Press, 1984.

Kaye, Anthony E. *Joining Places: Slave Neighborhoods in the Old South*. Chapel Hill: University of North Carolina Press, 2007.

Kelley, Sean M. *Los Brazos de Dios: A Plantation Society in the Texas Borderlands, 1821–1865*. Baton Rouge: Louisiana State University Press, 2010.

Kelman, Ari. *A River and Its City: The Nature of Landscape in New Orleans*. Berkeley: University of California Press, 2003.

Kerstetter, Todd. "Pipe Dreams and Fake Lakes: Engineering Water in Progressive-Era Fort Worth." In *Nature and Place in Texas: A History*, edited by Kenna Lang Archer, Char Miller, and Jason E. Pierce. Lubbock: Texas Tech University, 2026.

Kimball, Geoffrey. *Yukhíti Kóy: A Reference Grammar of the Atakapa Language*. Lincoln: University of Nebraska Press, 2022.

Kirby, Jack Temple. *Mockingbird Song: Ecological Landscapes of the South*. Chapel Hill: University of North Carolina Press, 2006.

Kirby, Jack Temple. *Rural Worlds Lost: The American South, 1920–1960*. Baton Rouge: Louisiana State University Press, 1987.

Kramer, Ken. "Texas Water Politics: Forty Years of Going with the Flow." In *The Living Waters of Texas*, edited by Ken Kramer. College Station: Texas A&M University Press, 2010.

Krauthamer, Barbara. *Black Slaves, Indian Masters: Slavery, Emancipation, and Citizenship in the Native American South*. Chapel Hill: University of North Carolina Press, 2013.

Lahiri-Dutt, Kuntala, and Gopa Samanta. *Dancing with the River: People and Life on the Chars of South Asia*. New Haven: Yale University Press, 2013.

Lassiter, Matthew D. *The Silent Majority: Suburban Politics in the Sunbelt South*. Princeton: Princeton University Press, 2006.

Leach, William. *Butterfly People: An American Encounter with the Beauty of the World*. New York: Pantheon Books, 2013.

Lewis, Ronald L. *Transforming the Appalachian Countryside: Railroads, Deforestation, and Social Change in West Virginia, 1880–1920*. Chapel Hill: University of North Carolina Press, 1998.

Lipman, Andrew. *The Saltwater Frontier: Indians and the Contest for the American Coast*. New Haven: Yale University Press, 2015.

Litwack, Leon. *Been in the Storm So Long: The Aftermath of Slavery*. New York: Knopf, 1979.

Majewski, John D. *Modernizing a Slave Economy: The Economic Vision of the Confederate Nation*. Chapel Hill: University of North Carolina Press, 2009.

Manganiello, Christopher J. *Southern Water, Southern Power: How the Politics of Cheap Energy and Water Scarcity Shaped a Region*. Chapel Hill: University of North Carolina Press, 2015.

Martin, Amy. *Wild DFW*. New York: Timber Press, 2023.

Martin, Howard N. *Myths and Folktales of the Alabama-Coushatta Indians of Texas*. Austin: Encino Press, 1977.

Massey, Mary Elizabeth. *Refugee Life in the Confederacy*. Baton Rouge: Louisiana State University Press, 1964.

Mauldin, Erin Stewart. *Unredeemed Land: An Environmental History of Civil War and Emancipation in the Cotton South*. New York: Oxford University Press, 2018.

McComb, David G. *The City in Texas: A History*. Austin: University of Texas Press, 2015.

McCurry, Stephanie. *Confederate Reckoning: Power and Politics in the Civil War South*. Cambridge, MA: Harvard University Press, 2010.

McCurry, Stephanie. *Masters of Small Worlds: Yeoman Households, Gender Relations, and the Political Culture of the Antebellum South Carolina Low Country*. New York: Oxford University Press, 1995.

McDaniel, W. Caleb. *Sweet Taste of Liberty: A True Story of Slavery and Restitution in America*. New York: Oxford University Press, 2019.

McFarlane, Scot. "The Legacy of Plantation Slavery on Texas Rivers." In *Nature and Place in Texas: A History*, edited by Char Miller, Kenna Lang Archer, and Jason Pierce. Lubbock: Texas Tech University Press, 2026.

McGraw, Seamus. *A Thirsty Land: The Fight for Water in Texas*. Austin: University of Texas Press, 2020.

Miles, Tiya. *All That She Carried: The Journey of Ashley's Sack, a Black Family Keepsake*. New York: Random House, 2021.

Miller, Char. *West Side Rising: How San Antonio's 1921 Flood Devastated a City and Sparked a Latino Environmental Justice Movement*. San Antonio: Trinity University Press, 2021.

Miller, Karl Hagstrom. *Segregating Sound: Inventing Folk and Pop Music in the Age of Jim Crow*. Durham: Duke University Press, 2010.

Miller, Thomas Lloyd. *The Public Lands of Texas, 1519–1970*. Norman: University of Oklahoma Press, 1972.

Milosz, Czeslaw. *Collected Poems, 1931–1987*. New York: HarperCollins, 1988.

Minutaglio, Bill. *In Search of the Blues: A Journey to the Soul of Black Texas*. Austin: University of Texas Press, 2010.

Mizelle, Richard M., Jr. *Backwater Blues: The Mississippi Flood of 1927 in the African American Imagination*. Minneapolis: University of Minnesota Press, 2014.

Moneyhon, Carl H. *Texas After the Civil War: The Struggle of Reconstruction*. College Station: Texas A&M University Press, 2004.

Morris, Christopher. *The Big Muddy: An Environmental History of the Mississippi and Its Peoples, from Hernando de Soto to Hurricane Katrina*. New York: Oxford University Press, 2012.

Muscolino, Micah S. *The Ecology of War in China: Henan Province, the Yellow River, and Beyond, 1938–1950*. Cambridge: Cambridge University Press, 2014.

Nash, Linda. *Inescapable Ecologies: A History of Environment, Disease, and Knowledge*. Berkeley: University of California Press, 2006.

Nathans, Sydney. "'Gotta Mind to Move, a Mind to Settle Down': Afro-Americans and the Plantation Frontier." In *A Master's Due: Essays in Honor of David Herbert Donald*, edited by William J. Cooper, Michael F. Holt, and John McCardell. Baton Rouge: Louisiana State University Press, 1985.

Nathans, Sydney. *A Mind to Stay: White Plantation, Black Homeland*. Cambridge, MA: Harvard University Press, 2017.

Needham, Andrew. *Power Lines: Phoenix and the Making of the Modern Southwest*. Politics and Society in Twentieth-Century America. Princeton: Princeton University Press, 2014.

Nelson, Megan Kate. *The Three-Cornered War: The Union, the Confederacy, and Native Peoples in the Fight for the West*. New York: Scribner, 2020.

O'Brien, Timothy, and David Ensminger. *Mojo Hand: The Life and Music of Lightnin' Hopkins*. Austin: University of Texas Press, 2013.

Ocampo, Emilio. *The Emperor's Last Campaign: A Napoleonic Empire in America*. Tuscaloosa: University of Alabama Press, 2009.

Ollson, Tore C. *Agrarian Crossings: Reformers and the Remaking of the US and Mexican Countryside*. Princeton: Princeton University Press, 2017.

Oubre, Claude F. *Forty Acres and a Mule: The Freedmen's Bureau and Black Land Ownership*. Baton Rouge: Louisiana State University Press, 1978.

Partlow, Miriam. *Liberty, Liberty County, and the Atascosito District*. Liberty, TX: Pemberton Press, 1974.

Pate, J'Nell L. *North of the River: A Brief History of North Fort Worth*. Fort Worth: Texas Christian University Press, 1994.

Penningroth, Dylan C. *The Claims of Kinfolk: African American Property and Community in the Nineteenth-Century South*. Chapel Hill: University of North Carolina Press, 2003.

Perkinson, Robert. *Texas Tough: The Rise of America's Prison Empire*. New York: Metropolitan Books, 2010.

Petty, Adrienne Monteith. *Standing Their Ground: Small Farmers in North Carolina Since the Civil War*. New York: Oxford University Press, 2013.

Phillips, Michael. *White Metropolis: Race, Ethnicity, and Religion in Dallas, 1841–2001*. Austin: University of Texas Press, 2006.

Phillips, Sarah T. *This Land, This Nation: Conservation, Rural America, and the New Deal*. New York: Cambridge University Press, 2007.

Pinkerton, Gary. *Bridles and Biscuits: Contraband Culture in Spanish East Texas*. College Station: Texas A&M University Press, 2025.

Pinkerton, Gary. *Trammel's Trace: The First Road to Texas from the North*. College Station: Texas A&M University Press, 2016.

Prather, Patricia Smith, and Jane Clements Monday. *From Slave to Statesman: The Legacy of Joshua Houston, Servant to Sam Houston*. Denton: University of North Texas Press, 1993.

Pruitt, Bernadette. *The Other Great Migration: The Movement of Rural African Americans to Houston, 1900–1941*. College Station: Texas A&M University Press, 2013.

Rawick, George P. *From Sundown to Sunup: The Making of the Black Community*. Vol. 1 of *The American Slave: A Composite Autobiography*. Westport, CT: Greenwood, 2013.

Richter, William L. *Overreached on All Sides: The Freedmen's Bureau Administrators in Texas, 1865–1868*. College Station: Texas A&M University Press, 1991.
Rothman, Adam. *Slave Country: American Expansion and the Origins of the Deep South*. Cambridge, MA: Harvard University Press, 2005.
Ruiz, Jose Luis García. *Texas: The False Origin of the Name*. Published by the author, 2016.
Saikku, Mikko. *This Delta, This Land: An Environmental History of the Yazoo-Mississippi Floodplain*. Athens: University of Georgia Press, 2006.
Salafia, Matthew. *Slavery's Borderland: Freedom and Bondage Along the Ohio River*. Philadelphia: University of Pennsylvania Press, 2013.
Saunders, Drew. *The Garden of Eden: The Story of a Freedmen's Community in Texas*. Fort Worth: Texas Christian University Press, 2015.
Schulman, Bruce J. *From Cotton Belt to Sunbelt: Federal Policy, Economic Development, and the Transformation of the South, 1938–1980*. New York: Oxford University Press, 1991.
Schultz, Mark. *The Rural Face of White Supremacy: Beyond Jim Crow*. Urbana: University of Illinois Press, 2005.
Scott, James C. *The Art of Not Being Governed: An Anarchist History of Upland Southeast Asia*. New Haven: Yale University Press, 2009.
Scott, James C. *Seeing Like a State: How Certain Schemes to Improve the Human Condition Have Failed*. New Haven: Yale University Press, 1998.
Shuck-Hall, Sheri Marie. *Journey to the West: The Alabama and Coushatta Indians*. Norman: University of Oklahoma Press, 2008.
Simmons, Ruth J. *Up Home: One Girl's Journey*. New York: Random House, 2023.
Sitton, Thad. *Backwoodsmen: Stockmen and Hunters Along a Big Thicket River Valley*. Norman: University of Oklahoma Press, 1995.
Sitton, Thad, and James Conrad. *Freedom Colonies: Independent Black Texans in the Time of Jim Crow*. Austin: University of Texas Press, 2005.
Smallwood, James. *Time of Hope, Time of Despair: Black Texans During Reconstruction*. Port Washington, NY: National University Publications, 1981.
Smith, F. Todd. *From Dominance to Disappearance: The Indians of Texas and the Near Southwest, 1786–1859*. Lincoln: University of Nebraska Press, 2005.
Stearns, Susan Gaunt. *Empire of Commerce: The Closing of the Mississippi and the Opening of Atlantic Trade*. Charlottesville: University of Virginia Press, 2024.
Stewart, Mart A. *"What Nature Suffers to Groe": Life, Labor, and Landscape on the Georgia Coast, 1680–1920*. Athens: University of Georgia Press, 2002.
Stine, Jeffrey K. *Mixing the Waters: Environment, Politics, and the Building of the Tennessee-Tombigbee Waterway*. Akron: University of Akron Press, 1993.
Stoll, Steven. *Larding the Lean Earth: Soil and Society in Nineteenth-Century America*. New York: Hill and Wang, 2002.
Sutter, Paul. *Let Us Now Praise Famous Gullies: Providence Canyon and the Soils of the South*. Athens: University of Georgia Press, 2015.
Szwed, Jon. *Alan Lomax: The Man Who Recorded the World*. New York: Penguin, 2010.
Taylor, Alan. *The Internal Enemy: Slavery and War in Virginia, 1772–1832*. New York: W. W. Norton, 2013.
Taylor, Amy Murrell. *Embattled Freedom: Journeys Through the Civil War's Slave Refugee Camps*. Chapel Hill: University of North Carolina Press, 2018.

Taylor, George Rogers. *The Transportation Revolution, 1815–1860*. New York: Rinehart, 1951.
Tiller, Jim, and John P. Evans. *Evolution of the Texas–Louisiana Boundary: In Search of the Elusive Corner*. Dallas: Southern Methodist University Press, 2017.
Torget, Andrew J. *Seeds of Empire: Cotton, Slavery, and the Transformation of the Texas Borderlands, 1800–1850*. Chapel Hill: University of North Carolina Press, 2015.
Truett, Joe C., and Daniel W. Lay. *Land of Bears and Honey: A Natural History of Texas*. Austin: University of Texas Press, 1984.
Ural, Susannah J. *The Soldiers and Families of the Confederacy's Most Celebrated Unit*. Baton Rouge: Louisiana State University Press, 2017.
Valencius, Conevery Bolton. *The Health of the Country: How American Settlers Understood Themselves and Their Land*. New York: Basic Books, 2002.
Walker, Melissa. *All We Knew Was to Farm: Rural Women in the Upcountry South, 1919–1941*. Baltimore: Johns Hopkins University Press, 2000.
Warren, Louis. *The Hunter's Game: Poachers and Conservationists in Twentieth-Century America*. New Haven: Yale University Press, 1997.
West, Elliott. *Continental Reckoning: The American West in the Age of Expansion*. Lincoln: University of Nebraska Press, 2023.
White, Richard. *The Organic Machine*. New York: Hill and Wang, 1995.
Williams, Heather Andrea. *Help Me to Find My People: The African American Search for Family Lost in Slavery*. Chapel Hill: University of North Carolina Press, 2012.
Williams, Kidada E. *They Left Great Marks on Me: African American Testimonies of Racial Violence from Emancipation to World War I*. New York: New York University Press, 2012.
Williams, John, and Andrew Sansom. *The Untold Story of the Lower Colorado River Authority*. College Station: Texas A&M University Press, 2015.
Woodward, C. Vann. *Origins of the New South*. Baton Rouge: Louisiana State University Press, 1971.
Worrall, Dan. *A Prehistory of Houston and Southeast Texas*. Flushear, TX: Concertina Press, 2021.
Worster, Donald. *Rivers of Empire: Water, Aridity, and the Growth of the American West*. New York: Oxford University, 1992.
Zhang, Ling. *The River, the Plain, and the State: An Environmental Drama in Northern Song China, 1048–1128*. Cambridge: Cambridge University Press, 2016.

## Journal Articles

Adams, Richard. "Basement Tectonics and Origin of the Sabine Uplift." *Gulf Coast Association of Geological Societies Transactions* 59 (2009): 3–19.
Ashburn, Karl E. "Slavery and Cotton Production in Texas." *Southwestern Social Science Quarterly* 14, no. 3 (1933): 257–71.
Baker, Andrew C. "From Rural South to Metropolitan Sunbelt: Creating a Cowboy Identity in the Shadow of Houston." *Southwestern Historical Quarterly* 118, no. 1 (2014): 1–22.
Baker, Andrew C. "Risk, Doubt, and the Biological Control of Southern Waters." *Environmental History* 24, no. 2 (2019): 327–50.
Bolton, Herbert E. "Spanish Activities on the Lower Trinity River, 1746–1771." *Southwestern Historical Quarterly* 16, no. 4 (1913): 339–77.

Cates, Madison W. "Homeplace Politics on the New River: Rural Environmentalism in Southern Appalachia, 1962–1976." *Journal of Southern History* 91, no. 3 (2025): 481–518.

Cervantez, Brian. "'For the Exclusive Benefit of Fort Worth': Amon G. Carter, the Great Depression, and the New Deal." *Southwestern Historical Quarterly* 119, no. 2 (2015): 120–47.

Du Bois, W. E. B. "The Negro Farmer." In *Negroes in the United States*, Bulletin 8, by US Department of Commerce and Labor, Bureau of the Census. Washington, DC: Government Printing Office, 1904.

Ekbladh, David. "'Mr. TVA': Grass-Roots Development, David Lilienthal, and the Rise and Fall of the Tennessee Valley Authority as a Symbol for U.S. Overseas Development, 1933–1973." *Diplomatic History* 26 (2002): 336–37.

Emberton, Carole. "Unwriting the Freedom Narrative: A Review Essay." *Journal of Southern History* 82, no. 2 (2016): 377–94.

Esmaeili, Delaraem, et al. "Rancid Rumors or Native Wisdom: Evaluating the Efficacy of Animal Fats as Insect Repellents Attributed to Historic-Period Native Americans." *PLoS ONE* 19, no. 7 (2024): e0301677.

Franco, Jere. "The Alabama-Coushatta and Their Texas Friends." *East Texas Historical Journal* 27, no. 1 (1989): article 7.

François, Mathurin, Terencio Rebello de Aguiar Jr., Marcelo Schramm Mielke, Alain N. Rousseau, Deborah Faria, and Eduardo Mariano-Neto. "Interactions Between Forest Cover and Watershed Hydrology: A Conceptual Meta-Analysis." *Water* 16, no. 23 (2024): 3350.

Griffin, Roger A. "Intrastate Sectionalism in the Texas Governor's Race of 1853." *Southwestern Historical Quarterly* 76, no. 2 (1972): 142–60.

Hasenmuller, Elizabeth, et al. "Stream Hydrology and Geochemistry Along a Rural to Urban Land Use Gradient." *Applied Geochemistry* 83 (2017): 136–49.

Holeman, J. N. "The Sediment Yield of Major Rivers of the World." *Water Resources Research* 4, no. 4 (1968): 737–47.

Johnson, Jack. "Nicholas Trammell's Difficulties in Mexican Texas." *East Texas Historical Journal* 38, no. 2 (2000): 15–39.

Luebke, Frederick C. "Regionalism and the Great Plains: Problems of Concept and Method." *Western Historical Quarterly* 15, no. 1 (1984): 19–38.

Manget, Luke. "Nature's Emporium: The Botanical Drug Trade and the Commons Tradition in Southern Appalachia, 1847–1917." *Environmental History* 21, no. 4 (2016): 660–87.

McCaslin, Richard B. "'A Curious War': Franklin A. G. Gearing in the Civil War." *East Texas Historical Journal* 53 (Fall 2015): 7–28.

McFarlane, Wallace Scot. "Defining a Nuisance: Pollution, Science, and Environmental Politics on Maine's Androscoggin River." *Environmental History* 17, no. 2 (2012): 307–35.

McFarlane, Wallace Scot. "Oil on the Farm: The East Texas Oil and the Origins of an Energy Economy." *Journal of Southern History* 83, no. 4 (2017): 853–88.

McFarlane, Wallace Scot. "The Wet Frontier of Slavery: Plantation Slavery and Freedom on Texas' Trinity River." *Slavery and Abolition* 42, no. 4 (2021): 733–54.

Miller, Thomas Lloyd. "Texas Land Grants to Promote Water Transportation." *Texana* 7, no. 2 (1969): 136–59.

Munoz, S., L. Giosan, M. Therrell, et al. "Climatic Control of Mississippi River Flood Hazard Amplified by River Engineering." *Nature* 556 (2018): 95–98. doi:10.1038/nature26145.

Murph, David. "The Search for Champ d'Asile." *Southwestern Historical Quarterly* 121, no. 2 (2017): 198–211.

Pearson, Charles, David B. Kelley, Richard A. Weinstein, and Sherwood M. Gagliano. *Archaeological Investigations on the Outer Continental Shelf: A Study Within the Sabine River Valley, Offshore Louisiana and Texas*. Baton Rouge: Coastal Environments, Inc., 1986. https://archive.org/details/doi-report_1-7212-2ar-2/mode/2up.

Perttula, Timothy K. "The Historic Caddo Archaeological Record in East Texas." Friends of Northeast Texas Archaeology, Special Publication No. 56 (2020). www.researchgate.net/profile/Timothy_Perttula/publication/337992442_SP_56_Historic_Caddo_Archaeological_Record_in_East_Texas.

Perttula, Timothy K., et al. "Archeological Investigations in the Upper Trinity River Basin in Parker County, Texas." *Index of Texas Archaeology*, Article 14 (2020): iv–46.

Richter, William L. "'The Revolver Rules the Day!' Colonel DeWitt C. Brown and the Freedmen's Bureau in Paris, Texas, 1867–1868." *Southwestern Historical Quarterly* 93, no. 3 (1990): 303–32.

Roane, J. T. "Black Ecologies, Subaquatic Life, and the Jim Crow Enclosure of the Tidewater." *Journal of Rural Studies* 94 (2022): 227–38.

Roberts, Andrea, and Maia L. Butler. "Contending with the Palimpsest: Reading the Land Through Black Women's Emotional Geographies." *Annals of the American Association of Geographers* 112, no. 3 (2022): 828–37.

Sánchez, José María, and Carlos E. Castañeda. "A Trip to Texas in 1828." *Southwestern Historical Quarterly* 29, no. 4 (1926): 249–88.

Scott-Chaber, Meghan. "'River of Death': Industrial Pollution and the North Texas Trinity River in the Progressive Era." *Journal of Texas History* 1, no. 2 (2025): 65–98.

Vincent, Louella Styles. "Governor George Thomas Wood." *Southwestern Historical Quarterly* 20, no. 3 (1917): 260–68.

Walker, Kenneth P. "The Pecan Shellers of San Antonio and Mechanization." *Southwestern Historical Quarterly* 69, no. 1 (1965): 44–58.

Woodward, Earl F. "Internal Improvements in Texas in the Early 1850s." *Southwestern Historical Quarterly* 76, no. 2 (1972): 163–68.

## Dissertations and Theses

Baker, Andrew C. "Southern Landscapes in the City's Shadow: Environmental Politics and Metropolitan Growth in Texas and Virginia, 1900–1990." PhD diss., Rice University, 2014.

Cervantez, Brian. "Lone Star Booster: The Life of Amon G. Carter." PhD diss., University of North Texas, 2011.

Davis, Edwin S. "The Movement for Trinity River Development." MA thesis, University of North Texas, 1964.

Loftus, S. E. "Postemancipation Landscapes and Material Culture: The Bethel Community and the Benjamin W. Jackson Plantation." PhD diss., Syracuse University, 2015.

Newland, Linda Sue. "The Persistence of Antebellum Planter Families in Postbellum East Texas." MA thesis, University of North Texas, 1998.

Orejel, Keith. "Factories in the Fallows: The Political Economy of America's Rural Heartland, 1945–1980." PhD diss., Columbia University, 2015.

Schiller, Joseph David. "Nature's Entrepreneur: Amon Carter and the Remaking of Texas." MA thesis, Texas Christian University, 2016.

Smith, David Paul. "Frontier Defense in Texas: 1861–1865," PhD diss., North Texas State University, 1987.

Sparkman, Michael D. "The North Texas Region and the Development of Water Resources in the Trinity River Basin of Texas, 1840–1998." MA thesis, University of North Texas, 1999.

Stull, Ernest. "The History of Navigation on the Trinity River." MA thesis, East Texas State Teachers College, 1955.

Wilson, C. W. "The Negro in Walker County, as Seen by Rev. C. W. Wilson, Former Chaplain, Texas Prison System." MA thesis, Sam Houston State Teachers College, 1934.

# INDEX

*Note: Italic page numbers refer to illustrations.*